# DRIVEN BY DIFFERENCE

# DRIVEN BY DIFFERENCE

*How Great Companies Fuel Innovation Through Diversity*

David Livermore

## AMACOM

### American Management Association

New York • Atlanta • Brussels • Chicago • Mexico City • San Francisco
Shanghai • Tokyo • Toronto • Washington, D.C.

Bulk discounts available. For details visit:
www.amacombooks.org/go/specialsales
Or contact special sales:
Phone: 800-250-5308
Email: specialsls@amanet.org
View all the AMACOM titles at: www.amacombooks.org
American Management Association: www.amanet.org

CQ is a trademark of the Cultural Intelligence Center, LLC.

Library of Congress Cataloging-in-Publication Data

Livermore, David A., 1967- author.
  Driven by difference : how great companies fuel innovation through diversity / David Livermore, PhD.
    pages cm
  Includes bibliographical references and index.
  ISBN 978-0-8144-3653-0 (hardcover) -- ISBN 978-0-8144-3654-7 (ebook)  1.  Diversity in the workplace. 2.  Cultural intelligence. 3.  Management--Cross-cultural studies. 4.  Diffusion of innovations. 5.  Technological innovations.  I. Title.
  HF5549.5.M5L583 2016
  658.3008--dc23
                              2015030410

**About AMA**
American Management Association (www.amanet.org) is a world leader in talent development, advancing the skills of individuals to drive business success. Our mission is to support the goals of individuals and organizations through a complete range of products and services, including classroom and virtual seminars, webcasts, webinars, podcasts, conferences, corporate and government solutions, business books, and research. AMA's approach to improving performance combines experiential learning—learning through doing—with opportunities for ongoing professional growth at every step of one's career journey.

Printing Number

18   19   20   LSCC   10   9   8   7   6   5   4   3   2

For Grace, Emily, and Linda . . . Discovering the world together has been among my greatest gifts in life.

# CONTENTS

Diversity has become a reality in the 21st century workplace. It offers incredible potential for developing innovative solutions, but it's not automatic. Groundbreaking research reveals that when cultural intelligence levels are low, diverse teams are unlikely to innovate as effectively as homogenous teams. But when cultural intelligence levels are high, diverse teams far outperform homogenous teams in coming up with innovative solutions.

## PART I: THE CLIMATE FOR CULTURALLY INTELLIGENT INNOVATION

Bringing together the seminal research on innovation, cultural intelligence, and social psychology, Part I explores the essential elements for creating a climate that promotes culturally intelligent innovation.

Your mind is your most powerful asset for innovation. See how consciously paying attention to innovation and the diverse perspectives around you primes you to come up with better, innovative solutions.

Learn how seeing from another point of view is a fascinating, critical part of developing innovative solutions that truly address the pain points of potential users.

Distraction and multitasking are the enemies of creativity. Discipline yourself to focus amidst the many possible distractions and challenges of pursuing innovation on a diverse team.

Discover how to take control of your space to help promote the right climate for innovation to thrive. Your surroundings are the incubator for developing and implementing new ideas with diverse colleagues.

Discover the five factors used to calculate trust and see how to build trust with diverse colleagues and clients as another essential part of creating a climate for culturally intelligent innovation.

## PART II: THE 5D PROCESS FOR CULTURALLY INTELLIGENT INNOVATION

Once you've created the ideal climate for culturally intelligent innovation, it's time to manage the process. The process for culturally intelligent innovation includes the steps covered in many innovation books, but Part II describes how to adjust those steps for a diversity of participants and users.

Learn the importance of creating a shared mental model for using diversity to create better, innovative outcomes. And gain leading practices for aligning diverse expectations on a team.

# DRIVEN BY DIFFERENCE

"**D**iversity leads to innovation!" That's the mantra repeated by many diversity proponents. I just heard it again a couple of weeks ago from a diversity guru who spoke before me at an international leadership conference in New York. It makes sense. Looking at a problem from a diversity of perspectives is likely to yield better solutions than viewing it solely from one myopic view. But this rose-colored view of diversity doesn't jive with reality. Just as two newlyweds quickly discover that vastly different perspectives on how to set up house don't necessarily lead to better results, the same is true for multicultural teams that are coalescing on a project.

I recently talked with a senior vice president from one of the largest global banks who told me his bank cut its diversity and inclusion budget by 90 percent because its leaders couldn't see any return on investment from their diversity efforts. A couple of months ago, a group of South African executives told me, "We're two decades post-apartheid and we've made very little progress in seeing better results from our incredibly diverse workforce." And many universities and governments around the world have abandoned affirmative action–type programs, suggesting it's time to move on.

Meanwhile, there's very limited diversity in many of the Silicon Valley companies lauded as examples of innovation. Jeffrey Sonnefeld of Yale University believes tech firms place a premium on young white males. He says, "It's sort of a throwback to an era we should be long past, which is the macho world of the giggling boys, with the hackers' sensibility that somehow we are living in a pure meritocratic world."[1] Google executive Nancy Lee agrees, at least in part. She admits that Google's workforce is predominantly white,

1

and 83 percent of its tech workers are male. Along with other Google executives, she is on a crusade to change that.[2]

Should tech firms, banks, and universities recruit a more diverse workforce simply because of pressure from stakeholders that it's the right thing to do? Or can a more compelling case be made for how a diverse workforce leads to greater innovation and success? Are there economic advantages to having a more diverse team, or is it simply a straw man argument?

There's no question that cultural diversity provides one of the greatest opportunities for global innovation. The potential is enormous. But it's a correlation, not causation. An organization that learns how to utilize the diverse perspectives from multicultural teams has a tremendous opportunity to come up with better solutions. In fact, when used strategically, diversity is one of the greatest resources for coming up with innovative solutions, which in turn leads to economic benefits. Learning the managerial steps for translating diversity into innovation is the primary objective of this book.

> **How can you utilize diverse perspectives to come up with better solutions? And what part of the innovation process needs to be adjusted to leverage diversity for better innovation?**

Those are the two primary questions this book will address.

Diversity by itself does not ensure innovation. Diversity combined with high cultural intelligence (CQ) does. Cultural intelligence is the capability to function effectively in culturally diverse situations. It's rooted in rigorous academic research conducted by scholars around the world. I've written much about the four capabilities required to work and lead with cultural intelligence.[3] But this book reflects the next stage in our research on cultural intelligence: implementing a culturally intelligent process to drive innovation. Getting diverse teams to function at the highest levels of productivity requires a leader and team members with high CQ and a plan for culturally intelligent innovation.

Chapter 1 introduces the core concepts behind a culturally intelligent approach to diversity and innovation, and it exposes many of the shortcomings of existing diversity paradigms. After that, the rest of the book is divided into two parts. Part I describes the *climate* needed for culturally intelligent innovation—both individually and for an organization as a whole. Part II describes the *process* for culturally intelligent innovation (see Figure X). The material in Part I stems from the research on cultural intelligence conducted by my colleagues and me, and from the seminal findings about creativity, innovation, and social psychology. Our research included surveys, interviews, and focus groups from every major industry, across 98 countries, and from more than 50,000 global professionals. That research informs the work I'm privileged to lead at the Cultural Intelligence Center, where we work with organizations and leaders around the world to help them assess and improve their work across cultures. The research on cultural intelligence reveals four capabilities consistently found in those individuals who can effectively work in culturally diverse situations. Given that I've written extensively about those four capabilities elsewhere, in this book I've simply provided a brief description of the cultural intelligence model and research in Appendix A. All four CQ capabilities (Drive, Knowledge, Strategy, and Action) are a part of culturally intelligent innovation, but the one that is most essential for creating a climate for culturally intelligent innovation is CQ Strategy—the degree to which you consciously address and use cultural differences to come up with better solutions. Many of the powerful ideas described throughout Part I—the power of perspective taking, freedom from distractions, the importance of trust—are relevant for any individual and team that is trying to innovate. But the more diversity on the team, the more important these practices are. Each chapter in Part I describes how to intentionally foster a climate that is conducive to generating and implementing better solutions for diverse groups. And each chapter ends with a brief "Climate Assessment," giving you a chance to evaluate your current climate for culturally intelligent innovation.

**Figure X: Culturally Intelligent Innovation**

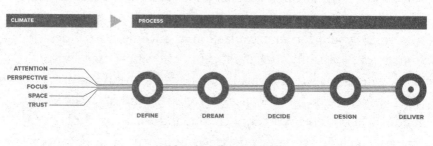

© Cultural Intelligence Center

Part II describes the *process* for culturally intelligent innovation. My bookshelves are overflowing with books on innovation, and nearly every magazine I read has articles on the topic. Do we really need one more book on the subject? Yes, because many of the current resources overlook the issues and opportunities that are relevant for innovation in a more global, diverse context. The innovation process described in Part II specifically addresses how the innovation process used by many leading companies needs to be adapted for culturally diverse situations. The material throughout this section combines our work in cultural intelligence with the world-renowned work of people like Clayton Christensen at Harvard Business School and the ideas and methods used at places like the d.school at Stanford University.

The first chapter in Part II is about how to align diverse expectations—the number one issue that derails most teams pursuing a new project (Chapter 7). Then we examine the specific challenges and opportunities of generating ideas from a diverse group (Chapter 8). Next, we look at how to select and pitch an idea in light of cultural differences (Chapter 9), at the implications of diversity on design and prototyping (Chapter 10), and finally, at a culturally intelligent way to implement better solutions (Chapter 11). Each chapter includes case studies and describes specific ways to approach the innovation process in light of cultural differences.

I don't view diversity primarily as a problem to be solved. Instead, I see it as a treasure trove, rich with innovative solutions waiting to be mined. When you see through another set of eyes, you gain the opportunity to see possibilities that you otherwise miss. The innovative potential of diversity is all over the place—but it's not automatic. It requires a deliberate, culturally intelligent process. And that's what we're going to tackle together in the pages that follow.

# CHAPTER 1

## DIVERSITY IS.

**A**mri Johnson, a senior executive at Novartis, is often asked what he thinks about the state of diversity in today's corporate environment. Amri laughs. "What do I *think* about diversity? Diversity is. That's it. It's not going away. It's here to stay and it's going to become more of an issue everywhere. *So what do we do about it? How do we optimize the opportunity?* That's the question I'm interested in discussing."[1]

Amri is right. These days, people are moving from everywhere to everywhere. First-generation immigrants are leaving Toronto for rural regions across Canada. Gay couples are moving into the suburbs. Chinese farmers are relocating to Australian suburbs, and Australian entrepreneurs are setting up agricultural businesses in China. Today, 36 percent of the U.S. workforce is made up of people of color, and by 2040, there will be no U.S. ethnic or racial majority. That reality is coming even more quickly to Canada. The shift is happening in more traditionally homogenous places like Denmark and Sweden as well. Similar trends exist most everywhere. And when you add the diversity of perspectives that come from one's gender, socioeconomic background, sexual orientation, profession, faith, and much more, indeed, "Diversity is." And there's no indication that the movement of people from everywhere to everywhere is going to lessen anytime soon.

If you wanted to visit the most culturally diverse country in the world, where would you go? India? The United States? Australia? The United Kingdom? Actually, you need to head to north central Africa, where Chad, the most culturally diverse country in the world, has 11.5 million people from more than 100 different ethnic groups. Erkan Gören from the University of Oldenberg in Germany studied the level of multicultural diversity in 180 countries. According to his data, the most culturally diverse countries in the world are Chad, Nigeria, the Democratic Republic of Congo, and a number of other African countries. The only Western country in the top 20 list is Canada. India is close behind, Mexico is just a bit further down, and the United States is in the middle of the list. The least diverse countries by Gören's measurements are Argentina, Haiti, Japan, and the Nordic countries.[2] The top 10 most culturally diverse cities in the world are less surprising: Dubai, Singapore, Hong Kong, Toronto, San Francisco, Sydney, Paris, Los Angeles, London, and New York.[3]

## The Diversity of Diversity

Diversity is sometimes used to broadly include any kind of difference, such as differences in personality, skills, working styles, tenure, and thinking. But if diversity includes everything, it ends up meaning nothing. On the other hand, diversity is more than just black versus white or German versus Chinese. Each of us is part of several different social groups, and there's incredible diversity within most countries.

Social categorization theory explains our human tendency to categorize people into "in-groups" and "out-groups." Subconsciously, we meet someone and within 10 seconds decide whether the person is "in" or "out." Think about how that influences the dynamics of a brainstorming session for a group tasked with developing an innovative solution! The way we determine who's in and who's out depends upon the context and the situation. For example, you might feel a loose sense of association with other people in your industry (e.g., teachers or engineers), with anyone who also works at your organization, or with someone who has the same disability as you. But for a group to truly have a "culture" of its own, it requires a shared pattern of beliefs, values, behaviors, customs, and attitudes.[4] Dutch psychologist Geert Hofstede says that culture is the collective programming of the mind that sets one society apart from another.[5] Therefore, in order to be a culture, there has to be a pattern of thinking and behavior that *distinguishes* it from other groups. Diversity is a way of describing any group that includes two or more cultures working and/or relating together.

That still leaves us with a very broad definition of diversity. Each of us is part of several different cultures, including our national origin, ethnicity, organizational and professional groups, gender, generation, sexual identity, socioeconomic status, religious beliefs . . . and the list continues. National culture is the cultural difference that most strongly shapes most people's behavior, though that's not as true in a place as diverse as Chad or in a newly formed republic where geopolitical boundaries have little to do with one's identity.

What culture most strongly influences the way you think and behave? It depends upon what you're doing, where you are, and who else is there. For example, many Indians working in Silicon Valley report that their workplace habits and preferences resemble North American norms, but when they go home at night, they behave in more "Indian" ways. Or think of it like this: You might not identify very closely with your hometown until you're away from it and meet someone who is also from the same town. Then suddenly that part of your cultural identity becomes relevant.

## Regional Perspectives on Diversity

A study conducted by the Economist Intelligence Unit found that executives across different regions of the world look at diversity differently. Gender and age were seen as the top diversity issues challenging workplaces in the Asia-Pacific region, and ethnic and religious differences were seen as the top challenges in the Middle

East and Europe. (See Table 1-1 for the top challenges identified by executives across five major regions of the world when talking about a diverse workforce.) This study examined what executives *perceived* as being the forms of diversity that were most challenging. Their perceptions may not be accurate. For example, even though Middle Eastern executives (mostly men!) didn't identify gender as a leading challenge, other studies suggest it should be one of their top concerns. But it's important to be aware of what executives from various regions perceive to be the most relevant challenges facing them.

### Table 1-1 Top Diversity Challenges by Region

|  | Ethnicity | Gender | Age | Religion | Language |
|---|---|---|---|---|---|
| **Asia-Pacific** |  | ✔ | ✔ |  |  |
| **Europe and Middle East** | ✔ |  |  | ✔ |  |
| **Latin America** |  |  |  |  | ✔ |
| **North America** |  |  | ✔ |  |  |
| **Sub-Saharan Africa** |  |  |  | ✔ | ✔ |

SOURCE: Based on data reported in Economist Intelligence Unit, *Values-Based Diversity: The Challenges and Strengths of Many* (London: Economist Intelligence Unit, January 23, 2014). http://www.economistinsights.com/sites/default/files/EIU_SuccessFactors_Values-based%20diversity%20report.pdf.

## What Kind of Diversity Matters Most

There are two kinds of diversity that most typically influence workplace behavior: visible diversity and underrepresented groups. The first one, visible diversity, refers to those differences that can immediately be observed when looking at someone. This includes differences that stem from ethnicity, gender, age, physical disabilities, and sometimes religion (such as a woman wearing a head covering). It's very difficult to disguise these cultural differences and as a result, they immediately influence the snap judgments made by others.

The second form of diversity that is most relevant for workplace contexts is any person from a culture that is underrepresented in the group, something Rosabeth Moss Kanter calls tokenism. Tokens are members of a subgroup who represent less than 15 percent of the whole group, and the disproportionate representation skews the ways they're perceived.[6] Being the only Southerner on a team of Northerners, the only marketer on a team of engineers, or the only "foreigner" in a department highlights cultural differences that might otherwise be overlooked. Many individuals reflect both forms of diversity, such as being the only person of color on a team and thereby being both visibly different and one of the underrepresented team members. But underrepresentation is also a factor for people with cultural differences that aren't as visible, such as having a particular sexual orientation, ideology, socioeconomic status, or level of tenure that deviates from the dominant norm in a group. An underrepresented group could also be a majority group that has limited power and voice, such as what black South Africans experienced for many years. In addition, underrepresentation is context-specific. Men are underrepresented among HR professionals, for example, and women are underrepresented among engineers. Each organization and team needs to consider what groups are underrepresented in their contexts.

For the purposes of this book, diversity refers primarily to those who are visibly diverse and/or underrepresented. You can rightfully apply the principles of the book to other differences as well, such as the diversity of thought or the diversity of experiences or skills. But visible diversity and underrepresentation have the most potential to create conflict and opportunity for developing innovative solutions.[7]

## WHAT KIND OF DIVERSITY MATTERS MOST?

1. Visible Diversity

2. Underrepresentation (Tokenism)

---

What ultimately matters is not the source of diversity but the different values and perspectives that emerge from it. The more diversity you have within an organization, the more ideas there are for how things *should* be done. Many intercultural training programs focus on the superficial manifestations of cultural differences such as how to exchange business cards or appropriate gift giving. *But the differences that most strongly influence innovation are the varied approaches for communicating, planning, and executing tasks. How do you align the values, expectations, and work styles of four generations, dozens of nationalities, and endless subcultures toward a universal vision and strategy for the organization?*[8] Answering that question is at the crux of our work on cultural intelligence because our interest has been to improve effectiveness working across cultural differences. And it's central to the purpose of this book—using different cultural perspectives to drive innovation. Cultural intelligence allows individuals to adapt their motivations, work ethic, and communication styles while learning from the different value perspectives to create better solutions.

Consider the diversity of generations in the workplace as an example of how competing values play out. This is the first time in history that four generations are working together, and a fifth one—Generation Z—is entering the mix. Many executives are working hard to attract high-performing young leaders. Upon recruiting them, they try to motivate Millennials with money, status, stability, and other things that may be entirely missing the values that drive them. As a whole, Millennials are less likely to value money for security and status and more likely to value it because it provides the resources they need to pursue their dreams. Many organizations miss this crucial point. Many executives got where they are by placing a high value on money and promotions, so they assume that's the way to do business with Millennials. When Millennials don't bite, the executives presume that means the younger workforce is entitled and unmotivated. But as Bill McLawhon, head of leadership development at Facebook, said to me:

> As a 56-year-old guy, I went through a period where I looked at these young kids and thought, "Wait until you get your butt kicked out in the real world." But I quickly realized this *is* the real world. And they're making it their own. This is the future of work. It doesn't look much like the world of work where I started. But I'm completely awed by the high-performing individuals I get to coach every day, most of whom are young enough to be my kids.[9]

Hiring a diversity of age groups is a start. But if you don't utilize the diverse perspectives of different age groups and instead try to mold them into all of your values, not only will you lose them but you will also lose their insights on what connects with consumers who share values with them.

Most of the research on the value differences across generations is biased toward Millennials from North America; however, generational differences are found in other parts of the world as well. The Asia-Pacific region is where generational differences have created some of the most conflict in the workplace because the area has a long history of centralized control in which flexible work structures and accommodating individualized preferences goes against the grain. Most Millennials in places like India, Taiwan, and Malaysia still have a strong measure of collectivism and filial piety—a loyalty to one's in-group and a sense of responsibility to defer to one's father or elders. But that orientation is tempered by the values these young people have for self-expression and flex-ibility.[10] Whenever you have multiple layers of cultural differences in one individual—such as a Millennial from Japan working in a U.S. company and reporting to an American baby boomer, there's all the more potential for value collisions.

Whether diversity is visible or not, what matters most are the vastly different values and perspectives that emerge from cultural differences. Culturally intelligent innovation begins with reflecting on and mapping the value differences that exist across your team. But before we can jump into describing effective ways to leverage those differences, we need to discuss some of the insufficient at-tempts that have permeated this discussion over the last 20 years.

## Diversity Fatigue

The other day I was working out at the gym and I overheard a guy say to his buddy, "So tomorrow I have to go to a diversity training workshop." "Oh God!" the other guy said. "That's right up there with getting a root canal!" to which his friend responded, "I don't mind diverse people as long as they agree with me!"

Many employees and executives have "diversity fatigue"—they've done the diversity thing and they're ready to move on. There's a lot of great work that has been done by diversity and inclusion professionals around the world, but something has to change in how we address this vital area of concern.

### Shame on You!

Employees sometimes walk away from diversity programs having heard one more shaming diatribe about racism or sexism, which they then shrug off as they struggle to see the relevance to their daily routines. Others leave diversity programs overly paranoid of saying something offensive, so instead of having real conversations with diverse colleagues, they walk on eggshells lest they be guilty of the kind of discriminatory behavior they heard described in their recent workshop. Shame and an emphasis upon punitive measures for not embracing diversity are too prevalent in many conversations about this topic. What's more, they rarely bring about lasting change.

One time, I was speaking to a group of U.S. real estate agents. Afterward, an older Caucasian woman walked up to me and asked, with a hushed voice, "Are you familiar with this group at the local university that brings together nonwhite, um, no, I mean, minority . . . No, that's not right either. I meant to say foreigners. Oh! Never mind! I don't know how I'm supposed to talk anymore. . . . " I assured her, "It's okay. I know what you're trying to say."

People are often scared to even enter the conversation about different cultures for fear they'll say something racist. Mind you, this woman had just listened to one of the other speakers at the real estate conference berate the agents for their consistent use of offensive, discriminatory language, including *walk-in-closets* ("How do you think that makes a disabled person feel?" he asked.) and *master bedrooms* ("Do you know how that sounds if your ancestors were slaves?"). Using appropriate language is a start, but it's far from what is really needed to build culturally intelligent relationships. We have to find ways to address the difficult, sensitive issues surrounding cultural differences without becoming paralyzed and failing to engage in the conversation.

## Representation and Compliance

Another thing many organizations do when addressing diversity is ensure they have diverse representation across leadership and staff. It's hard to imagine being a relevant organization today if people go to your website and staff listings and see only people from one ethnicity, gender, or age group; and compliance with legal guidelines for diversity is essential. But is hiring a representative team the best way to drive culturally intelligent innovation?

Once, I was in a meeting at the university where I taught, sitting next to my friend and colleague Christy. Christy was a vice president at the university and one of the most vocal women on campus regarding the importance of equal opportunities for female faculty, staff, and students. As the meeting got started, the guy chairing the group jokingly said to her, "I'm sure you'd love to take the minutes for us, wouldn't you, Christy?" He continued to make chauvinistic references throughout the meeting. I was waiting for Christy to level him, but she didn't. Instead, she engaged in the meeting in light of her responsibilities as a vice president, and she said nothing about the pats on her shoulder, the soccer mom jokes, and the chides about how she probably didn't get the sports analogies he was using. As we left the meeting, I said, "Christy! I can't believe you took that. Why didn't you say something?" She looked at me and said, "Because I was hoping you would speak up!"

Ouch! I could feel my face immediately go flush. I knew she was right. Everyone expects women like Christy to advocate for women, and people of color are expected to speak up on behalf of other underrepresented groups. But it's not enough to simply have women like Christy on the team. *Everyone* needs to own the value of building a culturally intelligent climate. It's not that Christy needed me to speak for her. It's that I could have voiced why the chair's behavior was unacceptable to *me!*

Intentionally hiring a diverse staff is a critical step in becoming a more culturally intelligent organization. But making the most of that diversity requires a commitment from everyone to utilize the differences effectively.

## Cultural Awareness Training

Another strategy typically employed to address diversity and inclusion is cultural awareness training. This kind of training usually emphasizes becoming more aware of one's own cultural background and understanding other cultures. Self-awareness is a critical step in the process of creating a culturally intelligent team. There's little hope that you can develop the skills to work effectively across cultures if you don't first have an awareness of how culture shapes your own thinking and behavior. One of the most effective ways to promote self-awareness is through the world-renowned work on unconscious bias—exposing ways we unwittingly favor certain types of people based upon our upbringing, experiences, and values. But self-awareness is not enough. The inevitable question after this kind of training is "Now what?" In other words, I know I'm biased and so is everyone else. What am I supposed to do about it?[11]

The other emphasis of most cultural awareness training programs is learning the basic stereotypes about large cultural groups. There's a place for understanding the cultural norms that are generally true of people from a particular context. However, these kinds of stereotypes have to be held very loosely. Let's assume you're being taught how to work effectively with Indians. But can you really generalize norms for more than 1 billion people? And do these norms apply equally to an Indian born and raised in Toronto, one who lives her entire life in Mumbai, and yet another who is from Delhi but working in Dubai?

None of us can be reduced to a single storyline. Our lives are far more multilayered than that. I'm an American, but my parents are Canadian. I have a Ph.D. I'm white. I'm a dad. I'm a Christian. Any one of those labels carries with it all sorts of connotations. But only as you and I get to know each other can we really understand how we've each been shaped by the varied cultures of which we're part. No one storyline defines you or me. One of the fundamental problems with most intercultural training is that it cannot substitute for direct knowledge from interpersonal interactions because cultural values alone are not a strongly predictive feature of human behavior.

## Kumbuya

Finally, many people grow fatigued from the diversity conversation because they perceive it as little more than a soft, touchy-feely topic filled with artificial Kumbuya moments focused on everyone getting along.[12] As with all these incomplete approaches to cultural diversity, there's an aspect of this emphasis that's critical. Cultural intelligence has to be rooted in something more transcendent than learning about other cultures to manipulate them. And respect and understanding are essential in the process of culturally intelligent innovation. But I understand why many leaders struggle to justify investing in diversity initiatives if they're simply framed as "do-good" programs and don't directly tie to the organization's strategic mission.

The Kumbuya approach is all about the "conversation" and helping people listen to each other. Intercultural dialogue and discussion certainly has a place. I was reared in a staunchly religious, fundamentalist subculture, and the first step in my seeing the world more broadly came from talking with people from different religions and backgrounds. I found that these people weren't as suspect as I had imagined them to be and discovered we had a great deal in common. But over time, I needed more than just conversation with my "Other" to sustain my growth and development in cultural intelligence.

I've grown increasingly fatigued and bored by unending conversation that doesn't lead to action. We need to move beyond politically correct, culturally sensitive agendas that minimize debate and overemphasize common ground. And we need to move toward action-oriented, robust discussions that lean as much into our differences as our similarities, for therein may lie our greatest insights for innovation and action.

## Diversity × CQ = Innovation

Diversity is here to stay. And it's going to continue to shape the way you operate internally and externally. Diversity by itself does not lead to better innovations. And many of the predominant diversity approaches miss the mark. But cultural intelligence is what makes the difference. The cultural intelligence of the individuals on a diverse team determines whether the team's diversity promotes or deters innovation. When you're involved in a situation characterized by cultural diversity, your CQ is the multiplying force that predicts whether you experience positive or negative benefits from diversity. Those with high CQ can manage the differences to come up with better solutions, while those with low CQ are continually frustrated when working with diverse colleagues and customers.

The top two reasons organizations need culturally intelligent personnel are the growing realities of increasingly diverse markets and the growing diversity among members of the workforce. For most organizations, the greatest opportunities for growth exist in expanding across a diversity of markets at home and abroad. Fortune 500 companies expect the greatest revenue streams over the next decade to come from emerging markets, and top universities are recruiting students from around the world and from groups previously underrepresented on their campuses. One of the best ways to effectively reach these diverse markets is through a diverse workforce. The convergence of consumer diversity with workplace diversity is the nexus of the greatest challenges and opportunities for a culturally intelligent approach.

## TOP TWO REASONS CULTURAL
## INTELLIGENCE IS NEEDED

1. Diverse Markets

2. Diverse Workforce

The convergence of consumer diversity with workplace diversity is the nexus of the greatest opportunities and challenges for a culturally intelligent approach to innovation.

How do you ensure that diversity leads to innovation and improved solutions rather than gridlock and inferior results? And how should you address this when there's already a significant level of diversity fatigue on the part of many in the workforce? Diverse teams *can* come up with far more innovative solutions than homogenous teams, but it's not automatic. The key lies in *minimizing the interpersonal conflict* from diverse groups and *maximizing the informational diversity* that exists in the varied perspectives and values.[13] This is what gave birth to our work in cultural intelligence at the Cultural Intelligence Center. We encountered leaders who had extensive understanding about different cultures but still couldn't effectively develop a plan for leading a culturally diverse team. We observed teams that were aware of their internal biases but still couldn't work together productively. And we saw organizations that successfully hired a more diverse population but found themselves stuck in gridlock. Cultural intelligence addresses these shortcomings by providing a more sophisticated approach for working across cultures.

Cultural intelligence, or CQ, is the capability to relate and work effectively in culturally diverse situations. Our research on cultural intelligence finds that the culturally intelligent have developed skills in four capabilities. The four capabilities (see Figure 1-1) are:

1. *CQ Drive (Motivation):* Having the interest, confidence, and drive to adapt cross-culturally

2. *CQ Knowledge (Cognition):* Understanding intercultural norms and differences

3. *CQ Strategy (Metacognition):* Making sense of culturally diverse experiences and planning accordingly

4. *CQ Action (Behavioral):* Changing verbal and nonverbal actions appropriately when interacting cross-culturally

**Figure 1-1 Four CQ Capabilities**

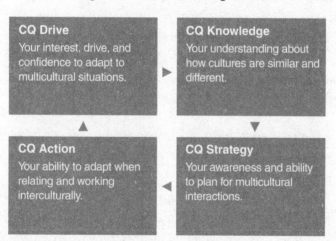

The research proves that all people can improve their CQ, and there are several promising results predicted by higher levels of CQ. (See Appendix A for additional information on assessing and developing the four capabilities of cultural intelligence.)

## ROI of High CQ for Individuals

Your CQ predicts how you will perform when working in culturally diverse situations—whether living or traveling internationally, working on a project with culturally diverse colleagues or customers, or working across two different organizational cultures. Meanwhile, 90 percent of leading executives from 68 countries identify cross-cultural skills as one of the most important capabilities needed in remaining competitive.[14] Therefore, the higher your CQ, the more likely you will outperform others, gain new opportunities, earn higher wages, and experience success working in the diverse, globalized context.

## ROI of High CQ for Organizations

The most important ROI for organizations with culturally intelligent individuals is that companies are more likely to accomplish their mission in culturally diverse situations. When CQ levels are low, diverse teams *underperform* homogenous teams. But when CQ levels are high, diverse teams *outperform* homogenous teams on several measurements—productivity, employee engagement, profitability, innovation, etc. More specifically, organizations that have employees with high CQ can expect:

- *Expansion into culturally diverse markets (global or domestic):* Adapting local delivery of products and services to diverse markets
- *High-quality service to culturally diverse customers, patients, or students:* Anticipating how to best serve culturally diverse customers and respond appropriately when mistakes and misunderstandings occur
- *Speed and efficiency:* Closing deals and accomplishing results effectively and efficiently in culturally diverse contexts
- *Productive global assignments:* Successful and sustainable international assignments
- *Becoming an employer of choice:* Attract and retain global talent when cultural intelligence is valued and modeled throughout the organization

- *Profitability and cost savings*: High-quality results and bottom-line performance when employees have high CQ
- *Multicultural team effectiveness*: Effective communication and performance as a diverse team.[15]

One of the ways we've examined the connection between diversity, CQ, and innovation is by looking at how diversity and CQ influence the degree to which individuals speak up on culturally diverse teams. Speaking up to express one's ideas and opinions is a critical part of the innovation process. But it's an exercise fraught with risk. A couple of my colleagues conducted research on how CQ influences whether a diverse team member speaks up. In one study, data were collected from 303 students attending an Asian university. All of the students were placed on teams that were assigned a complex, three-month project that represented a significant portion of their course grade. Some of the teams were made up of students from nationally diverse backgrounds, and other teams had students who were all from the same nationality. Students with low CQ were less likely to speak up if they were on one of the diverse teams as compared to if they were on a homogenous team. However, the students with high CQ spoke up as much or more on a diverse team as they did on a homogenous one. Their CQ attenuated the potential risks of voicing their input among a group of culturally diverse peers. As a result, the diverse teams that had students with higher levels of CQ came up with the more creative approaches to their group assignments.

The study was replicated by examining 205 supervisor-subordinate relationships across 41 offices of a multinational organization headquartered in Europe. The effects were similar to the study with the students. Subordinates with low CQ who reported to supervisors from a different cultural background were less likely to speak up and offer their ideas to their supervisor. But subordinates with high CQ consistently offered their input regardless of the cultural differences.[16]

Thus, high CQ predicts the degree to which individuals speak up in culturally diverse situations. In addition, individuals with high CQ are more likely to overcome the interpersonal challenges and anxieties created by cultural diversity. They build trust and engage in risk-taking behaviors such as voicing contrary opinions, and they do so in ways that are nonthreatening to others. We'll explore this critical finding further in Chapter 8 when we look at how to effectively generate ideas from a culturally diverse group.

The research on the potential benefits of diversity continues to grow. A growing body of evidence supports the idea that organizations that learn how to effectively obtain the ideas and input of a diverse workforce outpace those that are solely operating from a monolithic perspective.[17] Google's internal employment survey found that teams that were both diverse and inclusive were also the best at innovation. Sara Ellison, an economics researcher from MIT, conducted a study that demonstrated the improved business results that can come from teams with greater gender balance. The teams that had both genders equally represented and equipped participants to intentionally utilize the gender differences came up with more creative solutions than teams dominated by one gender. One professional service firm saw its revenue increase by 41 percent when it developed a plan to form teams with equal numbers of men and women and equipped them to utilize the value of their different perspectives.[18]

Jack Ma, the founder of Alibaba, says, "One of the secret sauces for Alibaba's success is that we have a lot of women."[19] Women hold 47 percent of all jobs at Alibaba and 33 percent of all senior positions—a stark contrast to what typically happens in tech firms. Women bring new knowledge, skills, and networks to the table and take fewer unnecessary risks. But the key lies in whether their female perspectives are effectively utilized with cultural intelligence.

Even following a diversity of people on Twitter has been proven to yield more innovative ideas than only following people who are similar to you.[20]

Novartis, the Swiss pharmaceutical giant, combines its commitment to cultural intelligence with utilizing multicultural employee resource groups to provide market research for launching new brands. The cultural perspectives offered by the staff provide a built-in resource that offers better findings than traditional market research findings and for virtually no cost. The research indicates that when a culturally intelligent team has at least one member who comes from the same cultural background as a targeted end user, the entire team better understands that user. In fact, one study found that a team with a member who shares a client's ethnicity is 152 percent more likely to understand that client than a team without someone from that background.[21] And because cultural intelligence is a multiplying force, the more cultural diversity and the higher the CQ among the team members, the greater the innovative potential. Novartis estimates that it has saved millions of dollars by using its built-in diversity while simultaneously using its culturally intelligent, multicultural teams to provide innovative solutions that improve and save people's lives.

The greater the diversity on your team, the more likely you can uncover potential problems and come up with creative solutions. True, it's a process that comes more slowly, and it's often much more difficult. When everyone sees things the same, there's an ease with which people can relate, work, and openly share their thoughts. Most teams find it more enjoyable, and it's more efficient in the short run. But that's a shortsighted view. When diverse teams draw upon their differences with cultural intelligence, it leads to better results. And with time, it's far more rewarding because you get to see the world in much more colorful ways.

## Conclusion

Diversity is. The convergence of consumer diversity with workplace diversity is the nexus of the greatest challenges and opportunities related to innovation. Homogenous teams outperform diverse teams when CQ levels are low. But when team members have high CQ, diverse teams are more innovative and productive than homogenous teams are.

I promise you more than empty platitudes about the benefits of diversity. Instead, we're going to look at empirical findings and best practices from leaders and organizations around the world that are tapping into the opportunities of culturally intelligent innovation. We'll begin with the essential elements for building a climate for culturally intelligent innovation; then we'll walk through the process for driving culturally intelligent innovation.

Managing diversity is a long-term game. Nancy Lee, Google's diversity chief, acknowledges how far her company has to go to change its white, male-dominated workforce. But she and her colleagues are committed to it. She says, "To succeed in business today, you need ideas coming from every perspective and background. Period."[22]

### DIVERSITY × CQ = INNOVATION

The cultural intelligence of the individuals on a diverse team determines whether the team's diversity promotes or deters innovation. Improve CQ to gain the benefits of diversity.

# Part I

The Climate for Culturally Intelligent Innovation

Innovation begins by looking at a problem from as many perspectives as possible. And diversity is the best way to do that. Bringing together the seminal research on innovation, cultural intelligence, and social psychology, Part I explores the essential elements for building a climate that promotes culturally intelligent innovation. These ideas are powerful for individuals and teams alike, and they're useful for anyone who is trying to be innovative. But these factors are particularly relevant when you want to leverage diversity to drive innovation. The climate for culturally intelligent innovation includes five powerful elements (see Figure I-1):

- Attention (Chapter 2)
- Perspective-Taking (Chapter 3)
- Focus (Chapter 4)
- Space (Chapter 5)
- Trust (Chapter 6)

**Figure I-1: Culturally Intelligent Innovation I Climate**

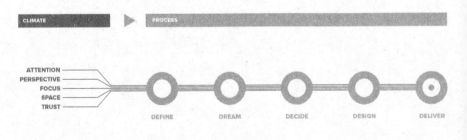

© Cultural Intelligence Center

# CHAPTER 2

........................................................................

## THE POWER OF ATTENTION

I f you buy a silver Honda, you start seeing silver Hondas everywhere. It's not that there really are any more silver Hondas on the road, but this simple reality demonstrates the power of the mind to more readily notice whatever you've been thinking about most. And the more you think about innovation, the more you'll do it.

Ellen Langer, a Harvard professor of psychology, demonstrated the power of attention by convening a group of 70-year-old men for a week. She put them in an environment that recreated life from 20 years prior, complete with 20-year-old magazines, music, and newspapers. After a week of this 20-year retro experience, the men grew visibly younger—not only in their attitudes and conversation but physically. Their medical exams showed that they stood straighter and were more flexible. Even their fingers, which typically grow shorter with age, grew longer.[1] There's tremendous power in what we pay attention to and what we don't. You can't force yourself or anyone else to have eureka moments. But the degree to which you *consciously* explore creative solutions is directly tied to the probability of producing innovative results.

The first critical element for building a climate for culturally intelligent innovation is paying attention to diversity and innovation. The amount you think about innovation is partially dependent upon your cultural upbringing and your organizational context. But before we explore that, let's redefine this word that appears everywhere nowadays: *innovation*.

## Redefining Innovation

For many, innovation equals mind-boggling inventions like space travel and the next iPhone. These kinds of innovations have a definite wow factor. But oftentimes, the most significant innovations are small, incremental changes that improve people's lives and create more efficient processes for getting work done. Innovation is creating something that is new and useful.[2]

IT programmers who collaborate to create a more user-friendly interface, teachers who work together to integrate students' personal interests with learning curricula, and administrative assistants who streamline communication among team members can make a world of difference, one small innovation at a time. These are the kinds of ideas and solutions, big and small, I'm after in this book—culturally intelligent innovation that leads to measurable change in the world. Some of the innovations that emerge may lead to big, audacious solutions like curing cancer and traveling to Mars. Most, however, will be small changes with real impact upon individuals and organizations across the world. These include *product innovations* like new gadgets, drugs, and apps. And they include *process innovations* like changing the way you do strategic planning, learning new ways to manage communication flows, and finding alternative ways to market ideas and solutions.

Culturally intelligent innovation is leveraging the power of a diverse team to meet the needs of an increasingly diverse population of users. The greater the diversity in a group, the higher its capacity to find problems and offer innovative solutions before someone outside the team does so first. Culturally intelligent innovation helped a diverse team of airline professionals work together to provide e-ticketing, a green innovation we all enjoy that required buy-in from companies as diverse as Lufthansa, Ethiopian Airlines, and Air China. But they did it, and the days of fretting about whether you've lost your ticket are over. This is a case study examined more thoroughly in Chapter 9. Swedish icon IKEA tapped its diverse team to help adapt store displays and furniture offerings for Hispanic customers who weren't interested in the neutral tones and small eating spaces that were typical of IKEA's design. And Procter & Gamble, consistently named one of the 50 top companies for diversity, also receives consistent recognition for having a highly innovative pipeline for household products. Innovative ways of working together across P&G's global enterprise are directly tied to the company's constant stream of new products.

## Think About Innovation!

You innovate to the degree you *consciously* think about innovation. This is the power of attention. Your experience of any situation or event largely depends upon what you choose to pay attention to or ignore. It's a physiological fact. Your life has largely been fashioned by what you've paid attention to and what you haven't. If you paid attention to other things, your reality and life would be very different.[3] And a great deal of research supports that we become what we practice. If you develop patterns of being mean and nasty, you will get meaner and nastier. If you practice being kind and caring, you will get kinder and more caring.[4] The same is true for an organization. The behaviors and respective priorities of a company or university shape what it does and how it operates. Our individual and organizational personalities become a composite of the things that grab our attention. The question is—when we're bombarded with endless stimuli, projects, and priorities vying for our attention—how do we choose where to direct our attention? And to what degree is developing new ideas, products, and services for diverse users a consistent part of what we think about? When we get stuck, is our default mode to give up or to persevere until we find a creative solution?

If you still aren't convinced of the power of attention, how does your back feel right now? That information was available to you all the time you were reading the previous paragraphs, but it's only when it's brought to your attention that you bring it up to the level of awareness. When you're driving and you become engrossed in the news on the radio or in a conversation, you become less aware of the scenery. You've turned down the sight dial in your brain so that you can allow the auditory inputs to capture your attention.

According to something psychologists call negative bias theory, you pay more attention to unpleasant feelings such as fear, anger, or the annoyance of a bad driver than to positive emotions be-cause the negative ones are more powerful.[5] Negative bias theory has enormous implications for a culturally diverse team. Imagine a team meeting that includes a working lunch. Because we're social-ized to eat in a certain way, watching someone eat in a different way can be jarring and strike us as rude or even barbaric. If you've learned that good manners include closing your mouth when you eat or breaking off small pieces of a roll rather than picking up the whole thing, seeing someone deviate from those norms immedi-ately surfaces on your attention. But when people eat the way we expect them to eat, their behavior largely goes unnoticed. You're unlikely to notice when someone eats "politely" but you most definitely notice when they don't. Good manners, respect, and appropriate professional behavior are culturally bound. Beware of too quickly assuming that someone isn't acting professional or demonstrating confidence. Similarly, we're less likely to notice a colleague's cultural differences when things are going well. He's just John or Jose when you're working without any conflict. But when something negative occurs, the first impulse is to view John or Jose in light of his culture. Suddenly, the thinking becomes: *You just can't trust people from that culture because they end up letting you down.* Giving undue attention to negative feelings shrinks your world and your breadth of perspective. Focus on the positive and you'll expand your view. This is the power of attention.[6]

## Culture Shapes Your Attention

How does culture influence where you direct your attention? Notice the similarity of preferences across your community. Most people drive cars similar to those driven by other people in their neighborhood or social groups. We decorate our yards and homes like our neighbors and friends do because we become socialized to accommodate the trends we encounter most often. We take vacations in similar places as friends, dress like others in our professional context, and most of us view academic achievement consistently with how our culture views it. For example, Asians are positively stereotyped as being smart, even though there's no conclusive evidence that the genetics of Chinese or Indian students makes them any more academically proficient than students from other cultural backgrounds. But many of the dominant Asian cultures place incredible expectations upon children to exceed academically as a way to bring honor to the family and succeed. As a result, because of the different level of attention placed upon academic proficiency in their homes and communities, a Chinese-American student with an IQ of 100 may achieve what a Caucasian-American student with an IQ of 120 achieves.[7]

How does your organizational culture shape your attention? When I walk across Facebook's sun-drenched campus in Menlo Park, California, I immediately pick up on an implicit message that people here are having fun while working hard. There are bowls overflowing with free candy and refrigerators full of Diet Coke. People are riding longboards from one building to the next, stopping in at the yoga studio and woodshop to relieve stress for an hour, or sitting at picnic tables with their laptops open. HACK is spelled out so large in the cement across the courtyard that you can read it from Google Earth. You get the idea that Facebook is a place where everyone is working at 100 percent capacity and having a whole lot of fun doing it. The environment is built to reduce the distractions of running off-site for lunch. Why leave campus when Mark Zuckerberg's favorite sushi and Mexican restaurants are right on-site? And there's no need to go to yoga before or after work when you can do it on campus with others who are just as ambitious as you are about coding something and getting it out to a billion people with the strike of a key.

In contrast, I pick up very different cues walking through the maze of corridors, offices, and desks in Tokyo at NTT, the largest telecommunications company in the world. There's a quiet, library-like atmosphere in the mammoth rooms where hundreds of people work fastidiously at their desks. The elevators have signs reminding people not to discuss business while moving from one place to the next lest an outsider overhear confidential information. And the lunchroom is a minimalist, functional space overlooking the sprawling city of Tokyo, where people talk quietly together eating traditional Japanese food. The environment at NTT effectively suits the Japanese culture and displays the high regard for minimalism and concentration that works well in the Japanese context. As a result, it's conducive for directing attention toward creativity. Your work environment shapes what you think about and how you behave.[8]

## Everyone Needs to Pay Attention to Innovation

When Luca de Meo, chief marketing officer at Volkswagen, was hired to transform the fragmented marketing unit at VW into an innovation powerhouse, he saw that innovation was the holy domain owned by VW engineers. De Meo believed marketers needed to be just as conscious about innovation as engineers, but the marketers weren't accustomed to that way of thinking. In their minds, the real innovators were the engineers and R&D people. De Meo worked relentlessly to get VW marketers to see that Volkswagen could never accomplish its vision to be the number one automaker in 10 years without marketers owning a key part of the innovative process. He told them, "Brand is not fluff. There is very concrete evidence of what great brands do. It's real business, not just magic."[9] He convinced them that VW's marketing approaches needed just as much innovation as the engineering behind the cars did.

With time, VW marketers began challenging other departments across the company to think and work innovatively. One of the programs that emerged was "Think Blue," a company-wide manifesto for environmental sustainability. Soon, all the employees across VW's 40 countries were working on their own Think Blue projects. De Meo knew that his role as chief marketing officer meant more than just ad campaigns and branding sessions. He needed to get everyone across the company paying attention to innovation, which in turn would support marketing VW.[10]

Don't underestimate the power of the mind. Simply getting a team *thinking* about innovation is the first step toward driving culturally intelligent innovation. The mere attention you're giving innovation by reading this book is the first step in creating a climate conducive to culturally intelligent innovation.

## Priming Your Subconscious for Innovation

Companies have long used the power of attention by priming customers' subconscious. Priming is the process of presenting a particular stimulus to make us feel and act in a certain way.[11] Few experiences better illustrate the power of priming than a trip to the supermarket. In many supermarkets around the world, "freshly cut" flowers are the first thing you see, priming you to think of freshness from the moment you enter the store, even if it's the middle of winter. Next, you see colorful fruits and vegetables, many of which have been carefully manipulated to get you to buy them. Dole, for example, issues a banana guide to grocers, illustrating the sales potential for bananas based upon their color. Vibrant yellow bananas are less likely to sell than bananas that are one tone of yellow warmer, because the latter are perceived to be riper and fresher. And for years now, supermarkets have been using a trend that started in Denmark—regularly sprinkling select vegetables with drops of water, which triggers a sense of freshness and purity. But our eyes are playing tricks on us. The dewy mist makes the vegetables rot more quickly than they would otherwise.[12]

So how does priming influence the way we work with culturally diverse colleagues and customers? Well, what if the following individual was joining your team: a 67-year-old woman, wearing a headscarf, who speaks English with a thick Russian accent? Any number of those descriptions—her age, gender, appearance, or nationality—triggers all kinds of responses in you. You might be indifferent to some of them, but you undoubtedly have some implicit assumptions about her, compared to, say, a 37-year-old blonde-haired woman who speaks English with a British accent. We all have implicit assumptions about certain cultures. And those preferences profoundly influence the way we engage in the innovative process. We're all biased, and we need bias to survive. It's the way our brains are wired to alert us to danger. But whether we act upon a bias is another thing altogether.

Left unchecked, unconscious biases are detrimental to leading effectively in the 21st century—whether it's hiring, marketing, or strategic planning. So companies, governments, and universities are investing millions of dollars in teaching staff about the implicit preferences they have for certain groups of people. In 2013, more than 13,000 of Google's 46,000 employees attended unconscious bias training to expose them to ways they unwittingly favor certain types of people based upon their upbringing, experiences, and values. Dow Chemical, PricewaterhouseCoopers, and Novartis are also seeing this as one of the most important ways to equip their increasingly diverse workforces; governments and military forces have jumped on the bandwagon too. Awareness of one's own culture and the potential biases one may have toward others is the first step toward improving your effectiveness with diverse colleagues and customers.

Take something as seemingly irrelevant as someone's accent. Two in five Americans associate a Southern accent with being uneducated. And it's not just the Northerners who think so. In one study, nine- and ten-year-old kids from Tennessee said people with Northern accents sounded "smarter" and more "in charge" than those with Southern drawls. Kentucky native Jim Rogers, the former CEO of Duke Energy, felt like an outsider at the start of his career. He says, "When I went to Washington to be a lawyer, I felt like I had to work harder, be better, and prove myself because I had a Southern accent and came from a rural state."[13] A similar innate bias toward accents exists in most places around the world where one regional accent is considered more sophisticated and intellectual than another one.[14]

One of the strongest biases found among Americans is a negative bias toward working with older people. On the whole, Americans view the elderly as rather benign and appealing, perhaps like kind, patient grandparents. But 80 percent of Americans surveyed demonstrated an implicit preference for working with someone young rather than someone who is older.[15] In many parts of the world, this is directly opposite. One of the first times I spoke at an event in Japan, the only question that came up during the Q&A was "How old are you?" The interpreter explained to me that my youthfulness caused the audience to question my credibility. Americans don't shout "Hurray for the young. Down with the old!" nor do Japanese say "Down with the young. Hurray for the old!" But these implicit assumptions strongly influence how people think and relate.

We need to discipline ourselves to do the hard work of identifying our implicit assumptions and train the brain to think differently. This comes with a great deal of practice and experience applying the kinds of strategies we'll review in the upcoming chapters.

## Why Are Some More Innovative than Others?

Conventional wisdom suggests that some personalities and cultures are better at innovation than others. There are some interesting dynamics to how one's personality and cultural background influence the innovation process. Every culture and personality can innovate effectively in some way. It's important, however, to understand how culture shapes creativity and innovation.

### Cultural Values

Paul Herbig and Steve Dunphy examined the influence of a nation's cultural values on its development of innovative technologies. They argue that several cultural values play a significant role in the innovative capacities found in a culture, including individualism, a willingness to take risks, a readiness to accept change, long-term orientation (focused on future more than present results), a non-hierarchical orientation (low power distance), a high tolerance for ambiguity (low uncertainty avoidance), and an openness to new information.[16] (See Appendix B for more on these cultural values.)

Another researcher, Scott Shane, measured innovation across different nations by calculating the number of inventions that have emerged from different cultures. His research suggests that the degree to which a culture tolerates ambivalence and ambiguity (uncertainty avoidance) is directly connected to the level of innovation that occurs. In fact, he suggests that a culture's tolerance for ambiguity is a far more significant factor in predicting innovation than per capita income, a variable more often used. And

Shane argues that individualist, egalitarian cultures are more likely to produce and promote innovation than collectivist, hierarchical cultures are.[17] This is an interesting claim given that most of the world is collectivist and hierarchical, including most of Asia, Africa, Latin America, and the Middle East.

The findings reported by Herbig, Dunphy, and Shane seem reasonable. A hierarchical culture that resists uncertainty does in fact seem like an environment that would deter creativity. But is it true? Japan, a very top-down culture that avoids uncertainty, disrupted the entire auto industry. And several Fortune 500 companies have invested big money in learning the Japanese idea of Kaizen—changing one small step at a time, which is a critical element of innovation. While Japan has faced some difficult economic challenges over the last decade, many indicators suggest the country is making a comeback through innovation. Singapore, also very hierarchical and a culture that resists uncertainty, is an incubator for innovation. The country has even come up with a way to purify sewage into safe drinking water. And Israel, one of the highest uncertainty avoidance cultures in the world, boasts the world's highest concentration of high-tech start-ups per capita of any country in the world. Nearly 1,000 new companies are launched there every year.[18]

According to the Global Innovation Index, the most innovative countries include Switzerland, Israel, the United Kingdom, Japan, the United States, and Singapore. These countries are spread across the continuum when it comes to their cultural value orientations around things like hierarchy and tolerance for uncertainty. So deciding whether a culture is innovative based upon its cultural values alone doesn't ring true with reality. However, cultural values do influence *how* a culture approaches innovation, something we'll address thoroughly in the upcoming chapters. In places like Japan, Singapore, and Germany, risky innovation is normal, but there are always several contingency plans for what will happen if the innovation doesn't work. But beware of thinking that some national cultures are innovative and others aren't simply because of their cultural values.

## Government Infrastructure

Another important consideration for the attention given by a culture to innovation is the role of government infrastructure. The first innovation priority for many governments is developing strong university systems, without which it's difficult to have the talent and research to drive innovation. Talented scientists and engineers are attracted to places with strong educational structures, resources, and support for new inventions and technologies. And places with strong universities produce additional skilled talent for driving innovation and growth. The governments that do this most effectively combine a strong educational infrastructure with a corresponding strategy for working with industry to ensure that academic findings move from labs and academic journals to the marketplace.

Intellectual property protection is another critical way governments promote innovation. And government incentives and regulations for growing diversity are another way that governments play a role in directing attention to innovation.

## Other Cultural Influences

There's a long list of other cultural differences that influence the degree to which you and the cultures of which you're part consciously innovate. Who is more likely to innovate—someone who is desperate or someone living with a secure quality of life? It depends. On the one hand, constraints can be a powerful driver of innovation. Being faced with life or death circumstances may motivate you to creatively determine a way to survive, whatever it takes. And amazing works of creativity have emerged from desperate situations, such as the artful masterpieces that were developed in World War II concentration camps. But the effort needed to survive may keep you from engaging in innovative thinking and planning. When you enjoy a certain quality of life, you have more freedom to consider ways to further improve life.

The origins of a country also play a part. Some studies indicate that people in the United States are far more likely to pursue entrepreneurship than people in the European Union are. This is often explained as a reflection of the pioneering roots of the United States, founded by entrepreneurs who left the stability of Europe to start over. One study found that more than one in four Americans were thinking about starting their own business, yet few Europeans ever consider the possibility.[19] It appears that entrepreneurship and self-directed survival are part of the consciousness of U.S. culture more than EU culture.

Other studies have pointed to the importance of nationalism and a sense of unity for promoting innovation in one country versus another. Indonesia, one of the most populated countries in the world, lacks a shared national identity across its vastly diverse islands and cultural groups. The nation typically scores low on innovation measurements, and some suggest there's a correlation between its lack of national identity and the absence of attention on innovation. In contrast, China shares a strong sense of unity across more than 1 billion people, and it's outpacing the United States and Japan for the number of inventions emerging annually.[20]

Still others have suggested that traditional cultures are less likely to innovate than contemporary ones are. Traditional cultures are devoutly religious, defer to authority, and retain strong family ties. Some research suggests this traditional orientation is negatively related to innovation.[21] Yet Herbig and Dunphy argue that it depends upon the religion itself. Protestants, for example, prioritize a strong work ethic, which leads to a thrust on continual reformation and improvement. In contrast, Hinduism and Buddhism highlight the importance of contentment, which may result in a more benign view toward innovation. And Herbig and Dunphy suggest that the Inshallah (if God wills) mentality of Islam may implicitly create passivity toward innovation since submission to what God wills is seen as more appropriate. These findings are inconclusive and require much more study, but it's worth thinking about how these variables influence one's approach to innovation.[22]

## Corporate Culture Trumps National Culture

National culture plays a powerful role in how you approach innovation. But the organizational culture where you work is the biggest factor for whether you successfully innovate. Look at the millions of different companies across the United States. The United States is traditionally viewed as one of the most innovative countries in the world. It's home to innovators like Apple, FedEx, and Nike. But it's home to as many or more companies that failed to innovate, from Kodak to Sears to Blockbuster. Corporate culture is a more important factor predicting whether you consciously think about innovation than national culture. Your national culture influences how you go about innovation, but whether you innovate is less related to where you're from and more related to where you work.[23]

Three characteristics are consistently found in organizational cultures that foster innovation regardless of the location: a willingness to cannibalize assets, a future orientation, and a tolerance for risk. Each of these is manifested differently, in part due to the cultural differences involved. But the consistency with which they appear is noteworthy.[24]

The first characteristic, a willingness to cannibalize current assets, is counterintuitive for many personalities and cultures. Why would you risk today's success for a possible innovation that is unproven? Most companies and institutions work hard to protect whatever provides their greatest profits. But an organizational culture that consciously promotes a willingness to sacrifice current profit-generating activities is an important part of conscious innovation. This may include encouraging competition between one internal unit and another. The degree to which the national and ethnic culture prioritizes harmony and collectivism may strongly influence the way this occurs, but internal competition can exist in companies from many different cultural backgrounds.

Second, organizations that consciously innovate usually have a stronger future orientation as part of their internal cultures. Leadership is continually thinking about where the organization will be in five years. Champions within the organization are empowered to come up with innovations that meet problems that are not yet felt but are looming on the horizon. A future orientation primes people in the company to realize the limitations of current technology and systems, and they more readily consider the emergence of a new generation of technology that may become dominant in the future. National culture definitely plays a role in how an organization approaches the future. Some cultures are far more future-oriented than others, with Confucian Asian cultures typically being the most long-term–oriented of any cultures globally. But an organization based in a more short-term–oriented culture, such as Russia or Argentina, can also take on a future orientation but may have to work harder to offer some short-term results and quick wins to avoid losing credibility.

Finally, innovative organizational cultures foster and promote a tolerance for risk. Innovative organizational cultures create a consciousness in people that views failure as an accepted, important part of the innovation process. They find concrete ways to demonstrate safety around the reality that not all innovations will lead to a guaranteed stream of profits. As already noted, some national cultures are much more risk-averse than others and failure comes with great shame in some contexts. So the larger context where the organization sits strongly shapes how a tolerance for risk is addressed. But no culture can really avoid risk—it's more about how they choose to deal with it.[25]

A long list of articles and books have been written about corporate culture and innovation. Clayton Christensen has devoted a significant amount of his career to providing some of the most important research on the drivers of disruptive innovation, including the correlation between how resources are allocated and where innovation occurs, matching technologies to markets, and the context-specific nature of innovation within a company. I'll continue to draw upon the work of Christensen and others with my purpose focused on how to specifically connect their findings to the opportunities and challenges presented by cultural diversity for innovation.

There's insufficient evidence to support that one national culture is consistently more innovative than another. What is clear is that the way innovation occurs varies across cultures. Some companies, like 3M, house their innovative teams in one location over another because of some of the unique cultural influences they perceive as being more conducive to innovation. But as global organizations become more interconnected, dispersed, and diverse, the way you raise the consciousness of innovation and the process by which you go about it will have to be adapted for the various motivations and perspectives represented.

## How to Pay Attention to Innovation

Your mind is your most powerful asset for innovation. Spend time thinking about innovation and it will help foster creative breakthroughs. Maintaining and developing a climate of culturally intelligent innovation among a diverse team requires a deliberate, ongoing effort. Our attention and therefore our companies are easily distracted. But there are a few practices that can help.

## Prime for Culturally Intelligent Innovation

To what degree do people across your organization share a vision for innovation and looking ahead? Do they view innovation like the VW marketers did prior to de Meo's leadership—a great idea that belongs to someone else? And to what degree is diversity consciously linked to innovation as a resource for new ideas?

Directing attention toward culturally intelligent innovation begins with leadership. Some companies actually appoint someone as the chief innovation officer, but not everyone agrees that's necessary or helpful. Google executives Eric Schmidt and Jonathan Rosenberg write, "The Chief Innovation Officer position is doomed to fail because it will never have enough power to create a primordial ooze . . . The CEO needs to be the CIO."[26] Aditya Ghosh, CEO of IndiGo, leads the charge on creating a culture of innovation at the fast-growing Indian airline, where employees at all levels are unafraid to make mistakes and think outside the box. The most important way to prime for culturally intelligent innovation is for the leadership to surround themselves with a diversity of perspectives, utilizing that breadth to drive their own innovative approaches. Innovation needs to be built into every person's role and across all the systems and processes for product development and implementation. Images, signs, town hall meetings, and written messaging need to be used to keep everyone's attention on the customers of tomorrow. What will diverse consumers' needs be in five years? What bold attempts (and failures) have been used to go after diverse users in the past? How can those be celebrated and used to inform the future? Discussion about these questions helps direct attention toward culturally intelligent innovation.

## Become Conscious of Blind Spots

Tap into the power of attention by becoming more aware of your subconscious. If you haven't been exposed to the groundbreaking work on unconscious bias, start there. Take one of the tests at Project Implicit (www.projectimplicit.org) and consider which groups of people you find most difficult to trust. How might that difficulty connect to a deeply rooted bias? And how might it be closing you off from innovative breakthroughs? Don't be too quick to answer. Check out Mahzarin Banaji and Anthony Greenwald's book *Blindspot*, the best book I've read on this subject, presenting this fascinating research in very practical ways. By becoming more aware of unconscious bias, you begin to retrain the mind to open yourself and others up to learning from the perspectives of people whom you may otherwise tune out.

## Train Yourself (and Others) to Think Differently

The brain is an amazing organ, and we can train it to be consciously thinking about innovation through things as simple as taking a different route to work or shifting around our morning routine. One of the best ways to consciously innovate is to disrupt your habits at least once a day. Make a habit of forcing yourself out of autopilot. Change up your morning routine. Drive to work a different way. Work from a different space. Don't always run your meetings the same way or in the same place. Ask team members to work differently from their typical patterns. When your team comes up with a solution, stop and ask each other whether this is the best option or whether a third alternative is worth exploring.

## Beware Your Gut

The gut can be a shockingly reliable mechanism for decision making. Our subconscious has been programmed over time. When assessing a familiar situation, the gut often leads to a better result than spending hours reviewing pros and cons. But the gut is subject to enormous error when the cultural context changes, and as a result innovative solutions are often missed. Consult with others and consciously suspend trusting your gut. Question your assumptions and proactively seek out third-way solutions.

## Conclusion

If all the world is a stage, where do you shine the spotlight of your attention? When you forget the name of the person you just met or can't find your keys, it's unlikely you're "losing it." It's more probable that you weren't paying attention when she introduced herself or when you set your keys down. The spotlight of your attention was turned elsewhere.

Is innovation nurture or nature? There may well be certain individuals who possess a unique capacity to think creatively and go beyond the norm. But all of us and our teams and organizations can become far more creative simply by becoming more conscious of innovation. Every time you make a decision, stop and ask yourself whether there's another way. If you lead an organization or team, create a culture that continually asks for a third solution rather than picking between either/or choices. Tap the brain's ability to see things in a new light and you'll be amazed how much more creative the results are, simply by spending more time consciously looking for alternative solutions.

And when you can't fathom why someone has just said or done what he did, remember that the spotlight of his attention is directed elsewhere. And that leads us to the next vital component of building a climate for culturally intelligent innovation: perspective taking.

### THE POWER OF ATTENTION

Your mind is your most powerful asset for innovation. By consciously paying attention to innovation and the diverse perspectives around you, you're primed to come up with more innovative solutions.

## Climate Assessment

| I'm surrounded by diverse people who pay attention to new and useful ways of doing things. | Almost Never | Sometimes | Almost Always |
|---|---|---|---|
| | | | |

# CHAPTER 3

## THE POWER OF THE EMPTY CHAIR
## | PERSPECTIVE TAKING

Jeff Bezos, founder and CEO of Amazon, frequently leaves one open seat at the company's most important meetings. It's there to remind executives and managers of the most important person in the room—the customer. Many organizations have emulated Amazon's empty chair practice. But if the people at the meeting don't have cultural intelligence, it's unlikely the chair will be of much benefit. The participants will simply assume the person represented by the empty chair values what they do. And if everyone in the meeting comes from the same cultural background, it's going to be tough to get a grasp of the preferences and opinions of the customer. So go ahead and add an empty chair to your most important meetings, but don't stop with that. Learn how to take on the perspective of a diversity of users, something known as *perspective taking.*

Perspective taking is "the capability to step outside [our] own experience and imagine the emotions, perceptions, and motivations of another."[1] It begins with realizing that two individuals can be presented with the exact same information and arrive at radically different interpretations. Most of us engage in perspective taking all the time. *What would my daughter like for a birthday gift? Where should I take this client for dinner? How will I convince them to close the deal?* But the more familiar an activity is to us, the less likely we are to do perspective taking because we assume others want what we want. *When I visit a website, I want it to look like . . . If colleagues need to contact me after hours, I prefer that they . . .* But my preferences might be the direct opposite from those of others. For every person who would rather you call than email, the opposite is also true.

Perspective taking is an essential part of culturally intelligent innovation. Once you learn to accurately take the perspective of others, you have a whole new ability to design products and services in a way that truly brings solutions. And with a diverse team, you have a built-in mechanism for taking on the perspective of your users.

## Core to Innovation

A critical part of successful innovation is finding a pain point and coming up with a way to alleviate the pain. Far too many attempted innovations overlook this. Take as an example the new energy-producing T-shirt. This is a shirt, currently being tested, that draws energy from your body. When you wear it, you can charge your electronic devices by plugging them into an outlet on the shirt! How cool is that? Or what about the new recently invented teeth sensors that automatically alert your dentist when you have too much bacteria and plaque buildup? But are these really the kinds of solutions we need and want? Do you really want to attach your devices to your clothes, and are most of us keen to tell our dentists: "Plaque alert! I haven't been flossing!"[2]

The reason most of us have a hard time keeping up with taking care of our teeth isn't because we aren't aware of plaque buildup; it's that we don't want to take the time to floss every day. We want in and out of the bathroom as quickly as possible. The new teeth sensor is really cool, but it assumes we'll voluntarily confess to our dentists that we haven't been flossing. A little more effort to take on the perspective of those who don't consistently floss would have led to a different innovation.[3]

In contrast, Esther Duflo, of the Abdul Latif Jameel Poverty Action Lab at MIT, found that offering Indian families a kilo of lentils if they immunize their children significantly raised vaccination rates. Duflo's idea is so effective because it's based on an understanding of what's meaningful to the families involved, on their terms. A bag of lentils may seem like a small idea, but it resulted in real, measurable impact.[4]

Few CEOs better demonstrate the power of perspective taking than A. G. Lafley of Procter & Gamble. Lafley insists on getting to know the tastes and interests of local consumers. In fact, he requires two things any time he travels internationally: an in-home visit with a consumer and a store-check. I've talked with some of his executives around the world who describe how important this priority is to Lafley when he visits. He sits with a couple in Santiago or a woman in Istanbul to watch them clean and ask what kinds of hassles they wish were removed from the process. He walks the aisles of the local stores and then quizzes staff to learn from their on-the-ground insights. He insists that this kind of up-close perspective taking is vital to him for effectively leading the company.

Culturally intelligent innovation requires the ability to take on the perspective of your colleagues and users. This requires not only learning how to read individuals one at a time but also learning how to see the tendencies, patterns, motivations, and connections across a particular cultural group. Cultural norms have limitations, but they provide a starting point for learning the motivations that are likely to exist among a group of potential users. Millennials' desire for instant feedback, Germans' quest for efficiency, and Latinos' priority of extended family are themes that ought to trigger reflection for how to pursue innovative solutions for these groups.

## The Danger of Minimization

One of the things that deters perspective taking is minimizing the presence or relevance of cultural differences. We're told that the world is flat and it's getting smaller. It is . . . sort of. You can find similar fashions, restaurants, and movies in many of the urban centers of the world. Many mosques in Istanbul look similar to the ones sprouting up in suburban North America. Starbucks has a similar look and feel in Sao Paulo, Beijing, and Berlin. Chinese students are studying in North America, and North American students are studying in China. Employees who may never travel far on business are working virtually with people 12 time zones away. It's easy to survey the global arena and assume the world is more similar than different. If your travel primarily consists of time spent in airport lounges, staying at four-star hotel chains, and interacting with others from your company, then the world looks remarkably similar. Even the locals you meet have often been trained to provide good service to international guests like yourself, which makes a faraway place seem like home. But when you stray away from these establishments, the world suddenly looks very different, wherever you go.

The tendency to overlook cultural differences and focus on the similarities is what Milton Bennett calls minimization.[5] It's one of the ways we cope with the dissonance of encountering different beliefs, preferences, and values. There's something very positive about minimization at some level. Rather than categorizing everyone as an "us" or "them," or referring to anything different as "weird," emphasizing what we have in common is a great starting point. And there is a whole lot we have in common, not the least of which is getting up every day, caring for our children, and finding ways to survive and find meaning. One of the first steps toward addressing our cultural biases is to see everyone as a fellow human being. Many human rights and peace advocacy groups capitalize upon this innate notion of finding common ground with each other. But we can't stop there. When we focus only on our commonalities, we fail to see the powerful discoveries that emerge from our differences.

Sometimes we're blinded to differences because of success. Success can make us overconfident that our business model and offerings address the needs and wants of customers everywhere. In 2004, Blockbuster was a $6 billion video rental enterprise with 60 percent profit margins and 60,000 employees. Six years later, it was bankrupt. For years, Blockbuster customers complained about skyrocketing late fees and the frustration of dwindling movie selections beyond new releases, but Blockbuster dismissed the complaints and forged ahead. Meanwhile, the company became well aware of Netflix, a start-up competitor that was offering home delivery and no late fees. Netflix had profit margins that were less than half of Blockbuster's. It surely didn't seem like taking Netflix's perspective was worth serious consideration, and Blockbuster executives were confident that they knew what their customers ultimately wanted despite what the customers themselves were saying. Blockbuster saw two choices: create a disruptive new approach requiring enormous cost and risk, or continue with the existing business. The *Harvard Business Review* reported, "The mildest application of a *different perspective*—stopping and considering what the world looked like to Netflix, or even what the world looked like to Blockbuster's customers—would have revealed that . . . their options . . . were to start the disruptive competitor—or go bankrupt" [italics added].[6] Blockbuster did experience rapid success in its first few years; the company met the growing demand by hiring managers who were committed to the existing business model. Blockbuster wanted leaders who would think and act exactly the same as the leadership in place. This led to the company's inability to innovate and its eventual demise.[7]

Perspective taking requires a willingness to lean into differences. It goes beyond emphasizing common interests to see what can be learned from the differences.

## Don't Overdo It!

On the other end of minimization is working so hard to take on the perspective of others that you lose yourself in the process. If you feel too deeply on behalf of the other, you might begin to submerge the interests of yourself and your own team. This is one of the things we discuss when teaching cultural intelligence to military officers. An effective military mission requires understanding the way your opponents think and behave, but at some point, if you become overly empathetic to their perspective, you may lose sight of your own. Perspective taking is not the same as empathy. Perspective taking is thinking like your potential user, whereas empathy evokes a more emotional, heartfelt response. To empathize is to put yourself in another's shoes and actually feel some sense of his emotions. There are certainly times when empathy is appropriate, but building a climate for culturally intelligent innovation is better served by perspective taking than empathizing.

Daniel Pink, author of *To Sell Is Human,* suggests that perspective taking enables the proper calibration between ignoring the other side and the danger of fully empathizing with the other side—allowing us to adjust and attune ourselves in ways that leave both sides better off.[8]

In one experiment, researchers simulated a negotiation over the sale of a gas station. The parties involved had mutual interests—one wanted to sell and the other was looking to buy. But as often happens in negotiating a deal, the highest price the buyer was willing to pay was lower than the lowest price the seller was willing to receive. The researchers set up one group of negotiators to imagine what the other side was thinking, one group to imagine what the other side was feeling, and a control group that wasn't instructed either way. The empathizers out-negotiated the control group and struck more deals. But the perspective takers did best of all. The "imagine what the other side is thinking" approach landed a better deal 76 percent of the time. Taking the perspective of one's opponent produced greater gains for both parties without sacrificing either party's individual interests.[9]

IKEA seems to have gained the benefit of perspective taking without losing itself in the process. The company's initial foray into North America was a *non-example* of culturally intelligent innovation. When IKEA first opened outlets in the United States, it provided customers with beds measured in centimeters, instead of describing them as king, queen, full, or twin-size. After buyers got the beds home, their sheets didn't fit. And the sofas were too small, the wardrobe drawers weren't deep enough, and the drinking glasses weren't large enough for the North American way. IKEA had failed to accurately understand the perspective of the U.S. buyer. "American customers were buying vases to drink from because the glasses were too small," recalled Goran Carstedt, the former head of IKEA North America, who helped engineer a turnaround.[10]

But IKEA learned its lesson. Today, research is at the heart of IKEA's expansion. The further the company goes from Sweden, the more time its people spend understanding the cultural differences. IKEA stores across Europe and North America are usually located in the suburbs. Customers drive to pick up their merchandise and carry it home. In China, however, IKEA understood that most people would come to the store using public transportation, so they set up their China outlets on the outskirts of cities, which are connected by rail and metro networks.[11] And by having anthropologists live with some Chinese families for a while, IKEA discovered that most of the families sat on the floor and used their sofas as a backrest. IKEA is using this insight to consider what kinds of innovations are best suited to the Chinese market.

IKEA used this same perspective-taking approach in targeting the Latino market across North America. The company sent designers to visit Latino homes, where they learned that Latino families are often larger than other North American families and therefore want larger dining tables and sofas to fit everyone. IKEA also learned that the Latinos wanted more color than the standard neutral tones that were popular in IKEA showrooms. This perspective changed the way the company designed and displayed furniture for the Latino market.

When IKEA first opened in Dubai, sales associates were taught about the need to do perspective taking based upon the profile of the customer. Sales associates were instructed to briefly greet Western customers, give them a cart, and let them be on their way. The do-it-yourself model of IKEA was built for them. But Asian customers were offered the service of having a sales associate follow them with a cart, helping them however they would like. And Arab customers were offered two carts, demonstrating a respect that the Arab customers could afford an abundance of merchandise if they so desired. This kind of profiling can be dangerous if not used carefully. But IKEA has learned to accommodate the perspectives of different markets while maintaining its overall do-it-yourself niche in the home-furnishing market around the world. Some customers have insisted on being able to purchase fully assembled furniture, something IKEA has not been willing to do because it violates their core business strategy. IKEA has learned the value of identifying with the customer's perspective and adapting as needed, while not losing sight of its core offerings and value proposition.

## Getting Personal

Perspective taking is personal. It creates a sense of dissonance and freedom when facing the reality that two people can view the same information and arrive at entirely different perspectives. And if not used responsibly, it can become a tool of manipulation to simply get people to do what you want.

The greatest challenges of perspective taking lie not so much in how we deal with entirely erroneous perceptions but how we deal with different, legitimate views and experiences that are each a part of the whole. Moving toward culturally intelligent innovation requires an ability to transcend pitting ourselves against those who have a different perspective from us; instead, it accepts the possibility that multiple perspectives can be equally valid.

It sounds easy enough on paper, but the challenge of holding together two seemingly different perspectives is one of the most disorienting aspects of personal development. Like many people, I grew up with a very insulated view of the world. Our family's social network revolved around people like us. We associated with people who looked like us, shared our religious beliefs, affirmed our political perspectives, and defined success and failure the way we did. We were convinced our way was the one right way to view the world.

In my early years, there was very little room for people who sized up the world differently from me. Different equaled "wrong" or at the very least "weird!" While there was an unusually strong religious orientation to my upbringing, a childhood with a focus upon one's family and networks versus others is typical for most people. And for the most part, this is a healthy way to begin life and development. Psychologists argue that a healthy sense of identity begins with understanding and appreciating one's self before being able to appreciate the world and reality of others. Protecting and caring for our own is not only okay but is central to how the world works.[12]

As a result, most of us start life with a pretty insulated view of the world that compares the world and others against our own perspective and experiences. And for most previous generations, you could easily be born, live, and die without ever having a significant encounter with people who view the world differently from your own upbringing. But that's getting harder to pull off. Muslims are moving next door to Christians, tribes are migrating to cities, and Easterners and Westerners have 24/7 Internet access to each other's behavior. The challenge now is how we embrace our unique perspectives and care for our own while simultaneously seeking to understand other legitimate ways of viewing the world. That's where this becomes personal.

The goal is not for all of us to abandon the social group and identity with which we were reared. Neither should we pretend we don't have legitimate self-interests. But how do we respect and care for ourselves while also broadening our scope of perspective and care to include others? Except in rare cases where one's upbringing is best dealt with by leaving it all behind, most of us find aspects of our upbringing that we want to bring with us into a broader, more global embrace. Clare Graves, a professor of psychology, studied the evolution of adult consciousness, something he described as spiral dynamics. It's a scientific theory that enumerates how and why our perspectives about the world change as the circumstances and problems we face shift up and down in complexity. Spiral dynamics provides a way of understanding how multiple perspectives can shed light on reality. The two words that best capture spiral dynamics are *transcend* and *include*. We want to transcend our existing perspectives without leaving them fully behind. As we broaden our scope by seeing through the eyes of others, we rarely abandon all our previous beliefs and ideas about the world; we transcend those perspectives to include others. The ability to transcend and include is an essential part of the culturally intelligent innovation process that we'll continue to revisit throughout the book.

## Use Responsibly

Getting personal means we use perspective taking responsibly. Some leaders use perspective taking simply as a ploy to predict where their opponent is going, not driven by any sense of altruism or transcendence. It's like the telemarketer who asks you personal questions and then turns the tables on you and uses what you've shared to try to pitch you something. If you can figure out what motivates others, it gives you a powerful edge. But a culturally intelligent approach to perspective taking has to be driven by a transcendent commitment to care for the interests of others as well as your own.

Adam Galinsky, a social psychologist at Columbia University, found that negotiators who used perspective taking may be more likely to resort to dirty tactics and behave unethically. Business negotiations often produce a sense of threat, and Galinsky found that if perspective taking isn't used responsibly, it can cause a negotiator to disproportionately focus on the potential of the other party's nefarious plans to cheat and cajole. He says: "When you're in an inflamed state, thinking about the other person's mind changes perspective taking from the glue that binds us together to the gasoline that worsens the competitive fire."[13] Part of using perspective taking responsibly is understanding the risks involved when emotions are high.

Use the power of perspective taking to see what you might otherwise miss and to develop innovations that truly strike at people's pain points. But resolve to be responsible in how you use the insights that emerge from gaining others' perspectives.

## Perspective Giving vs. Perspective Taking

Some research indicates those coming from a more dominant cultural perspective gain more from perspective taking than underrepresented populations do. Underrepresented cultures are usually pretty well in tune with the dominant perspective. For example, most employees already know leadership's perspective. In addition, the well-being of subordinates is often based upon the whims of what leadership decides to do, so staff members are often comparing notes on what they perceive their bosses are thinking. But who's telling the boss what everyone else thinks? And who's going to tell the boss that her jokes are stupid? People in power often have a harder time accurately taking the perspective of others. The same applies to cultures that are less dominant. Foreign workers in Qatar are well aware of the Qatari perspective, but the reverse is less likely. The same is true of Mexican immigrants in the United States. One study found that Caucasian Americans benefited significantly from hearing the perspectives of Mexican immigrants. They learned things they had never otherwise considered. But Mexican immigrants didn't have an equally positive experience when listening to the perspectives of the Caucasian Americans. It actually worsened their attitude toward them. A similar finding emerged between Israelis and Palestinians, where Israelis benefited from listening to Palestinians but not vice versa. The underrepresented groups benefited more from perspective *giving* than from perspective taking—that is, when offered a chance to describe their own experiences to attentive members of higher-ranking groups. Emile Bruneau, one of the authors of the study, says, "Nondominant groups express a strong desire to be heard or, in their words, to 'speak truth to power.' "[14]

If perspective taking is merely done to exploit other people, it's not going to lead to culturally intelligent innovation. It may lead you to some short-term benefits, but a truly innovative process strives to understand others' perspectives to come up with better solutions for ourselves, our teams, our customers, and—as much as possible—the world at large.

## How to Improve Perspective Taking

For highly diverse teams, perspective taking is a critical way to tap into the full range of information available through the breadth of perspectives. People with different sources of information, knowledge, and perspective are often isolated from each other—either in various functional units or psychologically in "us" versus "them" groups. There are several practices that can help you make perspective taking a regular part of your innovation process.

### Observing

Most innovators are intense observers. They observe people in a different environment and look for how they solved problems. They actively watch people as they use products. They observe people in real situations. They look for what's surprising. And they continually repeat the mantra of an anthropologist going into a new society: "Hmm . . . I wonder why that is!"

Observation happens best up close, not by simply reading reports about market trends. In a study on product innovation, researchers found that salespeople and R&D people weren't listening to each other. R&D people didn't accept what salespeople said was needed in the marketplace, even after reading extensive memos detailing all the needed attributes of a new and improved product. But when the R&D people were actually brought to meet with customers and listened to their needs and concerns, suddenly everything made sense to them.[15]

As you observe, continue to consider, *What is the pattern? Why is the pattern?* Notice as much as you can and pay attention to things that puzzle.[16] First observe, then interpret and explain.

When used appropriately, international travel is one of the best ways to go beyond our preconceived perspectives and observe the perspectives of others. Observe both the business and nonbusiness context. Send people to consumers' homes to observe products in use and uncover needs unrelated to the current product. As you travel, compare the different kinds of "normal" breakfasts eaten in China (porridge with "thousand-year-old" eggs), Mexico (an omelet with huitlacoche), Pakistan (goat soup), or Korea (fermented vegetables), and you have insights into how vastly different our perspectives are on something as simple as what to eat first thing in the morning. Observation allows you to better appreciate the discretionary nature of many of the choices we all make, and in turn, it's an effective way to shift your perspective to uncover alternative approaches. Noticing something as simple as the differences in what people eat for breakfast may change a global ad campaign you approve or a presentation you make.

## Listening

Perspective taking also relies on active listening skills. This is a natural complement to observation, but it's not automatic. Effective listening to gain the perspectives of others means intentionally hearing a customer's pain points and desires, and creatively getting them to share things that will enlighten how you go about the innovation process. Here are a few questions to inform the way you listen:

- How do customers order and purchase your product? Is there a way to make that easier and less costly?
- How do they receive it?
- What frustrations do they have?

In many cultures, you can't just ask these questions directly. It requires creativity to determine how you obtain this information. And if you want someone's opinion on a controversial issue, particularly if she comes from a conflict-avoiding culture that is driven to save face at all costs, ask her what most people in her demographic group might think about something, rather than asking her to directly weigh in on behalf of herself.

Tesco, the UK supermarket giant, listened to its customers in South Korea as a way to figure out how to grow its market share there. Listening allowed Tesco's executives to discover that taking the time to go grocery shopping added stress to the Koreans' already busy lives. So Tesco decided to bring the store to the shoppers—but not in the typical online/home delivery way. Tesco placed full-size images of its products in subway stations across Seoul. Using a smartphone, QR code, and credit card, people could shop while they waited for the train. They ordered their items from the train platform, and they were delivered directly to their homes. Customers loved it. Simply listening to the primary frustration of a diverse group of customers boosted Tesco's sales significantly.[17]

Morgan Friedman, who has made a career out of eavesdropping on conversations across New York City, says one of the best ways to expand your perspective is to become better at listening to the people around you. Friedman himself is obsessed with this pastime, and he has a full website, www.overheardinnewyork.com, where people can share things they've overheard while eavesdropping around New York, such as:

A guy on a cell phone says, "You asked me how I'm doing, and I tell you—and then you bring it back to yourself. You always do that."

An agitated man tells his buddy, "Then the tourists paused near the *New York Times* building . . . Their leader pointed to it and said, 'Everyone, that's Ground Zero.'" [Despite the fact that "Ground Zero," usually a reference to the World Trade Center, is four miles away].

You learn a lot about human behavior and how people think simply by listening to the conversations around you. Listen for what's being said and not said. Pay attention to what people find funny and what they complain about. And talk to senior citizens. They do a lot of remembering and many have lived between vastly different worlds—from growing up with the ice man bringing weekly deliveries to ordering groceries from a subway platform. Ask them what has changed most in their everyday lives since childhood, and press for details.[18] Young people have never been old, but old people have all been young. Listen and learn from their insights.

## Simulating the User's Experience

If you can't actually sit in the home of a customer like A. G. Lafley from P&G does, there are other ways to get the perspective of a diverse customer. The empty chair strategy at Amazon can be used by assigning someone to take on the perspective of a particular demographic and to role-play in the meeting as if he were someone from that cultural background.

Mark Zuckerberg is aware that the new Facebook campus designed by Frank Gehry is a world apart from where most Facebook users log on to view the site's newsfeed. He says that when you work at Facebook, "It's easy to not have empathy for what the experience is for the majority of people in the world."[19] In order to address this, Facebook engineers have simulated conditions that are on par with what Facebook users have in rural India. They keep an inventory of old low-end flip phones, and engineers have to prove that what they're coding works on a low-end phone using the network conditions that most of the world has. In fact, Zuckerberg doesn't allow Facebook staff to refer to these kinds of phones and network conditions as "low-end" because he wants them to understand that these aren't low-end phones—they're *typical* phones for most users.[20] So find ways to simulate the kind of experience your customers or prospective users have.

## Checking for Accuracy

One of the critical things we measure in assessing cultural intelligence is whether people check their assumptions. It is damaging to inaccurately assume someone's perspective, and it might be worse than never taking on another perspective in the first place. Perspective taking relies on your ability to consider other people's perspective accurately. If you don't really know what it's like to be poor, in pain, or at the bottom of the corporate ladder, or to have oil as your primary source of income, then the mental gymnastics of putting yourself in someone else's shoes isn't going to improve your innovation. It might make it worse. If your belief about the other side's perspective is mistaken, then considering that perspective magnifies the problems.[21]

Just look at the impact from having unending information at our fingertips. Many people believe what they want and don't have to look far for backup, even if what they believe had been proved to be false. Longtime journalist Evan Thomas writes, "These days a wild rumor in an email from your distant cousin can trump the *New York Times*."[22]

And beware of confirmation bias, the tendency to look for and favor information that confirms what you already thought. When was the last time you were surprised by new information and changed your mind as a result? If you can't think of a time, you may suffer from confirmation bias. Confirmation bias occurs when you interpret something that is ambiguous or anecdotal and automatically assume it further supports the viewpoint you already have. It is one of the reasons why international travel doesn't automatically lead to higher levels of cultural intelligence. Some travelers simply move from place to place, looking for evidence that their preconceived notions are accurate. You can almost always find something that will support your point of view—regardless of whether it's normative for the entire culture.

How do you know whether something represents a cultural norm or whether you're encountering an idiosyncratic perspective? Here are a few things you can do:

✔ How does this perspective compare with what research indicates about the norms for this culture?

- See Geert Hofstede's work on the norms for different national cultures (http://geert-hofstede.com/cultural-dimensions.html)

- Look up the average cultural values profiles for the 10 largest cultural clusters in the world (see *Expand Your Borders* by David Livermore)

- Review the findings of the GLOBE Leadership Study (see *Culture, Leadership and Organizations* edited by House, Hanges, Javidan, Dorfoman, & Gupta)

✔ What are other possible explanations for this perspective and/or behavior?

- Personality

- Circumstances

- Organizational factors

- Power struggle

✔ How do others who have experience and understanding with this culture perceive the situation?

## Conclusion

When you understand others' perspectives, you gain entirely new insights into what motivates them. Perspective taking is the bedrock of any good relationship because with it, you stop to consider what will cause the other person to feel understood. And it's at the core of culturally intelligent innovation. Perspective taking has been proven to be one of the recurring variables found among diverse teams that come up with and implement more creative ideas.[23]

Sadly, too many organizations and leaders operate with the implicit mindset "When I want your opinion, I'll give it to you." It's dangerous for any innovative team to assume they know what the user wants, but that's particularly true when the users come from a diversity of backgrounds.

Ralph Waldo Emerson wrote, "What is life but what a man is thinking of all day?"[24] Use the empty chair strategy and the diversity of perspectives on your team to understand what people are thinking and the pain points they wish to overcome. Then, you'll be well on your way to developing a climate for innovation that offers better solutions.

### THE POWER OF PERSPECTIVE TAKING

Don't assume others want what you want. Learn from the perspectives of your diverse colleagues and users to develop more novel, useful innovations.

### Climate Assessment

| I'm confident I understand a diversity of our users' perspectives. | Not Confident | Somewhat Confident | Very Confident |
|---|---|---|---|
| | | | |

# CHAPTER 4

## THE POWER OF 90 MINUTES | FOCUS

**D**istraction is one the biggest roadblocks to innovation. And the more globally dispersed your team, the greater the potential for distraction. From managing countless religious and national holidays to dealing with round the clock virtual team meetings, the interruptions and ubiquitous ping of technology, speed, and multitasking are often the enemies of culturally intelligent innovation. As a result, it's absolutely essential that we learn how to focus. Focus on a diverse team requires self-control, each person using his brain to its fullest, and learning how to regulate technology use. And it starts with tackling projects one 90-minute block at a time, the ideal amount of time to spend on a creative task.

MIT Professors David Foster and Matthew Wilson have devoted a great deal of study to the power of focus followed by mental breaks. In one study, they looked inside the brains of rats as the rodents ran through a maze. They paid particular attention to the brain activity in the hippocampus—the part of the brain that is most responsible for learning and memory in rodents, primates, and humans. Some of the rats were given a chance to relax in a calmed state after running through the maze, while others were nudged to keep running. The ones given a chance to relax showed better signs of learning and brain stimulation than the ones that had to keep moving.[1] The results corroborate what other researchers have found. Creativity and productivity are linked to sustained periods of focus, followed by a period for relaxation and disengagement.

Not convinced by a study done on rats' brains? Not to fear. Numerous other studies confirm the power of focus for driving culturally intelligent innovation. That's what we want to tackle in this chapter, along with how diversity on your team can be a key catalyst for distraction or focus—depending upon how it's managed.

## It Starts with Self-Control

Focus begins with self-control, and self-control requires focus. It's a symbiotic relationship that needs patience. Patience doesn't come easily to many of us, particularly in our constantly connected, instant gratification culture. Google slowed down the speed of search results by four-tenths of a second to see how it impacted our googling. The result: 8 million fewer searches a day! One out of four people abandon a webpage that doesn't load within four seconds. An email that doesn't get a response within 24 hours is considered unresponsive. And one *USA Today* study found that most Americans won't wait in line for more than 15 minutes.[2]

Ironically, many tribal cultures don't even have a word for "boredom." Cultural differences in time orientation are most often discussed in terms of punctuality, as in whether 9:00 really means 9:00. But the more challenging differences to address are conflicting expectations for how quickly something should be completed and the meaning of a "quick turnaround" or it's going to "take a while." Furthermore, impatience and working across cultures don't work very well together. Working with people and projects involving different cultures inevitably takes more time, effort, and patience. But can patience and self-control be learned? Or are they hardwired into us genetically? And does our cultural background influence our patience? Yes, yes, and yes!

Walter Mischel is best known for his renowned marshmallow experiment, conducted at a preschool on Stanford University's campus in the late 1960s. In the experiment, children were offered a choice between an immediate reward (e.g., one marshmallow) or a larger one (e.g., two marshmallows) if they could just wait 15 minutes. He discovered that children who could wait for the bigger reward fared better in their adolescent and adult lives than those who immediately took the treat. But long before this experiment, Mischel started his research on the connection between patience and self-control in Trinidad. He wanted to see whether there was a difference in the impulse control among African versus Indian children living in Trinidad. Similar to the marshmallow experiment, the children were given a simple choice: They could have a candy bar right away or wait a few days and receive a much bigger one. Mischel expected that the children's cultural backgrounds might influence their choices, but they didn't. Some kids from both cultures waited and some didn't. The kids' upbringing did play a role in their decision, however. For example, the kids from both cultures who lived with their fathers were better at being patient than those with no father at home. But culture itself didn't predict whether a child could patiently wait for the bigger candy bar.

Mischel's marshmallow experiment is his much better known research. Most discussion about the experiment focuses upon one primary implication: "Kids who can wait for a treat end up more successful." But further observation showed that *all the kids craved the extra treat.* What, then, determined the difference in self-control? Mischel's large data set from various studies allowed him to see that children who understood strategies for self-control were better able to delay gratification. "What's interesting about four-year-olds is that they're just figuring out the rules of thinking," Mischel says. "The kids who couldn't delay would often have the rules backwards. They would think that the best way to resist the marshmallow is to stare right at it, to keep a close eye on the goal. But that's a terrible idea. If you do that, you're going to [eat the marshmallow] before I leave the room."[3]

Mischel's conclusion was that the kids who waited learned how to direct their attention and focus elsewhere. Instead of getting obsessed with the marshmallow or the candy bar, the self-controlled children distracted themselves by covering their eyes, pretending to play hide-and-seek underneath the desk, or singing songs from *Sesame Street.* Their desire wasn't defeated—it was merely forgotten. "If you're thinking about the marshmallow and how delicious it is, then you're going to eat it," Mischel says. "The key is to avoid thinking about it in the first place."[4]

Did these kids learn this skill from their parents, or was it hard-wired into their genes? Mischel says, "Trying to separate nature from nurture makes about as much sense as trying to separate personality from situation. The two influences are entirely interrelated."[5] But the overwhelming evidence is that anyone can learn to be more patient by learning how to focus. The mind is a powerful tool.

Self-control, patience, and focus can be taught to anyone, but don't overdo it. Start with a 90-minute block, with no interruptions allowed. An interruption will cost you 20 minutes to recover. And then change tasks.[6] The same is true for collaborative work. Your team can focus on an issue together for 90 minutes, and then you all need a break. And ideally, the break should be truly a break—not a time for checking email and returning phone calls, but a 10-minute walk outside, a cup of coffee sitting quietly, or talking informally with colleagues. It's ironic that something so enjoyable and good for us takes such hard work. But the discipline is worth it. As the ancient African proverb says, "If you want to go fast, go alone. If you want to go far, go together." The power of focus for developing truly innovative solutions with a diverse team begins with learning self-control; and self-control often rests in simply distracting ourselves from distractions.

## Brain Control

Another critical part of leveraging the power of focus is learning how to manage your brain. Clayton Christensen, together with authors Jeff Dyer and Hal Gregersen, describes five skills that consistently characterize disruptive innovators: They associate, question, observe, network, and experiment. All five of these skills require a great deal of focus. It begins with the skill of associating, which is learning how to connect the dots. Real-life innovators agree with Christensen and his colleagues. According to Steve Jobs, "Creativity is connecting things." And Richard Branson says, "Always be connecting the dots."[7]

Some people seem to observe anything and immediately begin connecting the dots. We can all improve the skills needed for disruptive innovation by regulating the focus of our brains. Psychologist Norman Farb describes two kinds of focus: *narrative focus* and *experiential focus*. Both types are important. Depending upon your personality and cultural background, you probably emphasize one over the other. And chances are, if you're reading a book like this one, you're predisposed to the narrative focus of the brain. Narrative focus is the rational, didactic way of observing the world. We observe something, judge what's going on, and interpret what it means. It's a natural part of how we're wired as humans. It's using the medial prefrontal cortex of the brain and the memory regions, such as the hippocampus. It's called "narrative" because this is the part of the brain that holds together the story by which we view the world. Some might refer to it as our worldview. It's the network of our brain that is involved in planning, daydreaming, and ruminating on ideas.

I naturally default to the narrative focus in my brain. I journal almost daily, I regularly do SWOT (Strengths, Weaknesses, Opportunities, Threats) analyses, and I'm consistently reflecting on what something means and its broader significance. When operating from the narrative focus, we notice something and immediately think about how it connects with us and our view of the world. I was thinking about this one day (further proof of how quickly I default to the narrative focus) when I was walking with my daughter Grace across the frozen lake by our house. We were having a blast together. We had waited several weeks for the lake to be frozen enough to safely walk on it, and at last, we had a brisk, sunny day to go from our side of the lake to the shops on the other side. But while we were sliding across the lake together, I began to think about how quickly she's growing up and my desire to make the most of her time left at home, which made me wonder whether we're saving enough for college. And then I began to think about the upcoming kite festival that happens on our lake every February, which made me think about a speaking engagement I had the next month that I had to begin preparing for. I was lost in my thoughts, until Grace grabbed my arm: "Dad! Did you hear what I said?"

My consciousness was in the narrative focus mode, and she could tell I wasn't in the moment. I've often thought that living in my head, journaling compulsively, and reflecting on situations is a real asset to cultural intelligence—and it is a valuable component. But if we're not careful, it can actually be a roadblock to working and relating creatively with others, whether it's a fun walk across a frozen lake or working with someone a world away.

The other form of focus is experiential focus, which is sometimes described as direct experience. This is a way of experiencing the world that doesn't involve thinking intently about the past, the future, or what something means. Instead, this is the practice of simply taking in stimuli as they come to our senses in real time. This is how our pets function—responding to stimuli in the moment with little deepened consciousness about the deeper meaning. Neuroscientists find that during experiential focus, several brain regions become more active, including the insula (a region that relates to perceiving bodily sensations) and the anterior cingulated cortex (a region central to switching your attention).

When you activate your experiential focus, you aren't thinking intently about the past or future, about other people or ideas. In fact, you're not considering much at all. You're simply experiencing information and events coming to your senses in real time.

For me, this might have meant sliding across the ice with Grace, feeling the contrast of the warmth of the sun above us and the cold air from below. This would be consciously enjoying the experience of a spontaneous activity with my daughter, taking in her laughter and her questions about how the swans survive all winter . . . and holding at bay the deeper thoughts chafing for my attention. Using experiential focus requires a very deliberate choice to *not* move into the internal world of our own narratives and to focus instead on the moment at hand. It's a practice some talk about as being fully "present." As I learn to activate the experiential focus of my brain, I can consciously choose to stop myself from thinking about the work I need to do to prepare for my upcoming speaking engagement.

The brain operates much more quickly below the surface of consciousness. It reaches conclusions without immediately telling us why. Whenever we meet someone for the first time, interview someone for a job, or are faced with making a decision quickly under pressure, we use the experiential circuits of our brain. And experiential focus can also be a powerful force for generating new ideas and opening ourselves up to the power of collaborating with diverse teammates to drive innovation. We need to hold in tension the fact that on the one hand, our snap judgments can be better than ones well developed through rational decision making, and in other cases, our snap judgments can blind us from seeing beyond our cultural narratives.[8]

As we become more conscious of these two modes of focus—narrative and experiential—we can purposefully choose which brain circuitry is best suited to a task and situation (see Table 4-1). Farb found that the more people notice the two different paths of thinking, the more easily they can switch between the two. A narrative focus is well suited for organizing, planning, and developing goals. It's the focus that helps us to question our assumptions and to examine our cultural perspectives against others—hence the many years I've spent emphasizing this type of thinking as a part of developing cultural intelligence. It's an essential element for implementing an innovation because perspective taking, disciplined thinking, and execution require the reflective nature of narrative focus. But an experiential focus helps us get closer to the reality of any event, listening to the conversations around us and observing what's happening. This type of focus allows us to pick up on cues we might otherwise miss because it helps us perceive more information about the events occurring around us and better maximize the dynamics and perspectives of discussing a creative idea with a diverse team. It makes us less imprisoned by our own expectations and assumptions and allows us to be able to more actively respond to events and the ideas of others as they unfold.

### Table 4-1. Narrative vs. Experiential Focus

|  | Narrative Focus | Experiential Focus |
|---|---|---|
| **Definition** | Focus on what something means in light of our larger experience and understanding (Rumination) | Focus on what is happening in the moment and experience it through all our senses (Avoids rumination) |
| **Tasks** | • Reflection and questioning<br>• Connecting the dots<br>• Strategic planning<br>• Implementation plans<br>• Ideal for: Execution | • Observing<br>• Creative brainstorming<br>• Trust building<br>• Experimenting<br>• Ideal for: Ideation |
| **How to** | • Write—preferably with pen and paper<br>• Describe an experience; objectify it with details<br>• Explore the deeper meaning<br>• Transfer learning | • Meditation and mindfulness<br>• Breathe<br>• Walk in nature<br>• Pay attention to your body<br>• Take long showers |

Draw upon the diversity of your team to teach each other about the benefits of both brain processes. Introverts often default more quickly to the narrative focus than extroverts, and extroverts may more easily activate the experiential focus. You also need to consider monochronic cultures versus polychronic cultures. Monochronic cultures, most typically found in the Western world, are places where there's a linear approach to tasks and a high priority is given to handling one idea at a time. These cultures are well suited for the narrative focus. Polychronic cultures, found in many other parts of the world, are places where people more fluidly react to events and ideas as they come. This is similar to the experiential focus. When these differences surface on a team, it can either lead to immense frustration or, if used intentionally, it can be used to teach each other how to better activate the less utilized circuits in our brains. As you individually and collectively improve your cognitive control, and even intentionally ask one another to use one kind of focus for a task instead of another, you will have a greater ability to shape what you do, say, and produce.[9]

## Technology Is Not in Charge

Many of us pride ourselves on thinking we can multitask, but for the most part, none of us can. There are some limited situations where we can do so. We can walk and chew gum at the same time. We can go to a movie and listen, watch, and eat popcorn, feeling little strain from simultaneously doing all three tasks. But watching a dubbed movie or a movie with subtitles stretches you a bit further, and having a screaming baby nearby does so even more.

The real problem comes when we try to accomplish two tasks that draw upon the same part of our brain. When you try to type an email while participating in a conference call, something has to give. You might think you're doing both tasks, but you're actually switching back and forth between the two. And the absence of focus actually makes you less productive. Some studies suggest that lack of focus actually lowers your IQ the more you try to do more than one thing at once. At the very least, it wreaks havoc on productivity. Winifred Gallagher, who has written prolifically on the power of attention, says, "If your train of thought is interrupted even for a second, you have to go back and say, 'Where was I?' There are start-up costs each time you reload everything into memory. Multitasking exacts a price, and people aren't as good at it as they think they are."[10]

Technology has made it more difficult to focus than ever before. But your machines are not in charge of whether you focus—you are. When the machines become distracting, turn them off. Rather than feeling guilty about the lure of technology or shrugging it off as inevitable, you can do several things to responsibly leverage the power of technology to help you focus and allow you to expend more energy on innovation and benefiting from the diverse perspectives around you. For example, a carefully curated Twitter feed can gather key news, findings, and diverse perspectives for you. Purposely include news sources that provide a different interpretation of the same events. A diverse Twitter network exposes you to people and ideas you don't already know, which in turn helps generate better ideas.[11]

A well-managed online calendar can serve as a digital assistant reminding you when 90 minutes is up and keeping you on track with deadlines. In addition, effective crowdsourcing gives you the opportunity to gain global input on new ideas in a matter of hours. When used well, the personal assistant of technology can spark all kinds of creative thinking.

It's worth referencing the strategies often written on this topic as a way of ensuring that you control your technology rather than vice versa:

- Set specific times to check email.
- Remove push notifications so you aren't distracted by the lure of the ping.

- Put your phone on "do not disturb" during your 90-minute blocks. Most text messages are read within three minutes of their receipt, but they don't have to be.
- Take long showers and go for walks to activate the experiential circuit of your brain. These are great opportunities to free-associate away from your desk and technology.
- Use the power of the Internet's diverse resources to spark imagination; then shut it off, step away with pen and paper, reflect, and write or draw what lingers beneath the surface.
- Write down creative ideas on paper.
- Insist on all technology being switched off during team meetings.
- Take a technology fast for a week and see what it does to your ability to focus.

After stepping away, reconnect and share your creative ideas with a global network of online friends to gain their diverse insights and perspectives. It's not difficult to do any of these tasks, but it requires self-control and a conscious effort.

## Problem Finding

Albert Einstein said, "If I had an hour to solve a problem and my life depended on the solution, I would spend the first fifty-five minutes determining the proper question to ask, for once I know the proper question, I could solve the problem in less than five minutes." Focus is vital to problem finding. And clearly identifying and describing a problem is a crucial part of the innovation process. Unclear solutions begin as unclear problems. Yet far too many attempts at innovation are directed toward identifying and describing solutions for problems that are not clearly defined in the first place. When Steve Jobs set out to build the iPod, he defined the problem as "how to get one thousand songs in the pocket." The problem was very focused upon giving people an updated option for taking music on the go.

Many management practices focus on problem solving, but as bestselling author Daniel Pink notes, the crucial area requiring focus today is problem finding. In today's information age, if I know my problem, I can probably find a solution. The Internet is full of resources and information. But if I don't even know what my problem is, I need help finding it in the first place, and that requires patience, focus, and disciplined attention.

New services and products are most valuable when an individual or organization is mistaken, confused, or clueless about the problem. How do you get someone, coming from an entirely different cultural background, out of a confused state?[12] Answering that question requires focused reflection and thinking, ideally from a diversity of individuals. Clayton Christensen calls this the "job to be done" theory. He challenges the wisdom of spending inordinate amounts of time studying particular demographic segments and instead stresses the need to focus on providing a service or product that does a job for the user. He writes, "The mechanism that *causes* us to buy a product is 'I have a job I need to get done, and this is going to help me do it.'"[13]

Hindustan Unilever—a subsidiary of Unilever in India—was trying to identify how to develop a plan for expanded growth across India. The emphasis among most of Hindustan Unilever's competitors and in business journals was on the unending growth occurring in urban centers across India and the need to increase marketing to get customers in urban centers to buy more. But Hindustan Unilever identified a different opportunity: millions of potential customers living outside urban centers whom no one was reaching. The company identified a core problem that needed to be solved: How do you sell products in small villages without any access to traditional distribution networks, advertising, or infrastructure? Hindustan Unilever's focus on that problem led to the development of a direct selling approach. It partnered with NGOs, banks, and the government to recruit women across rural India to become direct-to-consumer sales distributors for soaps and shampoos. The company provided extensive training for the women as micro-entrepreneurs, and by 2009, 45,000 women were selling Hindustan Unilever products across rural regions in India. The innovation emerged from having a diverse team step back and focus on identifying the problem itself.[14]

What does it look like to focus on problem finding? To identify the problem, focus on the pain point. Then ask as many questions as you can. Write down at least 50 questions about that problem. Ask questions like: What is? What caused? Why? Why not? What if?

If you're doing this as a team, follow these guidelines:

- Have one person write down all the questions so that everyone can see them and reflect on what is being asked.
- No one can ask a new question until the previous one has been written down.
- No long qualifiers or preambles are allowed before asking the question. Just ask the question.

And don't answer the questions yet. For now, the point is to focus on the problem. Leverage the diversity of perspectives on your team to get the widest view of the problem possible.[15]

Questioning is a way of life for innovators. Christensen and his associates, Dyer and Gregersen, found that not only do innovators ask more questions than non-innovators, they also ask more provocative ones.[16] But you have to manage the art of asking questions carefully. The cultural values of saving face, promoting harmony, and respecting authority often prevent some team members from asking questions or cause them to be offended by those who do. Not wanting to look stupid or avoiding any suggestion of being viewed as an uncooperative or disagreeable person also deters the process of asking questions for certain individuals. So you have to utilize cultural intelligence in thinking about how to get at this. Also, be clear that the questions are being asked of the entire team to enhance focus and problem finding, not to interrogate anyone. We'll come back to some specific ways you can get people to speak up and ask questions, as well as offer input, in Chapter 8. But don't let the challenges keep you from this important aspect of problem finding.

Focus on questions that will help you get at otherwise overlooked problems. Consider questions like:

- If the disposable income of our current customers dropped by 50 percent, how would our product or service have to change?
- If air transportation was no longer possible, how would we change the way we do business?[17]

Take the time to clearly articulate the problem and utilize the diversity on your team to see the problem from multiple perspectives. The clarity of the innovative solutions you come up with is directly connected to the clarity of understanding around the problem itself. As Einstein said, "The formulation of the problem is often more important than its solution."

## How to Increase Focus

Taking time to focus is something many of us readily acknowledge as valuable but easily overlook because of our busy lives. We're rarely held accountable to focus, at least not directly. But the impact of focus is enormous. As with each of these innovation practices, it has relevance for any innovation project, but the potential of distraction and the importance of focus are magnified when working on a project involving a diversity of cultures. Here are a few ways to get started as you build focus into your climate for culturally intelligent innovation.

## Do Creative Work First

We often start the day with mindless tasks like responding to email and scheduling meetings and save the toughest tasks for later in the day. But each task drains your energy and lowers your focus. Just as exercise tires the body, tasks like these tire the brain. Many team meetings are the same way. They begin with covering administrative details and updates and save the big collaborative work for the end.

David Rock, a thought leader in neuroscience, says, "An hour into doing your work, you've got a lot less capacity than [at the beginning]. Every decision we make tires the brain."[18] Change the order. Start with the tasks that require a greater measure of creativity and concentration and then move to the easier work. Whenever possible, I protect mornings for creative work and schedule meetings and other management tasks for later in the day.

## Get Out of the Office

There's recurring evidence that many people do their best independent thinking outside the office. The interruptions in the office are constant. If you have the option to get outside the office for your most creative tasks, do so. Figure out what environment works best for you. The same goes for your team. When you need to tackle a creative task, change environments. Simply being in a different surrounding can stimulate the experiential circuits of the brain, something we'll explore further in Chapter 5.

## Mind Your Breath

Mindfulness courses and stress management programs routinely emphasize the importance of mindful breathing. In fact, 70 to 80 percent of our energy is supposed to come from our breathing.

And simply paying attention to our breathing is another way to exercise the experiential circuitry in our brains. Paying attention to breathing is also a way of automatically putting life back into perspective by putting focus on our most essential function. Being mindful of our breathing for a few minutes brings the diverse team together around the most fundamental human similarity—we all need to breathe.

## Write

If breathing helps awaken the experiential circuits, writing helps awaken the narrative circuits. Thinking and writing are very different. Thinking is somewhat unstructured, disorganized, and even chaotic. But writing encourages you to create a story line and structure that helps you make sense of what has happened and work toward a solution. Writing provides a more systemic, solution-based approach.[19]

Amazon founder Jeff Bezos is known for requiring his leaders to come to meetings with a full written description of what they need to discuss. Bullet points are not sufficient. "Full sentences are harder to write," he says. "They have verbs. The paragraphs have topic sentences. There is no way to write a six-page, narratively structured memo and not have clear thinking."[20] When I read something from a leader that isn't clear, it raises a red flag about the individual's clarity of thought or causes me to consider whether a language barrier or cultural difference might be impeding clarity.

In several studies on people who have experienced a traumatic event, participants have been encouraged to spend just a few minutes each day writing a diary-type account of their deepest thoughts and feelings about the event. In one study, participants who had just been laid off were asked to reflect on their deepest thoughts and feelings about their job loss, including how it had affected their personal and professional lives. There was a remarkable boost in the psychological and physical well-being of participants, including a reduction in health problems and an increase in self-esteem and happiness.[21]

You don't have to write a tome. Even a few sentences or words to describe an experience, some questions for exploring more deeply, and some possible learning outcomes can be a valuable aid for tapping into the power of reflection.

## Set Three Priorities

What three priorities are you focused on this week? If you can't list them right off, that's a red flag. Every weekend, part of my journaling routine is to reflect upon key insights from the past week and anticipate what's coming up the next week. I've made it a practice to identify the top three priorities that need my attention in the coming week. My to-do list usually far exceeds those three priorities. And with an extensive travel schedule, one of the priorities may include delivering a keynote presentation with excellence at an upcoming conference. But many times, when I've lost focus, it's because I either didn't take the time to identify my top three priorities or have allowed the tyranny of the urgent to crowd them out.

## Conclusion

The more personalities and cultures you have working together on an innovative project, the easier it is to lose focus. Left unchecked, competing ideas and work styles take things out of focus. The default is to focus on the interpersonal challenges and friction rather than on defining a problem and solving it. But when a diversity of perspectives and styles coalesce around a shared objective, and each individual does the hard work of keeping focused on achieving that objective, the colorful solutions that result are well worth the effort.

I've been working on this chapter for 90 minutes, so it's time to take a break. It's cold outside, but I'm going for a walk. And having spent the last 90 minutes in the narrative focus, I'm going to strive toward functioning in the experiential focus of my brain and simply soak in what I see, hear, and smell.

## THE POWER OF FOCUS

Discipline yourself to overcome the increased distractions that come from a diverse team and focus on defining the problem and solving it.

### Climate Assessment

| I feel very focused on the problems I need to solve and what I need to do. | Almost Never | Sometimes | Almost Always |
|---|---|---|---|
| | | | |

# CHAPTER 5

## THE POWER OF TREES | SPACE

**W**hat kind of space is most conducive to culturally intelligent innovation? If you put the same team in two different environments, how will the outcome change? Or if you put two teams from different cultural backgrounds in the same space, how will their diverse backgrounds shape what happens there? Few companies have spent as much time considering the power of the work space as Google. Its open office environment, on-site massages, all-you-can-eat gourmet kitchens, and flexible work spaces have been featured in many discussions about how the workplace environment influences innovation and productivity. And while these distinctions are most evident at the company's Silicon Valley campus, similar elements appear in Google offices around the world. Google Singapore is housed in a slick skyscraper that is home to a number of corporate offices. The lobby of the building looks pretty much like most corporate lobbies found in major cities across the world. But when you ascend 30 stories and step into the Google suites, you enter a whole different universe. The bright colors, the eating areas within 100 feet of any workstation, the foosball tables, and the working pods are all part of creating an open, flexible space to cultivate creativity.

Or walk into any number of Novartis labs and offices around the world, and you see vast swaths of natural light, an abundance of plants, and large community areas intended to promote collaboration and innovative research across an incredibly diverse group of researchers and project managers. Do these kinds of work spaces promote innovation for everyone who works there? Or are they biased toward the U.S. and Swiss cultures from which they emerge?

Teams that meet in spaces with natural light report a more positive team experience than those who work together in windowless spaces. And people who look out at natural environments from the workplace feel less pressured and more satisfied with their jobs and suffer from fewer ailments such as headaches.[1] Nature, light, temperature, and noise have a consistent impact upon how diverse teams engage in productivity. These are universals that need to be factored into any space in order to most effectively leverage the potential of diversity for driving innovation.

On the other hand, not everyone responds the same way to the physical environment. Some work productively in complete silence, while others can't think without some external stimulation. Some are disoriented when there isn't a corner office for the boss, and others find it inspiring when everyone gets the same kind of work space. Japanese engineers approach office and home design in a remarkably different way from Chinese or Korean engineers, not to mention European or Latin American ones.

So does the environment shape the culture or does the culture shape the environment? Both. And diversity is reshaping the very world of design itself. As more companies adopt the open work spaces of Google and the functional minimalism of Scandinavian design, more thought needs to be put into the connections between diverse teams and their space as part of the innovation process.

## Universal Influences

Children who play in tree-lined playgrounds engage in more creative activity than those who play in treeless ones. Patients who recuperate at home recover more quickly than those who stay in the hospital. And, as previously stated, people whose work areas look out on natural spaces feel less pressured and more satisfied with their jobs.[2] In fact, according to the findings of psychologist

Marc Fried, environment is the second strongest predictor of an individual's quality of life, with a good marriage being first.[3] This seems to be true regardless of one's cultural background.

Cultural differences seem to matter in the associations we make with various spaces based upon our socialization. Our brains are continually making associations between our environment and our previous experiences in similar contexts, and that in turn influences our mood and the degree to which we're primed for generating new ideas. Different spaces cue us for different responses. We're socialized to act professional in the office, casual at the pub, and quiet in a concert hall or museum. But the way you're socialized to behave in each of these contexts differs based upon your upbringing. For those of us from monochronic cultures (e.g., in Germany)—where time is approached in a more linear fashion and work and personal life are dealt with separately—if you receive a work-related phone call when you're out at dinner with a group of friends, you may have trouble accessing the information and skills required to engage in a work-related conversation, even if the solution involves something you know really well. The reverse can happen when you're fully engaged at work and suddenly get a personal phone call or text message. Polychronic cultures (e.g., in the Middle East) approach time more fluidly and are less conditioned by the environment for what kind of interactions and thinking should take place in certain spaces. Taking a personal phone call in the middle of a work meeting is less likely to disorient someone from a polychronic context, but their monochronic peers may perceive them as distracted.

Culturally intelligent innovation must account for the power of space. The work space influences the generation of ideas, the building of trust, and the overall quality of life for individuals and teams as a whole. Forward-thinking organizations are investing a lot of time and money to develop spaces that promote improved levels of employee engagement and innovation. Let's look at some of the important variances in how space influences different individuals and cultures. But first, we need to briefly review some environmental factors that exist for all of us: nature, light, temperature, and noise.

## THE FOUR UNIVERSAL ENVIRONMENTAL FACTORS

1. Nature
2. Light
3. Temperature
4. Noise

The way these factors influence the innovation process varies according to personalities and cultures. But everyone should consider how to maximize the influence of these four factors for supporting innovation.

### Nature

There are city-lovers and country-lovers, but nature is good for all of us. The more of it you get, the better off you are. Nature works its magic in easing the mental fatigue that plagues us. One researcher in Basel, Switzerland, treated people depressed by winter weather by insisting they take an hour walk no matter how bad the weather was. The participants saw a drastic improvement in their outlook, health, and sense of well-being.[4] People recover from surgery faster if they can look out on a natural environment. Nature is essential for our survival and well-being.[5]

Environmental psychologist Winifred Gallagher describes the growing importance of natural surroundings given the mental fatigue that's endemic to a generation that spends inordinate amounts of time immersed in high-tech, artificial spaces. The soothing influence of rippling water, drifting clouds, rolling meadows, trees, rocks, and flowers is a refreshing contrast to the constant ping of email, text messages, and sitting through PowerPoint presentations. Being absorbed in nature increases our flow. Even in the middle of a city, it's possible to benefit from the powerful influence of nature by stepping from a busy street into a nearby park.[6]

I facilitate sessions and speak at conferences in a variety of venues around the world. Some event organizers determine a venue primarily based upon cost and convenience. But others prioritize finding a venue that promotes innovation, connection, and the benefits of nature. When there's natural light, easy access to the outdoors, and a view of gardens, mountains, water, or trees, the delegates end up with a far different experience than if they attend a conference in a basement for a couple of days straight. I've intentionally arranged my home office so that I get optimum stimulation for creativity. My desk is surrounded by large windows and faces a beautiful landscape of woods and water. Even when I travel, which typically ends up being in large urban areas, I work hard to find some time to get into nature—even if it's just running through a park or taking a walk by a river. Nature has a profound impact on our physical and mental well-being.

## Light

When I walk into a hotel room during the day, the first thing I do is whip open the curtains. I need light. The mind and body are triggered by exposure to light. Nothing better reveals this phenomenon than jet lag. Jet lag is mostly about how the mind and body respond to light. We're equipped with an internal light meter that sets our 24-hour circadian rhythms. We're programmed to be alert and active during the brightness of the day and restful and dormant during the darkness of the night. The internal clock is set by the body's reading of sunlight. Certain things happen in the body every day at certain times—the release of particular neurochemicals and the rise and fall of body temperature. For those who live in places with short days in the winter and long days in the summer, the internal clock is further calibrated around seasonal differences. These internal timing mechanisms are so important to your functioning that they tick away even in the womb. Therefore, when you upset the sequence of day and night, it takes time for your body to reset to the cycles of light and darkness in a new time zone.[7] Jet lag is not all in your head. It's your body and mind's response to light.

The best type of light to promote culturally intelligent innovation is natural light. The human mind and body have evolved in response to daylight. Both the central nervous system and the neuroendocrine hormonal system are influenced by the powerful stimulus of light.[8] The proper use of natural light decreases occurrences of headaches, seasonal affective disorder (SAD), and eyestrain.[9] When you remove these physiological barriers, you're better primed to think creatively and to engage with diverse perspectives. Natural light also shapes your level of focus. It is more than just a nice-to-have. It has a direct impact on productivity and your overall well-being, regardless of your cultural background.[10]

Being exposed to sunshine is the best way to help you become or remain alert and engaged, but good artificial lighting can also be useful. In addition, a 15-minute walk outside, even on a cloudy day, may do more to help you generate ideas than two hours facing a whiteboard. Figure out ways to incorporate light, preferably natural light, into the spaces where you're doing your innovative work.

## Temperature

Temperature is another essential influence to consider for everyone. Just as your body learns to adjust to different light rhythms, you physiologically adapt to different temperatures. People often joke about their blood having thinned if they've moved from a cold environment to a tropical one, but this is very real. The body adjusts to different climates and usually does so quickly. Gallagher writes, "No matter where we are from, we can physiologically adapt to the Sahara or the Amazon basin in a few weeks, mostly because our bodies will 'learn' to sweat sooner and more efficiently."[11]

Cold is a stimulant and heat is a sedative. It's pretty simple: To decrease your body's heat production, you have to stop activity. To get warm, you need to move. One study found that an hour of exposure to temperatures exceeding 32° C (90° F) tends to impair physical performance, and exposure of two hours or more begins to significantly interfere with difficult mental tasks.[12]

Many of us today have little need to adjust to vastly different temperatures because we spend the majority of our time indoors. Over the last 50 years, most people working in the developed world have spent the majority of their time in a perfectly temperate climate—heated during wintery temperatures and evenly cooled in the warmth of summer. The indoors is the primary work space of the 21st century. But it's still important to be mindful of how temperature influences people's creative contributions. The temperature in a room influences the way people are able to engage. A team member's complaint about the meeting room being too hot or cold can seem like a petty concern. But these kinds of discomforts are the very distractions that impede optimum performance when we're trying to nurture culturally intelligent innovation.

## Noise

If nature, adequate light, and a comfortable temperature are the ideal elements of an environment to promote innovation, noise is the biggest roadblock. Noise is any sound you dislike. In our beeping, buzzing, smartphone world, we can all use more quiet.

The degree to which sound acts as a stimulant or a distraction differs among individuals. Some come up with their most creative ideas with some music playing in the background, while others are distracted by that. But the universal principle is to stop and consider how sound and noise shape the way different people engage in collaborative work. Quieter spaces typically produce higher productivity, but you have to find just the right degree of quiet. Too much quiet can be a sedative.

These four environmental factors—nature, light, temperature, and noise—are universally important considerations for anyone engaged in innovation. Conscious planning around these factors will directly influence the creative process.

## Do You Need More or Less Stimulation?

Culturally intelligent innovation must also account for individual and cultural differences when it comes to the power of space. Some function best studying in the quietness of a library, while others work better in the middle of a busy coffee shop. And sometimes it depends upon the project and your mood. A familiar place such as home typically generates a secure feeling, while a novel place provides a potential sense of danger and adventure. But for certain personality types, some sense of novelty and uncertainty is exactly what is needed to generate new ideas. Others need a sense of security to generate their best ideas. The key is striking the balance between being interested and relaxed and helping others find that for themselves.

One of the most important individual differences to understand about yourself and others is the level of stimulation that will be most conducive to getting a task accomplished. Broadly speaking, extroverts direct their attention outward to the greater world because that's what stimulates their thinking and behavior. Introverts focus mostly upon their own thoughts and feelings and receive stimulation from within. Both personality types need people and both need alone time. Having an understanding of what kind of stimulation is needed from one's space is a helpful tool for strengthening the ability to generate new ideas.

The dazzling array of amenities at tech firms like Google, Facebook, and LinkedIn is an intentional use of the power of space to simulate a context similar to a university, where students play hard and work hard. Google executives Eric Schmidt and Jonathan Rosenberg say, "What most outsiders fail to see when they visit Google is the offices where employees spend the bulk of their time. Follow the typical Googler . . . from the volleyball court, café, or kitchen back to their workspace and what will you find? A series of cubicles that are crowded, messy, and a petri dish for creativity."[13]

Schmidt and Rosenberg argue that most organizations' work spaces are designed to keep people quiet and to demonstrate authority. Entry-level staff members are put in cubicles and CEOs get a big corner office walled away from everyone else. In contrast, Schmidt and Rosenberg maintain that the ideal context for innovation is a highly interactive, boisterous, crowded office space busting with hectic energy. Google offers places where individuals can take a private phone call or get some alone time, including outdoor terraces and nap pods. But the norm is keeping everyone surrounded by teammates so the minute you have a eureka moment, you can tap someone on the shoulder and get her perspective on it.[14]

While most organizations don't provide the gourmet meals, free massages, and nap pods offered by Silicon Valley's big tech firms, more than 70 percent of today's workforce have an open office plan where walls and cubicles have been removed. The average amount of space per employee shrank from 500 square feet in the 1970s to 200 square feet in 2010. This is also happening in schools, where traditional rows of seating have been replaced by pods of four or more desks pushed together.[15]

Susan Cain, author of the book *Quiet*, challenges the notion that group work, collaboration, and brainstorming are always the best ways to promote innovation. Cain argues that introverts come up with far more innovative ideas when they're offered regular bouts of solitude. Personal space is vital to their ability to deliberately focus and generate ideas. As I walk through the maze of people at places like Google, I definitely sense a high-energy vibe among many. But I also notice that nearly everyone has ear buds drowning out the chitchat around them. It's important to consider how open office environments shape the work that needs to be done.

Many individuals from hierarchical cultures wonder what kind of respect a company has for its executives if the senior leaders don't sit in an office that is different from where an entry-level associate sits. Companies have every right to go against the cultural norms; but beware of assuming that ego is the only reason an executive should be given a corner office. In many hierarchical cultures, the honor given to an executive reflects upon the organization and society as a whole. If an organization is going to replicate the Google office space, its leaders need to consciously consider how this will affect the engagement of different individuals and cultures.

Pay attention to the kind of space that best allows talent to do the work they need to do. Monitor when you personally need more stimulation and when you need less. After several weeks of travel, speaking to large groups of people, and meeting with individuals, I covet the chance to work from the refuge of my home office for a while. But after a long stretch of writing in solitude, I need the stimulation of larger systems than those that exist in my private work space. A critical aspect of creating a space for innovation stems from making conscious choices about where and how we work.

## Culture ←⎯⎯→ Environment

Nature, light, temperature, and noise are environmental factors that influence everyone. But the way you respond to these natural elements is partially shaped by your cultural socialization. Furthermore, culture itself is something that is largely developed as a society's response to its natural environment. It's impossible to separate culture from environment.

There's a long-standing relationship between culture and environment. Traditionally, anthropologists studied cultures by examining what people did in order to survive in their environment. This survival stems from the most basic need: How will we feed ourselves? Societies develop norms, values, and preferences based upon whether they hunted or gathered to survive. Hunting is a more independent task than farming. It requires going off by yourself or in small groups to search for your prey; then you come back to the homestead to feed yourself and others. But farming requires a much more collective effort. You need several people to work a field and harvest the crops, and the result is that people have to work together more collaboratively. You can't do it on your own. Therefore, societies don't arbitrarily decide to become "individualist" or "collectivist" cultures. They organize themselves based on what's needed to survive, and over time, that behavior shapes how they think and behave. Cultural values stem from how a society has learned to survive within its environment.

Societies also develop norms and practices that lead to the creation of an economic system. Tribes and communities determine how to exchange goods with each other, and they figure out how to obtain the materials and goods they cannot get from their own environment. A society has to answer the question "How should we trade goods with other societies?"; the system that develops becomes its latent economic system.

The same kind of survival-oriented responses to environment lead a society to develop myriad other cultural systems, including family systems (who should marry whom and how should children be cared for and integrated into society?), order (how will we govern ourselves?), mobility (what modes of transportation will get us from one place to another?), and security (how are we going to protect ourselves?). Each of these cultural systems is developed in response to surviving the demands of the environment. Culture does not merely develop as a cognitive abstraction. Instead, culture is the pattern of life that emerges from how a group of people learns to survive in response to the geography, weather, and overall natural environment of the surroundings. The relationship between culture and environment runs deep. It spills over into food. People in tropical climates are more likely to eat spicy foods, with the spices sometimes used to preserve the food longer and eliminate bacteria. And in northern environments, cultures have built diets around things like potatoes, apples, and beets that stay fresh for a long time in cold storage.

You see the impact of environment upon culture by looking at the contrasts in behavior between country folk and city folk. People living in rural regions often refer to how cold and rude people are in the city. In one study, fewer than 40 percent of urbanites shook hands with a stranger, but almost 70 percent of small-towners did.[16] But are city people "meaner" than country folk? Studies show that city people are just as affectionate and accommodating with those they know as small-town people are. But the cosmopolitan chill is a behavioral shield that protects city folk against the overstimulation of strangers. If you stopped to greet every person who walked by in the city, you'd never survive.

The inability to explain the behavior of others is one of the biggest sources of conflict among diverse groups. Some enhanced understanding about how people's cultural backgrounds influence how they behave can go a long way toward developing a more culturally intelligent team. Organizations can prime the way diverse teams collaborate by giving careful attention to space. Do marketers engage with their spaces differently than engineers? Does your function in the workplace change how you react to your space? Absolutely! Goethe wrote, "It is a pity that just the excellent personalities suffer most from the adverse effects of the atmosphere."[17] Individuals working in the creative fields—including designers, musicians, writers, and artists—are more prone to the highs linked to abundant light and the lows caused by too little. The great composer Gustav Mahler experienced highs in the summer and lows in the winter, but spring and fall were his most productive seasons. Artist Vincent van Gogh seemed particularly obsessed with light and color, with some of his paintings dark and ominous and others full of sun. This has caused some to believe he suffered from seasonal affective disorder.[18]

Don't discount the power of space for the kind of innovative work generated by your team. Large investments in innovative office design may be worthwhile for some. But even a planned gathering in a natural environment can be an inexpensive, strategic way to utilize the power of space to drive culturally intelligent innovation. Forget the forced team-building programs and just go have fun. Do outdoor group activities in a new place, far enough away from the office to feel like a real trip but still doable in a day, and provide an experience that people couldn't or wouldn't have on their own. A day like this is likely to do more for the innovative process than a year of one-hour meetings in a conference room.

## The Virtual Space

How does working virtually influence the power of space? Building trust, managing conflict, and sharing ideas are all more difficult when done solely through technology. One study of 30,000 employees working for a variety of multinational companies found that 46 percent of those working on virtual teams had never met their virtual team members. Another 30 percent said they only met them once a year. Cultural differences make trust building and collegiality difficult on any team, but it's all the more difficult on a virtual team.[19] On the other hand, a virtual space allows individuals to adjust their work environments to ideally suit their personal preferences (temperature, amount of visual stimuli, etc.). And virtual connections allow most any team to tap a global network of diverse team members.

The absence of a shared physical space is a large part of why being on a virtual team is so difficult. When you work with people in the same space, you see them, socialize with them before the meeting or during a break, and are aware of them even when they aren't speaking. You also have tacit information about things going on that may influence their behavior (e.g., a storm that made getting to work extra difficult for everyone or the fact that everyone will be off tomorrow for a national holiday). Most of this information is lost on a global virtual team. You lose the input from nonverbal cues and informal conversation. Team members working from vastly different spaces can even have a different psychological mindset when reading an email in one setting versus another.

Virtual team meetings are one of the most challenging exercises. For most global virtual teams, some participants are calling in late at night, others early in the morning, and still others somewhere in between. And some might be listening to a loud lawn mower going by outdoors, some might be dealing with the smell of paint fumes in an adjacent room, while others might be drinking coffee and enjoying a good pastry. The temperature and light is varied in each location, as are the possible distractions. All of these environmental factors influence what occurs. As we move into the process for culturally intelligent innovation, I'll describe some specific practices that will help address these challenges on a virtual team. For now, consider the way different spaces change the way your virtual team members engage in innovation. This includes the kinds of specific environmental factors I just mentioned—different lighting, temperature, smells, etc. But it's also things like the influence of working on a project in the middle of Chinese New Year, Ramadan, or Christmas. And it most certainly includes the way the actual technology used influences the kind of collaboration and innovation that takes place.

## How to Use the Power of Space

Some people like very little external stimulation when working on an innovative idea, and others want all kinds of it. Some cultures are very sensitive to the environment, and others aren't. So what's a culturally intelligent way of utilizing the power of space to support the innovative process?

### Determine Need for More Stimulation or Less

Begin with yourself. Monitor whether you need more stimulation or less. This includes awareness of the kind of space that best supports creative thinking for you, which may vary according to your current flow, mood, and the project at hand. Some individuals find that the chatter at the coffee shop isn't as distracting as the conversation around them at work because coffee shop discussions can be tuned out as irrelevant. As you engage in creative work, look at the task and consider when you need complete silence to focus and when working from a more active environment would help you better accomplish your goal.

### Create the Space You Need

I've managed to work on creative projects in some pretty unusual contexts—from standing on a subway and scribbling down ideas to sitting under a tree in Liberia while waiting a couple of hours for my host to pick me up. Sometimes, an idea comes to you and you make the most of it wherever you are. But becoming mindful of how to leverage the power of your space will enhance the creative process and the interactions you have with others.

Set up your space intentionally. Eliminate distractions, arrange for exposure to natural light, allow for the physical breaks needed, and pay attention to the temperature and how it influences the way people engage. Most work spaces are not set up for encouraging culturally intelligent innovation, but do whatever you can to change that.

## Allow Flexibility

Understand the diversity of preferences among the people on your team. Just as some people prefer urban life and others prefer life in the country, people have very different responses to physical environments. Look for the space that works best for your team, and empower individuals to take control of making the space most conducive for them. Begin with the universals of light, nature, noise, and temperature. Then allow for some flexibility in how people interact with the space. When people are surrounded by prompts to think creatively and come up with innovative solutions, they are more inclined to think and behave that way.

## Go Minimalist

A minimalist workspace is different for each person. Moreover, creativity and minimalism operate in dynamic tension. On the one hand, creativity is often fueled by having ready access to a number of ideas—which might be found in books, magazines, or product samples. On the other hand, an abundance of information and visual stimulation may make it difficult to focus. On the whole, eliminating unnecessary clutter is advantageous for culturally intelligent innovation. The degree to which you want to minimize is highly personal and varies widely across cultures, but there's increasing evidence that clutter and an abundance of visual stimulation get in the way of the creative process.

Clear the walls, toss the knickknacks and trinkets, and clear desks and tables. Organize and simplify the way you capture ideas so that you can actually find them when needed. When meeting together around a table, declutter the space as much as possible. Provide only the printed materials that are necessary, and ask everyone to reduce summaries to one page or better yet a diagram.

## Conclusion

I recently facilitated two similar sessions with two different groups of executives. The first session was held in a dowdy banquet hall with dim lighting, décor straight out of the 1970s, no windows, and "easy-listening" music playing through the speakers while people came in. The next day, I facilitated another session with a different group of leaders. This one was held in a brightly lit, chic room with windows all across the back wall and upbeat music pumping through the speakers as people found their seats. The difference in how people engaged was remarkable. Part of it may have been the difference I felt personally as the facilitator. But I'm convinced the different space was the biggest factor in what changed.

Take control of the innovative process by managing your space. The stimuli that come from your environment are ripe with opportunities for discoveries about ourselves and the world. Beware of the differences among your team and leverage the universal power of light and nature.

### THE POWER OF PHYSICAL SPACE

Take control of your physical space in order to create the ideal climate for culturally intelligent innovation.

### Climate Assessment

| I am aware of the kind of physical space that is most conducive for me to do creative work. | Not Aware | Somewhat | Very Aware |
|---|---|---|---|
| | | | |

# CHAPTER 6

## THE POWER OF TRUST

**W**ang, a local Chinese leader, has a hard time convincing his German headquarters that they should buy some needed equipment from a manufacturer in China. The German office insists that the equipment should be imported from Europe to ensure quality. When Wang can't get anywhere, he involves his European colleague Hans. Hans agrees with Wang and tells headquarters that the source in China is far cheaper and can offer equal quality to what's available in Europe. Corporate listens to Hans and not only agrees to purchase the equipment for China locally, but makes China the primary sourcing agent for the equipment globally, at a huge savings to the company.[1]

Why did corporate trust Hans and not Wang? Was it just a matter of their different abilities to persuade corporate leadership, or did their respective cultures have anything to do with it? There's compelling evidence that culture played a significant part in why headquarters more quickly trusted Hans than Wang. And this works both ways. Not only are Germans more likely to trust Germans, but Chinese are more likely to trust Chinese. One study revealed that Chinese workers consistently describe their expat managers as empty vessels—all talk and no content. One Chinese worker described his expat manager by saying:

> I mean he has no knowledge in this industry and he told something to me [and] it's very stupid . . . he's just talking, talking . . . he doesn't know . . . Actually other people are saying he's dumb.[2]

Innovation involves risk, both for organizations and their employees. And it's unlikely individuals will make themselves susceptible to risk unless there's a climate of trust. When individuals feel trusted, they know they can take the risks required to pursue innovative projects. Failure is expected and the key is whether bold attempts are made and lessons learned.

Most diverse teams describe trust as the make or break issue for whether they can be creative and productive. We all know intuitively that trust is a crucial component in order for any relationship to succeed, and innovation is unlikely without it. But how do you effectively build trust across diverse teams? And what does the research reveal about how cultural diversity influences the trust-building process?

## The Role of Trust in Innovation

Edwin Land, the inventor of the Polaroid camera, popularized the idea that failure is a critical part of creativity and innovation. He said that individuals and organizations that are afraid to fail are doomed. Serial entrepreneur Richard Branson says, "The very idea of entrepreneurship . . . conjures up the frightening prospect of taking risks and failing."[3] Branson should know. In the early years of Virgin Records, Branson's two partners were split on how to handle the desperate need for cash to sign bigger artists. One partner, Nik Powell, wanted to conserve resources and slowly earn money through retail sales. But Simon Draper, the other partner, wanted to invest heavily in signing big artists. They went with Draper's riskier option, which turned out to be a profitable decision, but it set them up for a possibility of massive failure.

Branson's most recent risk has been the investment in commercial space travel. The crash of a test flight of the Virgin Galactic SpaceShipTwo in 2014, in which one of the pilots died, might be Branson's biggest failure yet. But Branson won't give up. He says he'll be on the first commercial flight Virgin Galactic takes to space.

Branson has far more appetite and tolerance for risk than most of us ever will. But anyone who wants to innovate has to embrace the possibility of failure, and your willingness to fail is directly tied to the level of trust involved. This works both ways. Management can't trust teams to innovate if the teams haven't proven themselves as trustworthy. And teams won't attempt something that could end in failure if they don't trust management and feel that management trusts them.

Trust means different things to different cultures. It comes down to whether you believe somebody is dependable. It's a subjective evaluation, but it's crucial for innovation to occur. The very same behavior can elicit trust for one individual and erode it for someone else, depending upon how the behavior is interpreted. For example, a leader from a culture oriented toward egalitarianism might earn trust from her subordinates by sharing an example about when she failed; but disclosing those failures, especially early on with a group, might erode trust and credibility with followers who come from a culture with a top-down orientation to leadership. Trust is based on different values and therefore has a complex nature.

There are many layers of complexity to how we're socialized to think about success, failure, and trust. In many cultures, failure not only reflects upon you as an individual but also reflects on your entire corporation and most of all your family and parents. This is what happened to Heather Cho, former vice president at Korean Airlines, after she threw a fit on a flight because she was served nuts in a bag rather than in a dish. Cho demanded that the flight attendant be removed from the flight and ordered the plane to return to the gate. The media got hold of the story, and Cho was forced to resign for her unacceptable behavior and was later imprisoned for it. Her father, the chair of the airline, held his head in shame as he described his daughter's "foolish conduct." He said, "I beg the people to blame me for the current situation, because everything is my fault . . . I failed to properly educate my daughter."[4] What a view of failure! The father of a senior executive owns his adult daughter's failure because he didn't teach her better as a child.

Not all failure is equal. Some failures should cost people their jobs, regardless of the cultures involved, but that is highly dependent upon the circumstances and context of the culture. I'm simply suggesting that helping diverse teams become comfortable with failure and learning to trust one another in the midst of risk is going to require more than a few team-building activities. A willingness to trust is deeply rooted in our psyche.

And the obstacles toward building trust are compounded when working virtually. When working with someone in the same location, trust is built through a series of experiences and observations over time. Based upon the way you get along around the office, your behavior at lunch, and your interactions in team meetings, your peers form opinions about whether they can trust you. If you have a bad day and don't show up for a meeting, your colleagues have a larger context from which to interpret your behavior. But when collaboration is all virtual, trust is almost entirely dependent upon follow-through and reliability. There's no watercooler conversation to create a larger picture of who you are. People from Western cultures find it relatively easy to trust a culturally dissimilar colleague as long as they follow through, whereas people from many other cultures (Asian, Middle Eastern, Latin) face significant barriers trusting someone they've never met. Therefore, on a virtual team, trust is built or destroyed by one or two factors. I'm a strong proponent of virtual collaboration. A great deal of the work we do with our team around the world is conducted virtually, and it allows us to bring in a far more global, diverse perspective. But if culturally intelligent innovation is going to be a reality, the cultural dynamics of trust building have to be addressed on any diverse team, and especially on virtual ones.

## It Starts in Your Head!

Many people deny that someone's ethnicity or culture has anything to do with whether they trust them. Yet the consistent response I hear when I ask people whom they trust most is "I trust people who are like me." One young woman told me, "I look for whether they share my morals and beliefs"; another individual said, "I trust people like my friend Katie because I know she'll do the job the same way I would."

We trust the familiar, and that tendency emerges in infancy. In one study, 10-month-old American and French infants were offered two equally attractive toys. One was offered by an English-speaking adult and the other by a French-speaking adult. The American babies consistently reached for the toy offered by the English speaker, while the French babies did exactly the opposite. Even babies gravitate toward people like themselves because of the safety of the familiar.[5]

What's remarkable is how slight the similarity needs to be for a sense of trust and attraction to occur. Brett Pelham is renowned for his research on this tendency to favor people with even the slightest similarities to ourselves. Women are more likely to marry men whose last name shares the first letter of their maiden name. People named Louis are more likely to live in St. Louis, just as people named Paul, Mary, and Helen are more likely to live in St. Paul, St. Mary, and St. Helen.[6]

Research consistently reveals that we're implicitly biased toward people who are similar to us. It's not so much that we feel explicit hatred or dislike toward others—it's that we reserve our admiration, sympathy, and trust for our in-group.[7]

Fundamental attribution error is a psychological phenomenon that explains our tendency to view our own behavior based upon the circumstances involved and to view the behavior of others based upon their personality and cultural background. The greater the cultural difference, the more likely we are to engage in fundamental attribution error. In other words, we're more likely to give ourselves and people like us the benefit of the doubt. If my phone rings in the movie theater, clearly everyone should understand that I'm waiting for a call from my daughter who is traveling alone. But if your cell phone goes off, my default thought is: *What a jerk! He didn't turn his phone off.* This works the other way too. If I succeed at something, my implicit response is to give myself credit for making it happen. But if you succeed, particularly if you're from a different background, I'm more likely to credit the circumstances that enabled your success rather than giving you personal credit. The more different you are from me, the more likely I am to resort to fundamental attribution error to interpret your behavior.

We implicitly trust people like ourselves. We're all biased. Some implicit favoritism is inevitable. But acting upon that bias is not. We can consciously learn to trust people who differ from us and help others do the same. And we can leverage the power of in-group bias by creating bonds within a team striving toward innovation. But before we lay out some of the leading practices for doing this, we need to examine the variables that most consistently influence whether we trust someone.

## Calculating Trust

How do you decide whom to trust? For many people, trust revolves around someone who does what he says he will, follows through on promises, and isn't a "crazy" person. But for others, trust is more likely to be derived from shared social networks—who knows whom, the individual or company's reputation across those networks, and a leader's ability to build harmonious teams. So when the leader of a diverse teams says "We just need to build trust," there may be multiple understandings of what that means.

Coca-Cola expects each of its 139,000 employees around the world to earn and maintain trust by being "honest and transparent in [their] dealings."[8] Neeraj Garg, a Coke executive in South Asia, is an ardent supporter of the company's commitment to honesty and transparency. However, he says, "The path to that understanding can vary in different cultures." When Garg works with Westerners, he knows that building trust means getting down to business quickly, but many of the South Asians he works with expect trustworthy business dealings to begin with a friendly conversation over coffee or tea. Garg says, "In India, don't expect quick decisions or actions because everything is a journey."[9] Trust takes a long time to build, but it can be lost overnight.

What goes into calculating trust? Five factors consistently emerge when calculating trust: likability, competency, intentions, reliability, and reputation.[10] The degree to which these factors influence whether you trust someone depends upon the task involved, your personality, and your culture. Whom I trust to design a website is much different from whom I trust to care for my kids or whom I trust to provide financial advice. Think about the importance of these five factors for you and then consider how others on your team might value them differently.

## 1. Likability

One of the first things many managers intuitively look for when screening job candidates is an individual's likability. Is this the kind of person we want to bring into our organization? How "nice" is she? People often say, "Only hire someone you'd want to have a beer with." But Eric Schmidt and Jonathan Rosenberg of Google say, "Truth be told, some of our most effective colleagues are people we most definitely would *not* want to have a beer with . . . You must work with people you don't like because a workforce comprised of people who are all 'best office buddies' can be homogenous, and homogeneity in an organization breeds failure."[11]

Some of your best teammates might annoy you. This is one of the most important lessons I've learned throughout the years. An intuitive sense of chemistry has often been important to me in selecting people with whom to partner. But I've sometimes learned the hard way that they weren't always the best partners. In contrast, there have been times when I was part of a team that selected a partner who wasn't overly likable to me, but without question, the individual became an incredible asset to the project.

Furthermore, likability is culturally bound. Individuals coming from cultures that prefer indirect communication, saving-face behaviors, and a deferential posture may like someone who is indirect and deferential more than someone who is direct and confident. And individuals coming from cultures that prefer charisma, friendly banter, and sarcasm may distrust someone who is more reserved and poised.

U.S. voters care more about whether their elected officials are likable than German voters do. U.S. presidential candidates are presented as likable through sharing personal stories and taking time to connect with the everyday person at the local diner. However, people like Angela Merkel and her advisers don't seem to put too much effort into making her appear likable to the general public. She comes off as matter-of-fact, modest, efficient, and someone who gets the job done. Ironically, given the dominant values in German culture, those are the very things that make her more likable to many Germans, so perhaps likability is just as important but is defined differently for Germans versus Americans. However, less effort is put into presenting Chancellor Merkel as a warm, likable person you'd want to invite to dinner.

## 2. Competency

An individual's competency to complete a task successfully is another crucial variable that influences whom you trust. You might like someone a great deal, but at some point, you question whether the individual has the skills to do what needs to be done. How many times have you heard "He's a nice guy but I'm just not sure he's the right fit for this job"? This factor correlates most with the specific task that needs to be completed. There are people who are very dear to us whom we wouldn't trust to do a certain job because they lack the skills to do it.

Competency is less subjective than likability, but it's still influenced by cultural differences. If you have a low tolerance for ambiguity (high uncertainty avoidance), you might evaluate a team member's competency based upon how seriously he has weighed the pros and cons of a proposed idea. Does he demonstrate an understanding of the risks and has he suggested a structured plan for implementation? However, someone who prefers to be more spontaneous (low uncertainty avoidance) might view a team member who takes a great deal of time to work through all the details as lacking the insight, confidence, and intuition to quickly make a decision.

One's competency to program a software solution is less subjective than the competencies of effective leadership. But even technical competencies can be interpreted differently based upon cultural orientations. Some of the cross-cultural conflicts experienced by IT workers aren't always a right versus wrong approach in programming but simply different. The designers of some computer languages are dogmatic about the need to use procedural coding, whereas others use what's called declarative language or an object-oriented approach. Like anything, each language has its strengths and weaknesses, but our inclination is to view those who use our preferred approach as being more competent.

## 3. Intentions

Trust involves risk. Part of opening ourselves up to that risk is putting our confidence in the intentions of others. Do I perceive you as someone with whom I can safely share my creative idea, or will you ridicule it or steal it and take the credit for it? This comes down to your perception of whether you feel psychologically safe with a fellow team member or supervisor, and it has a strong, direct effect on interpersonal cooperation and teamwork. It's the belief that you will not be rejected or humiliated and that you can trust the positive intentions of your co-innovators.

People coming from universalist cultures, where it's expected that the same rules and policies should apply to everyone, often distrust the intentions of people from particularist cultures, where preferential treatment is given to some based upon relationship and circumstances. Universalists are afraid that particularists are going to show favoritism to some and not others. These conversations quickly lead to discussions about bribes and corruption. But the reverse is also true. Individuals who come from particularist cultures, which are organized around social obligations and relationships, have a hard time trusting an individual or organization that ascribes to a seemingly arbitrary set of rules and policies with no regard for the immediate circumstances and relationships involved. And many underrepresented groups in various societies don't trust the intentions and discernment of the judicial system of the dominant culture to arbitrate fairly and in a trustworthy way, despite claiming they use universalist policies and laws.

The issue of intentions can be further exacerbated by the very real differences that emerge on teams as a result of variance in the time allocated by each team member to the project. Some individuals may be expected to devote 40 percent of their time to a project, while others are spending only about 10 percent of their time on it. This changes the level of priority the project has in each team member's mind and can cause subconscious evaluations of one another when some members are putting less time into it. And particularly if these different time allocations are not made explicit to everyone, some distrust may emerge based upon the limited priority some seem to be placing upon the team's shared project.

## 4. Reliability

Reliability is another part of how we calculate trust. This is one of the most important variables for many Westerners. When Western managers are asked about their experience leading staff in various places around the world, it usually comes down to deliverables. Do they deliver in a timely and consistent manner? Do their innovative ideas translate into results?

Reliability looks different depending upon the culture and organization involved. At Facebook, reliability is not doing something perfectly but it's following through and getting it done or "shipping it," as they say. In fact, the company has posters all around its campus that say things like "Done is better than perfect" and "Move fast and break things." Hackers are welcomed and bad press is just a part of being a high-tech, fast-moving company. Trust is built based upon whether you ship it.

In contrast, reliability in many other cultures means having completed a task with precision, even if it takes longer than originally expected. Akbar Al Baker, CEO of Qatar Airways, insists on the highest level of perfection and attention to detail before he trusts a new product. When Airbus first debuted the A380, the largest passenger jet, to Qatar Airways, Al Baker rejected it. The plane had some cosmetic shortcomings he perceived as unacceptable, and therefore in his mind it was completely unreliable.

## 5. Reputation

Finally, an individual's or organization's reputation is one more significant part of the trust calculation. Particularly in face-conscious cultures like most of Asia and the Middle East, an individual's reputation is paramount when people are assessing trustworthiness. This is an area where I've often experienced some of the greatest cultural differences with some of my colleagues. For me, the top two factors that go into my calculation of trust are the chemistry with a person (likability) and a confidence that he will follow through according to plan (reliability). But for many of my colleagues from other cultural backgrounds, the individual's reputation is at least equally important as his follow-through and certainly more significant than his likability. Even if someone's reputation has been smeared unfairly by disgruntled employees or a competitor, some of my colleagues are much more conscious of how the individual's reputation will influence the perception that he's trustworthy, particularly in places like Asia.

For many North American organizations, working with an innovative start-up that no one has heard of is a nonissue, as long as the start-up has the capacity and competency to do what it promises. But for many companies in other parts of the world, hiring a new vendor that is unknown is a huge hurdle to overcome. There's no established reputation, and that adds a high level of risk. What's this group like under pressure? How long will they stay at it? Who do they know and where have they worked before?

The five trust factors—likability, competency, intentions, reliability, and reputation—show up in most any individual, organization, and team around the world. The difference is in the level of importance they have for an individual, a culture, and the respective team. Take a moment and think about a situation where you need to trust someone. Then put the five trust factors in the order of priority they are for you in trusting someone with this situation. If you're leading a team, ask members to put them in order of importance. Or give each person on your team 20 votes to be distributed according to the level of importance each factor has for her in calculating trust. This can create a useful dialogue on a diverse team about the different needs and perceptions you have about what it means to trust each other.

## FIVE TRUST FACTORS

Five factors consistently emerge when calculating trust. The degree to which these factors are relevant for whom you trust depends upon the task involved, your personality, and your culture. Think about an innovative project you're working on. Put these in the order of importance they have for you as you think about trusting others to do their part on the project:

☐ Likability                    ☐ Reliability

☐ Competency               ☐ Reputation

☐ Intentions

Trust is crucial across all stages of teamwork and development, but it's most crucial during the forming/bonding stage. And given that diverse teams have fewer commonalities upon which to immediately build mutual trust, this has to be addressed intentionally from the start. Without sufficient trust from the beginning, team members may not be willing to share critical information with each other or accept the risks associated with relying on others. Notice that the majority of the trust factors discussed in this chapter are things that need to be established before much work together even begins. But it has to be factored in continually throughout the innovation process because people inevitably default back to their implicit notions of trust. When conflict hits, the default is to go back to in-group and out-group categories, which leads us to distrust someone who is unlike us. And when trust is lost, the innovation process deteriorates.

## How to Build Trust on a Diverse Team

Global leaders need to demonstrate trust-building capabilities in two ways. First, they need to *gain trust* from members from different cultural backgrounds. In some cultures, trust is gained primarily by the leader's formal position. In other cultures, a leader can best earn trust by demonstrating his competency and by how he relates to others.

Second, global leaders need to *build trust among team members.* The culture and personality of individuals on a team influences how the participants calculate trust according to the five trust factors, so culturally intelligent strategies are needed. A great deal of this comes down to whether team members feel like they can relate to each other. Team leaders often focus most upon aligning tasks and results as the sole driver for creating team spirit. The differences according to various functions and cultures are overlooked, but they're still there, lurking beneath the surface. People still do not feel as if they are a team, and therefore they are not willing to go that extra mile for each other. Structure by itself does not make a team. The organizations that can create mutual trust and a sense of relatedness despite cultural differences have a clear competitive advantage.

Here are a few leading practices for building trust across a culturally diverse team.

### Leverage the Power of In-Group Bias

One of the most startling aspects of in-group bias is how easily it is triggered. Henri Tajfel discovered what is called the "minimal group procedure"—an experimental technique in which people who have never met before are divided into groups on the basis of minimal information (e.g., a preference for one type of painting versus another, places everyone in the group has visited, or even just the toss of a coin). Tajfel discovered that groups formed on the basis of almost any distinction are prone to in-group bias, even if the distinctions are created randomly, such as the "green group" versus the "blue group."[12]

Work on developing some in-group identity as quickly as possible. I use this judiciously when I speak. I try to find something I have in common with the audience; then, I work on identifying with them in contrast to others who are not part of the group in attendance. This has to be done very carefully or it erodes cultural intelligence and promotes an unhealthy "us versus them" mentality. But once you create a sense that you're an in-group together, it allows you to have greater authority in challenging some of the potential blind spots of the group, rather than doing so as a perceived outsider. Once people perceive me as being "one of them," they may be more open to me speaking as a friendly critic from within the group about ways we might need to improve our approach to cultural intelligence and global leadership.

The less competitively oriented a culture is, the more cautious you want to be in using this tactic explicitly with a team. And there may be an impulsive resistance and distrust of someone who comes in and tries to create a bond that doesn't really exist. But given the reality of our default preference for people "like us," help the group establish likability by accentuating the shared characteristics across the team.

## Build Team Competence

Once a team bonds around what they have in common, lasting trust requires that the team is competent enough to accomplish their task. This stems from something described as group efficacy—the degree to which each individual on a team thinks the members of the group are able to perform the behaviors required of them. This assumes that you've put the right team together in the first place. It's also connected to self-efficacy, an individual's sense of confidence that she has the capability to accomplish a task. Group and self-efficacy are critical parts of cultural intelligence because without some self-confidence in your capabilities, it's difficult to persevere through the inevitable challenges of cross-cultural work and relationships.[13]

Find ways to demonstrate the value of the different skills and perspectives represented by your team members. Give some short-term manageable goals that are possible to achieve only with the shared competencies on the team, and then create a workflow that reflects the respective competencies and expertise among team members.

Shared competency gets built on a team when the leader uses a culturally intelligent approach to draw out the strengths of various team members and the added synergies from when those strengths are combined with others. Without that, team members may default to their personal preferences and cultural values. The individualists on the team are most likely to perceive the highly productive, autonomous team members as the most competent people on the team. However, the collectivists are more likely to perceive the team members who can commit to shared goals, work collaboratively, and contribute to consensus as being the most competent team members. In reality, the most competent team is one that brings together the best of autonomous initiative with a collective sense of working toward the same goal. Strive to develop team successes that wouldn't be possible without both of these.

## Develop Team Results

Next, grow the team's confidence in its ability to reach results. This is something referred to as group potency—the extent to which everyone on the team thinks the group can deliver results.[14] Teams that score high on group potency are more consistently perceived as highly effective teams by the managers who work with them.[15]

Group efficacy (confidence in the team's competence) and group potency (confidence that the team can achieve results) are related but different. Among teachers at a school, group efficacy is the perception that they have the skills needed to effectively teach the students. Group potency, however, is the teachers' perception that their efforts will result in students successfully achieving learning outcomes. You might perceive that the teachers are competent, but if there's inadequate budget or a dysfunctional administration, it might prevent you from having confidence that the skilled teachers can successfully accomplish the shared outcomes. Both group efficacy and group potency are important for building and sustaining trust.[16]

Create some small wins early on and allow the team to experience successes that they couldn't have had without being together. Provide regular feedback and be sure to set measurable goals that are challenging enough to motivate team members but not so difficult that they end up defeated. A culturally intelligent leader helps teams work interdependently when task uncertainty is high. And the more collectivist a team member is, the more important that he has a sense of confidence in the team's ability to pull off what you've set out to do.[17]

## Create Psychological Safety

Psychological safety is a group climate where team members are comfortable that they will not be negatively judged or ridiculed if they speak up with an idea. This is a critical part of developing a trusting climate for diverse teams to pursue innovation. In a psychologically safe environment, diverse team members can coalesce around creative ideas rather than around protecting themselves.[18] Perceptions of psychological safety tend to be similar among people who work closely together. In some cultures, leaders nurture this kind of safety by explicitly inviting input and feedback, being inclusive, and modeling openness and fallibility. In other cultures, leaders may nurture it by showing strength, personal confidence, and limited fallibility. Psychological safety is a climate where members are confident their teammates won't embarrass, reject, or punish them for speaking up with their ideas.

Psychological safety is often lacking between airline pilots. If a young pilot in training believes the captain and cocaptain may have made a crucial misjudgment, without psychological safety, she may not say anything given her junior status, and all the more so if she comes from a hierarchical orientation. Not only is she less experienced, she's being evaluated by these captains on every flight. The prospect of speaking up to the superior officers brings significant emotional costs, even though all three of the pilots are viewed as an interdependent team in the cockpit. The junior pilot chooses silence, even though it could cost her her life. The anticipated discomfort of being chastised or ignored distorts her judgment.

To create psychological safety, a culturally intelligent leader creates a team culture that builds trust based upon some shared values and practices agreed to by each member of the team. The leader needs to actively silence more dominant, powerful team members and draw out those who are less likely to speak up—something we'll address more fully in Chapter 8. In the end, psychological safety can enable team diversity to be utilized more effectively, thereby reaping the benefits of diversity.[19]

## Conclusion

Many organizations spend a lot of money to bring in consultants and facilitators to guide an innovative process of brainstorming and strategic planning. But there's little the best facilitators can do for you if the team members don't trust each other. Culturally intelligent innovation comes from a climate of trust where differences are perceived as an asset rather than a liability.

I work with many colleagues from cultures where ambiguity and uncertainty creates a lot of anxiety (high uncertainty avoidance). When we're interacting together socially, it's not a big deal. But when I'm asked for the 15th time for assurances about the plan for an upcoming project, I start to think: *Why don't you trust me?* Meanwhile, when I provide a less than detailed explanation and response, they begin to think: *Why can't you offer us more thorough plans? Can I trust you to do this?*

Trust begins with a spirit of positive intent. When encountering behavior that seems out of the ordinary or potentially untrustworthy, start with assuming the best and seeking to understand what's behind the behavior. There will be times when it becomes clear that we shouldn't trust someone. There are some individuals who are unreliable and incompetent and whose intentions cannot be trusted. But we need to arrive at that judgment carefully, particularly when cultural differences are involved.

## THE POWER OF TRUST

Learn what builds trust among your diverse colleagues and users in order to accept the risks that are necessary for successful innovation.

### Climate Assessment

| I know what trust factors are most important to my diverse colleagues and clients. | Strongly Disagree | Somewhat Agree | Strongly Agree |
|---|---|---|---|
| | | | |

# Part II

The 5D Process for Culturally Intelligent Innovation

Culturally intelligent innovation is most likely to emerge from a *climate* that includes the powerful elements we covered in Part I: attention, perspective taking, focus, space, and trust. These elements create the ideal ecosystem for culturally intelligent innovation. Once the climate is in place, you need to manage the *process* for culturally intelligent innovation. This process includes the steps covered in many innovation books (e.g., define, ideate, test), but we'll look at how to adjust these steps for a diversity of participants and users. The process (shown in Figure II-1) is something I refer to as the 5D process for culturally intelligent innovation:

- Define: Align Diverse Expectations and Goals (Chapter 7)
- Dream: Generate Diverse Ideas (Chapter 8)
- Decide: Select and Sell Your Idea (Chapter 9)
- Design: Create and Test for Diverse Users (Chapter 10)
- Deliver: Implement Global Solutions (Chapter 11)

**Figure II-1. Culturally Intelligent Innovation I Process**

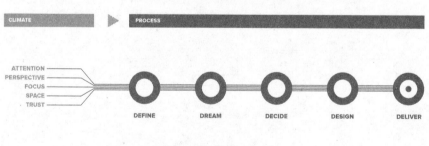

© Cultural Intelligence Center

Each chapter in this section reviews the importance of each step in the 5D process and the implications of cultural diversity for how you manage the process. Each chapter concludes with a segment called "Fusion Lab," which outlines leading practices for driving innovation through differences.

The 5D process applies to individuals as well as teams. Anyone seeking to innovate will benefit from going through each step of the process and collaborating with a diversity of individuals to come up with more creative solutions. For example, although I'm the author of this book, I tapped my diverse network of colleagues and friends all throughout the writing process, and their perspectives significantly shaped the outcome.

The 5D process is most directly relevant to diverse teams working on an innovative project together. Breakthrough innovations are rarely a solitary act. The innovations of Steve Jobs, Thomas Edison, and Jack Ma all stem from teams that experimented with them. Furthermore, because this is a book about how to leverage diversity to come up with innovative solutions, the 5D process is intentionally developed to harness the interplay of ideas that occur during the interactions of people with diverse backgrounds, experience, or points of view—something that most often occurs within the context of a multicultural team. Some of these may be intact teams that work together for a long period of time, others may be convened solely for the purpose of a specific project, and still others might be only a loose network of diverse individuals who informally shape your innovation. Several parts of the 5D process also include how you work with a diversity of customers or partners at home or overseas. Most of the strategies and practices offered are oriented toward application with a multicultural team, but you can adapt them to fit your situation and context.

# CHAPTER 7

## DEFINE: ALIGN DIVERSE EXPECTATIONS AND GOALS

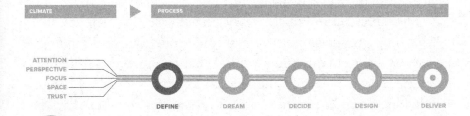

O ur team at the Cultural Intelligence Center was recently working with a Fortune 50 company to develop an innovative global leadership program. The objective seemed clear: to create a new leadership program focused on one of the company's newest leadership competencies—"Act like an owner." I immediately resonated with the priority of helping leaders think and act like owners. My business partner and I want our team to make decisions and engage in their roles as if it were their business and money at stake.

At the first meeting with this Fortune 50 company, the individual facilitating the meeting started by restating the objective: to create an innovative leadership program focused on helping leaders "act like an owner." Several participants affirmed how vital it is to ensure that the company's leaders view themselves as vested stakeholders in the company. However, at the first break, a couple of the participants came up to me and said, "Perhaps you can help our colleagues understand that 'Act like an owner' doesn't necessarily communicate the same thing everywhere." One of them said, "With my team in Bangkok, owners are perceived as guys who spend all day on the golf course getting drunk and randomly call-

ing in their orders to the office." Regardless of whether the perception she identified was accurate, it immediately demonstrated that
the stated objective was not equally understood. If there are widely
different expectations about what it means to act like an owner,
there's little hope of creating an innovative program for developing that leadership competency. I diplomatically shared the input
with others on the team and we stepped back to reconsider what
"act like an owner" actually means.

Most intercultural challenges begin with clashing expectations.
What one group views as honest and straightforward, another
views as disingenuous and myopic. What an individual from one
culture sees as "efficient," another sees as "shortsighted." What an
individual from one culture views as respectful, another views as
rude.

Think about a team you're part of. It might be a team at work,
a volunteer board, or a sports team. What expectations do you
have of your team members? What do they expect from you? And
to what degree does everyone on the team have a similar understanding of the overarching goal? If you were to ask each person
what the team was trying to achieve, what would you hear? Once
you've created the climate for culturally intelligent innovation, the
first step of the innovative process is aligning diverse expectations
around a shared, defined goal.

## A Shared Mental Model

Clearly defining the goal is the first step of any innovation process.
But the more diverse the team is, the more important it is to take
time to ensure that everyone understands the goal. The goal might
sound straightforward, such as coming up with an innovation to
help leaders act like an owner. But when working toward innovative solutions across cultures, additional time and effort is needed

to create a shared mental model where everyone understands the goal.

Toyota, for example, has a long-stated goal of being cost-conscious, even down to the pennies. As the company expanded across cultural and geographic borders, there were extremely varied expectations about what it meant to effectively control costs. Many non-Japanese leaders who joined Toyota expected that cost-consciousness would include reducing staff during an economic downturn. But that wasn't the expectation at all in Tokyo. Toyota's Japanese executives would no sooner terminate employees because of a temporary recession than any of us would put our kids out on the street because the stock market went bad. There's a long-term expectation at Toyota that says cost-consciousness is directly tied to protecting and nurturing personnel, even when times are tight.[1]

Jeffery Liker of the University of Michigan interviewed Fujio Cho, president of Toyota Motor Corporation in Kentucky, and asked him about the differences between managing manufacturing plants in the United States and in Japan. Both Toyota locations had the same goal of making quality cars and doing so with as little cost as possible. But Cho said his number one problem in the United States was getting team leaders to *stop* the assembly line. The U.S. team assumed a successful month was one when the assembly line never had to be shut down. Cho sent his team leaders the following memo:

> If you are not shutting down the assembly plant, it means you have no problems. All manufacturing plants have problems. So you must be hiding your problems. Please take out some inventory so problems surface. You will shut down the assembly line but you will also continue to solve your problems and make even better-quality engines more efficiently.[2]

When the goal is to reduce costs, what does that mean? When you insist that leaders act like an owner, what are you hoping to accomplish? How should a leader most effectively align expectations on a diverse team? As more organizations adopt a matrix structure where leadership is less clearly defined, explicitly identifying the goal becomes more important than ever. Here are a couple of important facts to consider:

- 80 percent of team conflicts can be attributed to unclear goals.[3]
- The top three stress factors for teams are uncertainty, ambiguity, and time pressure.[4]

The global companies that most successfully and consistently innovate are the ones that spend more time developing a specific goal and strategy up front.[5] Everyone on the team needs to be able to answer the who, what, why, when, and how questions related to the innovation at hand. Even in a command-and-control environment where the goal is stated from the top, a culturally intelligent innovation process begins with devoting space and time to having diverse participants truly understand the goal. Ask each participant to demonstrate his expectations of the goal by requiring a written description of what successful achievement of that goal might look like. In more collaborative contexts, the team itself can help construct and clarify the goal.

One study found that team members' clarity about the task they need to accomplish is the most important factor of whether culturally diverse teams perform well. The more clarity brought to the issue or problem being addressed, the higher the quality of input from diverse participants.[6] A high level of specificity around the task attenuates the confusion from cultural differences. The task itself provides a concrete way for diverse team members to compare their understanding and responses. In contrast, a goal or task that has been ambiguously described magnifies cultural differences because members of different cultures fill in the blanks using their own cultural values and norms for interpreting it. The more diverse the team, the more time you need to devote to defining and clarifying the goal.

In addition, with a shared mental model, team members with less load and more margin can help those who are overloaded. This is less likely to happen when there hasn't been a concerted effort to develop a shared understanding of the joint goal you're trying to achieve. Collaboration is impossible if you don't agree on what the problem is.

## Paradigms for Global Innovation

One way to gain a shared mental model is to discuss what paradigm for cross-border partnerships best characterizes what you want to develop and how. Who adapts to whom? Should Germans adapt to the Chinese or vice versa? Should engineers defer to sales when designing a product? And what generational culture should dominate the organizational ethos?

The most common paradigms for working across borders are internationalization, localization, and globalization. We'll cover each of these briefly as they relate to driving innovation, and then we'll look at fusion, an additional paradigm that is more ideally suited to culturally intelligent innovation. While these paradigms have the most direct relevance to how an organization innovates internationally, they also provide direction for how to innovate across cultural differences in a domestic context.

### Internationalization: Do It Our Way

History is filled with examples of the first paradigm: internationalization. This is when Culture A expects Culture B to adopt A's way of doing things (see Figure 7-1). This can occur among individuals—for example, Dave insists that Javier adapts to Dave's preferences for speed and autonomy. Or it can be among organizations—for example, Walmart sets up stores in Germany and insists on replicating the same kind of big-box store model used in the United States, right down to the greeters at the front door.

### Figure 7-1. Internationalization Paradigm

Culture A                                    Culture B

Colonization was primarily built upon the internationalization paradigm. The Portuguese Empire insisted that its colonies in places like Macau, Brazil, and Mozambique adopt Portuguese religion, educational practices, family customs, foods, etc. But internationalization is also the paradigm many companies have used to expand internationally. Traditionally, multinational companies sent their top performers overseas on expat assignments. This ensured that the overseas operation was run by someone who did things the way they're done at home—"ethically" and "efficiently."

Most of the criticism written about foreign policy, international business, global expansion, and overseas charitable efforts has focused on the ills of an imperial "Do it our way" mentality. I've done extensive research observing and describing the liabilities of this model, particularly as it relates to charitable volunteer efforts and other international programs.[7]

On the other hand, there might be a place for the cultural penetration of the internationalization approach for some innovations. Everyone loves the iPhone pretty much the way it is. Some minor adjustments might be needed in how Apple develops contracts with phone companies in different markets, but consumers want to be able to buy the same phone in London, Shanghai, and Cape

Town that they can buy in San Francisco. And a key dimension of the global success of McDonald's has been in the standardization of how to efficiently make a hamburger and fries using the company's equipment and processes all over the world to provide quick service. In turn, customers know what to expect any time they order McDonald's fries.

An internationalization paradigm sets the course for how the innovation process unfolds. A team working together on creating a new product will primarily follow the dominant culture's approach for what and how they pursue innovation.

## Localization: Do It Your Way

The next paradigm, localization, often emerges as a knee-jerk reaction to the perceived ills of internationalization. In this case (Figure 7-2), Culture A decides that the best way to relate to Culture B is to allow B to fully retain its own cultural values and way of doing things. I sometimes refer to this as the "go native" approach where individuals or organizations decide that the ideal way to expand globally is to fully localize their presence wherever they go. Culture A needs to fully adjust to the preferences, values, and norms of Culture B when going there, and vice versa.

**Figure 7-2. Localization Paradigm**

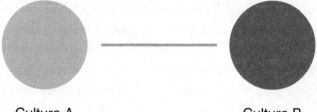

Culture A                    Culture B

Starbucks followed the localization model to a certain degree when it first opened up in China. The company focused more heavily on tea offerings, but many of its strong coffee drinks were not offered, and the inside of the coffee shops was altered to better resemble Chinese teahouses. But the Chinese customers didn't like it. They could easily find any number of excellent teahouses without Starbucks trying to pull that off. What they wanted at Starbucks was the unique Starbucks experience, complete with Frappuccinos, venti-size mochas, and overstuffed chairs.

Sometimes when I'm in Singapore, I use Singlish, a colloquial form of English spoken among Singaporeans with each other. Some of my Singaporean friends and colleagues find it jarring when I suddenly throw in an "okay-lah" or refer to myself as an "ang mo"—a pejorative epithet used for Caucasians. My use of Singlish is unnecessary and can come off as insulting. This shows that adjusting fully to the other culture is not always best. It's important to consider the context, the situation, and the shared objectives to discern how much adjustment should occur.

There are aspects of localization that are required for most innovations that span international borders. Written material needs to be offered in local languages, HR policies have to account for legal requirements, and calendar-driven rollouts have to adapt to regional holidays and seasons. When determining how much of the localization paradigm to adopt, one of the most important considerations is determining whether the local culture is tight or loose. This refers to how strong the social norms are within a given culture. Tight cultures are places where there are very prescribed expectations of how people should behave, such as Saudi Arabia and Japan. There's a prescribed view about what kind of behavior is and isn't appropriate. Loose cultures are typically more cosmopolitan; in order to absorb the heterogeneous makeup of a place, these societies are less dogmatic about what kind of behavior is acceptable. Nations like Thailand and the Netherlands are loose cultures where you're free to behave as you wish, as long as it doesn't infringe on the rights of others to do the same.[8]

Some adaptation to local cultures is almost always valuable both at a personal level and organizationally. But going too far can reduce the distinctive value you offer or, worse yet, it can be offensive by making it look like you're trying too hard. Your cultural differences may well be what make your products or services most innovative to another culture.

## Globalization: Find Where Our Approaches Intersect

The globalization paradigm is the approach most frequently promoted in the cross-cultural management models that are taught today. This is usually a better way of moving toward culturally intelligent innovation than internationalization or localization because it can draw the best from each culture involved. Think of the globalization paradigm as a Venn diagram where cultures overlap at the point of an intersecting goal or interest (Figure 7-3).

**Figure 7-3. Globalization Paradigm**

Culture A    Culture B

Many successful global brands have used an approach like this. They've figured out a way to remain true to their core brand identity while also making tweaks for the local taste. McDonald's has internationalized its fast-food system and brand but globalized its menu offerings. They don't serve beef burgers in India and they serve beer in Germany with many overlapping food items most everywhere in the world. KFC has larger dining areas in Chinese restaurants than North American ones because Chinese customers want to dine in while eating their chicken rather than get it as a takeout meal, as the majority of North American customers do. And the software company SAP's success is largely built upon how it has integrated information systems around the world. These companies all assure customers of a consistent standard of products and services while offering localized adaptations as needed.

Globalization isn't only a paradigm that guides how a company innovates with its customers in local markets. It also guides how the company adapts its own policies and practices with its staff around the world. Few companies have an organizational culture that is as strong as Google's, but Google has made a conscious effort to find overlapping goals with its employees around the world. For example, the longtime practice at Google of giving employees the autonomy to work from wherever they like and the chance to spend 20 percent of their time innovating are Google practices that have been core to the company's organizational DNA. Employees get to work where they want on projects that interest them. In return, the company gets motivated employees who come up with things like Gmail and Google Glass. But these practices were a tough sell in the Asia-Pacific region. Googlers there had been socialized during their upbringing to defer to the group and to follow the ideas of the most senior members; they were disoriented by not being offered more direction about where and how they should work and innovate. Yet for Google to have fully changed these practices would have eliminated a central part of the organizational culture. In addition, some of the locals working for Google in places like India, Singapore, and Japan have told me, "We don't want Google to use a top-down, highly directive approach like many local companies do. The autonomy they offer is why we wanted to work for Google!" Google has been looking for ways to find intersecting interests for the sake of pursuing its core mission to organize the world's information and make it universally accessible and useful.

The globalization paradigm makes sense for a lot of reasons. But the more different the cultures involved, the less the cultures overlap, and therefore the shared space and resulting innovation might be very limited. Might there be another way to make the most of the differences and similarities?

## Fusion: Discover a New Way

The greatest opportunity for innovation comes from creating and sustaining a fusion paradigm for working together that utilizes the best of the differences involved. Most approaches to working cross-culturally seem to work from the assumption that only one or two cultures are working together (i.e., when you're working with individuals from a hierarchical culture, use a more top-down approach; when you're working with individuals from a more egalitarian culture, use a flat, empowering approach). But in reality, most 21st century teams have members from several different cultural backgrounds, so it's not as simple as one culture adapting to the other one. It's an abundance of cultures coming together on the same team. This is where the greatest challenges and opportunities for innovation lie. *The fusion approach seeks to minimize the interpersonal conflict that comes from the cultural differences and leverage the informational diversity that exists from them.* (See Figure 7-4.)

**Figure 7-4. Fusion Paradigm**

The fusion paradigm leads to a whole new way of working together that is different from what any of the respective partners would do on their own. It requires everyone giving something up in order to gain something better. The reality is that diverse people have different starting points and ways of doing things. This is true whether we're talking about national and ethnic cultures or different cultures organized around gender, religion, or function. A fusion approach doesn't mean that each individual and culture is fully stripped of its distinctive values and contributions. That would rob diverse teams of one of the greatest benefits of diverse perspectives. But it does mean that there's an intentional attempt to develop alternative practices and policies together to benefit from the fusion that results.

Fusion cuisine provides a helpful metaphor for this paradigm of global innovation. Fusion cooking combines and substitutes ingredients from different cultural traditions while preserving some of the distinct cultural flavors and traditions involved. From kimchi tacos in Los Angeles to udon soup with rashers of bacon in London, the best fusion dishes don't just mix all the ingredients together. Some of the ingredients remain distinct, but they all have to work together to become one dish. The fusion approach to innovation allows for the coexistence of different approaches and perspectives while coalescing around a shared goal.[9]

The fusion model is rooted in paradox. It combines creativity with realism, and it purposely amplifies the differences through passionate discussion and disagreement rather than simply focusing on what you have in common. Fusion allows different cultural norms to coexist, and each person is invited to transcend and include her personal preferences as part of the team process. Some norms are used to accomplish certain objectives and others are used for other purposes. For example, individualists are allowed to use the autonomy that works best for them rather than assuming they aren't committed to collaboration. They're consulted for helping the team take personal initiative and to consider the question everyone is considering at some level: *What will this project mean for me if we do this?* Likewise, collectivists are allowed to work more collaboratively rather than having others assume they're shirking personal responsibility as they might sometimes be viewed by individualists. And collectivists on a fusion team are ideally suited to help move the team toward consensus around a shared goal. (See Table 7-1 for more examples, several of which will be built upon in the upcoming chapters.)

### Table 7-1. Fusion of Cultural Values

| Individualism | Collectivism |
|---|---|
| Emphasis on individual goals and rights | Emphasis on group goals and relationships |
| ✔ Personal initiative | ✔ Consensus building |
| **Low Power Distance** | **High Power Distance** |
| Emphasis on equality; shared decision making | Emphasis on differences in status; decisions made by superiors |
| ✔ Bottom-up ideas | ✔ Top-down intervention |
| **Low Uncertainty Avoidance** | **High Uncertainty Avoidance** |
| Emphasis on flexibility and adaptability | Emphasis on planning and predictability |
| ✔ Unexpected opportunities | ✔ Deliberate strategies |
| **Cooperative** | **Competitive** |
| Emphasis on collaboration and nurturing behavior to get results | Emphasis on competition, assertiveness, and achievement to get results |
| ✔ Social good | ✔ Results |
| **Short-Term** | **Long-Term** |
| Emphasis on immediate outcomes (success now) | Emphasis on long-term outcomes (success later) |
| ✔ Immediate viability | ✔ Long-term sustainability |

*(continued)*

| Low Context (Direct) | High Context (Indirect) |
|---|---|
| Emphasis on explicit communication (words) | Emphasis on indirect communication (tone, context) |
| ✔ Explicit processes | ✔ Holistic understanding |
| **Being** | **Doing** |
| Emphasis on quality of life and working smart | Emphasis on being productive and meeting goals |
| ✔ Fulfillment and well-being | ✔ Productivity and speed |
| **Universalism** | **Particularism** |
| Emphasis on rules; standards that apply to everyone | Emphasis on specifics; unique standards based on relationships |
| ✔ Global standards | ✔ Local customization |
| **Neutral** | **Affective** |
| Emphasis on nonemotional communication; hiding feelings | Emphasis on expressive communication; sharing feelings openly |
| ✔ Negotiating strength | ✔ Warmth and rapport |
| **Monochronic** | **Polychronic** |
| Emphasis on a linear approach to time; work and personal lives kept separate | Emphasis on multitasking; can combine work and personal lives |
| ✔ Timeliness and focus | ✔ Flexibility and spontaneity |

✔ *An example of what this cultural value contributes to the fusion approach to innovation*

Andrew Ouderkirk, a leading scientist from 3M with more than 165 patents, uses a fusion approach as an essential part of how he innovates across the globe. He says, "I've found that different team members from different cultures are ideal for different parts of a project. For example, our Japanese counterparts like having us [as Americans] along in customer meetings since we can get away with asking questions that they could not. And, if we need highly detailed data or information, our German or Asian colleagues are the best ones suited for this challenge."[10] Ouderkirk says this has been a critical part of his role in making 3M one of the most innovative companies in the world.

How do these four different paradigms for global innovation apply to a company that wants to expand its presence to another region of the world?

*Internationalization:* Set up an office overseas, send personnel from the home country to manage the operations, and hire and train local labor to do things the way they've been done successfully at home.

*Localization:* Work with an overseas partner to set up an office overseas to make sure the management, staff, and processes are thoroughly localized. Or find an existing factory overseas to be a supplier, let the people there do things their way, and clarify what the deliverables should be like.

*Globalization:* Set up overseas facilities and/or acquire overseas companies to expand global presence. Develop a matrix structure to centralize shared functions like IT, HR, etc., and allow regional-specific processes to remain autonomous from the whole.

*Fusion:* Use any of the above expansion methods (set up a new site, partner with an existing supplier, and/or acquire a local company) and identify all the resources, connections, and possibilities that exist between the partners involved. Spend time identifying the core differences from the cultures and regions involved and do a SWOT (Strengths, Weaknesses, Opportunities, Threats) analysis of the differences. Find ways to use the differences to make a better whole.

Fusion begins at the most senior level of leadership where leaders from the respective regions consciously work together to develop something that would be impossible without the diversity of inputs. People from the home office may be placed overseas and people from overseas are placed in leadership positions in the home office. Leaders are expected to have local expertise along with global sensibilities. There might be a move away from a "home office" completely, where a shared culture transcends regional differences across all the offices while also utilizing the differences as part of the shared organizational ethos.

The fusion paradigm offers the most potential for innovation. We'll look more specifically at what a fusion approach for global innovation looks like throughout the rest of the book. A critical part of aligning expectations is determining which paradigm best reflects what you're doing together. There are times when internationalization, localization, or globalization are best suited for what you're trying to accomplish. But when possible, look for the more creative solutions that can emerge from using a fusion paradigm to leverage the diversity around you.

## Fusion Lab: Define

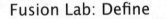

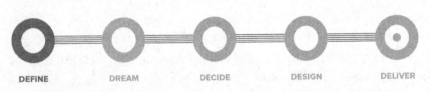

DEFINE          DREAM          DECIDE          DESIGN          DELIVER

Each chapter in Part II concludes with leading practices for using the fusion paradigm for culturally intelligent innovation. In contrast to the typical intercultural approaches that emphasize how to work with one culture versus another, these strategies are specifically designed for teams and projects that include a fusion of cultural values and backgrounds.

The Fusion Lab begins with coming up with a shared goal and aligning expectations. Keep at it until everyone is in agreement with what the goal means. Use the diversity in your team to get a fuller understanding of the goal. When pursuing culturally intelligent innovation, "where we are is where we've never been."[11] Here are a few leading practices to use when defining the goal and aligning expectations on a culturally diverse team.

## 1. Map Your Differences

Stephen Covey wrote, "The best response to someone who doesn't see things your way is to say, 'You disagree? I need to listen to you!' "[12] This is counterintuitive because we're hardwired to more readily like, trust, and cooperate with people who are similar to us. Many books on negotiation emphasize finding points of agreement and common interest. This is what leads to the Venn diagram mentality behind the globalization paradigm shown in Figure 7-3. But culturally intelligent innovation insists on exploring and capitalizing on the *differences* as much and more than on the areas of agreement.[13] Christensen says the blockbuster idea is almost always disruptive where there is a rich interplay of diverse viewpoints and odd connections. It does not come from the mainstream, homogenous thinking that goes on in most corporate offices.[14] Disagreement and differences represent an opportunity for new insights and a chance to learn about new perspectives.

Identify each team member's differences. Create a list with names and the most relevant differences each member brings to the team. Start with the two kinds of diversity that are most relevant for how you work together: visible diversity and underrepresented groups (Chapter 1). Consider other differences that might also be relevant such as personality styles, skills, and industries previously worked in. Calculate the relative importance of the five trust factors for each team member (Chapter 6).

Many of the organizations I work with use the CQ Assessments available through the Cultural Intelligence Center, which not only provide feedback on an individual's intercultural skills, but also profile the individual's cultural value orientations. The teams create a composite of each individual's cultural profile and each person posts it by his desk as a visible reminder of the different values and orientations each team member brings to the team. (Figure 7-5 is an excerpt of such a composite.)

### Figure 7-5. Team Cultural Values: Excerpt from CQ Assessment Report

### Mapping Your Cultural Values

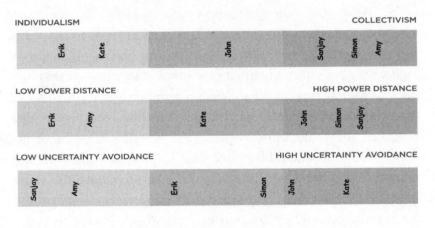

© Cultural Intelligence Center

## 2. Compare Your Expectations

Next, compare your expectations for the job that needs to be accomplished, including a list of criteria for a successful outcome. What would "better" look like for reaching this goal? Find ways to get input from diverse groups that allow you to hear from more than just the verbal, dominant contributors. (More ideas on how to accomplish this are in Chapter 8.)

Avoid trying to convince each other at this point. The purpose right now is to understand the different expectations that exist. Solicit contrary opinions, listen, and seek to understand. Encourage absurd thinking to foster an environment that is open to considering the end-goal from as many angles as possible. Keep opposing options on the table for the time being. This requires cultural intelligence from everyone because appropriately voicing opposing views is rooted in cultural norms. But don't avoid the value of gaining these divergent expectations.

Some of the research teams at Genentech, part of the Roche pharmaceutical company, use what they call a *pre*-mortem review. At the very beginning of a clinical trial for a new drug, each team member is asked to imagine that it's two years from now and the trial was a complete failure. The drug doesn't work and it can't go to market. The team is asked to forecast why it failed. Not only does anticipating failure allow the team to engage in preventative planning, it also reveals the goals, priorities, and definitions of success and failure held by various team members. Have the team do this independently or in subteams and then compare the responses.

You can also use the opposite approach. Ask your teams to imagine future success: *It's 10 years from now and you're receiving an award for the work accomplished as a result of your innovation. What does the individual announcing the award say about the innovation and what's been accomplished as a result?* Ask each individual to write her vision of future success independently, then look at them together as a group. Pay as much attention to the differences as to the recurring themes that emerge.

## 3. Take Each Other's Perspective

Once you've mapped your differences and expressed your varied expectations, try to empathize with each other's perspectives. Set personal expectations and preferences aside for a moment and ask everyone to take on the perspective of someone who views the goal or project differently from how he does. Ask each person to role-play the perspective of someone else. For example, tell Kate to take on Ravi's perspective and ask her to share with the team what she believes is most important to Ravi for this project. What are Ravi's expectations and concerns? Then allow Ravi to clarify whether Kate has accurately understood his perspective. Repeat the process by having Ravi take on Kate's perspective.

For some participants, the time devoted to mutual understanding may seem like a distraction from getting to the task at hand. But it's a critical part of aligning expectations and defining the goal. The time spent empathizing and understanding each other at the beginning will play a strategic role in helping the team function effectively. And the more you understand the diverse perspectives on your team, the better you will anticipate the diverse values and expectations of your potential users.

## 4. List What You Have in Common

After amplifying your differences, discover what you have in common. Begin with the obvious (e.g., all working for the same organization, all serving on the same innovation team) and then explore some of the other shared similarities that might be easily overlooked. For example, look for similarities in educational backgrounds and previous work experiences or whether everyone (or no one) is native to the places where you currently live. Look for some of the nonwork similarities that exist too (children the same ages, shared hobbies, favorite coffee shop, etc.). Set a timer for five minutes and see how many things the group can come up with that everyone has in common. This can be a useful way of developing a sense of team, and you might find some creative ideas that lie implicitly within some of the unique similarities you share. Then be sure to discuss any potential blind spots from what you have in common. For example, if you're designing an innovation for cleaning the shower and none of you clean your own shower, then it's important to determine how to account for that shortcoming.

## 5. Define a Common Goal

Finally, define the shared goal for the innovation at hand. You want each individual to have a sense of personal ownership while also seeing the goal as something that is bigger than any one person can pull off alone. The best goals on a fusion team are viewed as "mine" and "ours."

Get agreement around a one-sentence summary of the goal. Don't move on until you have consensus. Describe what successfully achieving the goal would look like. Revisit the varied expectations shared previously and see how you can address those as part of the common goal shared by everyone.

George Doran developed the popular idea that goals should be SMART: Specific, Measurable, Achievable, Relevant, and Time-bound.[15] Each one of these is influenced by cultural differences. The level of specificity (S) needed for someone coming from a culture that strongly values certainty is different from how much specificity is needed by someone coming from a culture that is more comfortable with ambiguity. What to measure (M), the expectations surrounding what can realistically be achieved (A), and the sense of whether the goal is relevant (R) are also aspects that are culturally conditioned. And agreeing upon timing (T) and the expectations of what kind of flexibility should surround established milestones and deadlines is one of the biggest challenges faced by many multicultural groups. The top line of the goal needs to be shared by everyone, but the ways it gets further defined can reflect the cultural differences represented. That brings out the best of a fusion of cultures because you get to see the goal through a kaleidoscope of perspectives.

Test the understanding of the objectives by asking each individual to paraphrase how she would explain the objectives in her context. For example, how would you explain "act like an owner" in your context? You'll learn from the diversity of explanations as well as clarify whether you've really reached a fusion approach that transcends and includes the preferences of individual functions, cultures, and personalities.

Work through these strategic questions in developing and clarifying the objectives:

- What are our overarching aims and aspirations? Allow for the diversity of personalities and perspectives to be reflected in what is expressed and how.
- Where will this innovation play? In which part of the organization and/or in which markets or contexts? Where will this *not* be implemented?
- What are our tangible goals (e.g., $1 million in profit; seamless, online payment system)?
- What are our intangible goals (e.g., to have a reputation for being *xyz*)?

Ask for a willingness to go for a solution that is better than any of you have reached yet. This disarms the defensiveness that often emerges when talking about differences because you aren't asking anyone to abandon his ideas. You're simply asking everyone to work together to come up with a third alternative that is better than any individual idea or approach.

## Conclusion

Judith Orasanu, a psychologist at NASA, studied the communication strategies used by airline pilots in the cockpit, a place consistently characterized by cultural diversity. She found that the best crews have prepared to cope with emergencies by developing a shared mental model during periods of low workload and stress. Then, during times of high workload, stress, and potential danger, the pilots implicitly draw upon their previously established mental model to guide what they do. The extent to which crews had clear mental models and ground rules for working together, the more effectively they performed under stress. Teams that did not have a shared mental model performed less effectively.[16]

High-performing teams communicate *less* during intense, high workload times than low-performing teams do. That's because they're relying upon an implicit coordination that emerged at the beginning during times of low stress. Think about a sports team. During a game, most teams don't have much time to explicitly discuss their strategy. And the closer the game gets to the end, the higher the stress, particularly if the score is close and it's a significant game. But the team is unlikely to be successful without some regular strategy sessions to lay out expectations, individual responsibilities, and a plan.

When working with a homogenous group, a shared mental model often exists implicitly. It's valuable to spend time defining the expectations and understandings shared across any group before engaging in the innovation process. But taking the time to create a shared mental model and define your goal is a nonnegotiable for a diverse team.

## DEFINE: ALIGN DIVERSE EXPECTATIONS

Keep working on the goal until it represents a diversity of users' perspectives.

✔ Describe the problem you are trying to solve and identify at least three different ways diverse users experience this problem.

# CHAPTER 8

# DREAM: GENERATE DIVERSE IDEAS

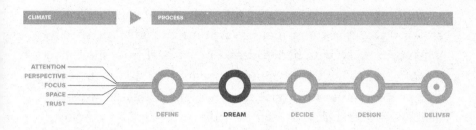

Atsushi Saito, a Japanese executive with Coca-Cola, says that in a Japanese context, asserting oneself too bluntly or assertively may drive people away. However, when he was a 20-something working in the United States for the first time, this worked against him. He was overly conscious of not making mistakes and worked hard to speak correctly, and as a result, he rarely spoke up and few people paid any attention to him. Several years later, he's learned to state his opinions and ideas clearly when he's in the Atlanta office, even if those ideas aren't yet fully developed. But he still spends more time listening to various opinions before speaking up in meetings with Japanese clients.[1]

Many Western leaders believe they're doing something positive when they ask team members to "speak up." It's management's way of saying "Your opinion is important and we want to hear from you." But for many individuals like Atsushi Saito, being asked to speak up runs against the very grain of what they've been taught as a collectivist: *Blend in. The nail that sticks up gets hammered down.* Furthermore, English is a second language for many diverse team members, making it even more difficult for them to speak up confidently.

One of the greatest opportunities that comes from diverse networks is access to a broader repository of ideas. When confronted with a problem, we scan our brains for solutions that have been used to solve this kind of problem in the past. Ideas are the holy grail of innovation. When used with cultural intelligence, a diversity of perspectives almost always trumps individual perspectives when coming up with better ideas. Ronald Burt from the University of Chicago has done a number of empirical studies indicating that people with more diverse sources of information consistently generate better ideas. In contrast, the more insular employees' connections, the lower the quality of their ideas and subsequent solutions.[2]

Yet the more diverse the team, the less likely the participants are to offer their input and perspectives. A popular Chinese saying is "One is bound to have a slip of the tongue if he talks too much." So a guiding Chinese assumption is: *It is better not to talk than talk too much.* In many Western classrooms, however, students are rewarded for participating and offering comments, even if they aren't fully developed. At Harvard Business School, 50 percent of a student's grade is based upon classroom participation. Is it any wonder that generating ideas from culturally diverse teams is extremely challenging? The effort to get people to participate and contribute to creative ideas and innovative implementation requires a culturally intelligent approach. Team members need to manage their contributions so that their input is neither too much nor too little.

How can you effectively get diverse teams to dream together about creative ways to solve a problem? The second step in the process of culturally intelligent innovation is learning how to effectively leverage one of the greatest assets of diversity: a wealth of ideas for innovative solutions.

## The Brainstorming Challenge

Brainstorming is the primary way most leaders try to generate ideas from a group. The dominant brainstorming approach is guided by rules that emphasize the *quantity* of ideas rather than the quality. The criticism and evaluation of anyone's idea is highly discouraged. Groups are told, "No matter how ridiculous your idea might seem, share it because it might spark another idea for someone else."

Even homogenous teams experience some barriers to using brainstorming successfully. Some research indicates that brainstorming can actually lead to a smaller number of ideas for solving a problem than if everyone just worked on the problem independently. One reason brainstorming doesn't always work is because of something called "production blocking." This is what happens when you have a breakthrough idea but you have to wait to express it because someone else is talking. By the time you have a chance to share it, you might decide it's no longer relevant, the facilitator may have moved on, or you may have lost the idea altogether because you were asked to discuss something else.[3]

In addition, brainstorming sessions create "evaluation apprehension." This is the fear of what others will think about your idea. Those who are not part of the dominant culture are all the more likely to hold back on offering their input for fear of negative implications from speaking up.[4] Despite all the ground rules about not criticizing any idea, no one wants to look dumb. Brainstorming is a social situation and inevitably, some participants are self-conscious about how others will perceive them if they say what they're really thinking. Conformity, confidence, and power all play a role in who says what. Evaluation apprehension is particularly relevant when an influential person with power is present. German psychologists Andreas Mojzisch and Stefan Schulz-Hardt found that more often than not, the first idea presented in a brainstorming session ends up being the idea most likely to be accepted. And usually, the first idea comes from the most assertive and often the most powerful participant in the group. So conformity quickly crowds out the benefit of learning from the diverse perspectives around the table.[5] In addition, most groups tend to focus on the common knowledge shared as a team rather than highlighting the knowledge differences that exist. Yet the unique knowledge possessed by various members offers the greatest benefit for innovation.[6]

Finally, most brainstorming sessions include "social loafers." These are participants who don't engage because they know other people will speak up and do all the talking. The social loafers sit back and let others do the work. In addition, some participants, either because of an introverted personality or as a result of their cultural values, prefer an approach that allows them to independently consider the issue and work through the problem in their heads first.

## BRAINSTORMING ROADBLOCKS

1. Production blocking
2. Evaluation apprehension
3. Social loafing

These may exist on any team, but they're magnified on a culturally diverse team.

The potential barriers of production blocking, evaluation apprehension, and social loafing exist in any brainstorming session, but they're magnified on a diverse team. For example, if you're from a hierarchical culture and your boss asks you during a brainstorming session what you think about her idea, your default response is likely to be "That's an excellent idea, boss!"—even if you think it's ridiculous. However, if you're from a more egalitarian culture, you're more likely to tell your boss what you really think. Granted, you probably do so diplomatically and avoid being too harsh, but individuals from egalitarian cultures have been taught that respect is earned by offering constructive feedback, not by simply being a "yes man." However, if your boss is from a hierarchical culture and you offer a dissident perspective on her idea, her default assumption will be that you're being disrespectful, rude, and possibly even insubordinate.

Brainstorming might seem better suited for collectivists than individualists since it's built around the power of shared ideas. However, collectivists often find brainstorming much more challenging than individualists do because it usually goes against the collectivist priorities of harmony, conformity, and not standing out with a unique idea. Brainstorming is largely predicated upon an individualist perspective where everyone is encouraged to contribute, and the more divergent the ideas the better.[7] In individualist cultures like the United States and Germany, the unique idea is the sought-after prize. Individualists have been socialized to see the value of autonomous thoughts and ideas and often enjoy the chance to brainstorm. Global teams with individualists and collectivists need to create standards for how teams can promote unique ideas in a way that accommodates the best contributions of everyone.

In Chapter 1, I referenced a study conducted by my colleagues that found CQ is the moderating difference for whether participants in diverse groups voice their perspectives. So diversity creates a barrier for speaking up for those with low CQ.[8]

When CQ levels are low, homogenous groups generate more ideas than diverse groups. But when CQ levels are high, diverse groups come up with far more innovative ideas and solutions than homogenous groups. CQ is what makes the difference. A diverse team made up of individuals with high CQ and facilitated by a leader with high CQ can utilize the benefit of everyone's input and perspective. Leaders and associates with higher levels of CQ will be less likely to assume someone is cocky or incompetent based upon whether he speaks up in a meeting.

The reality is that most teams have people with varying degrees of CQ. Next, we need to address the specific communication barriers that magnify the challenges of brainstorming and generating new ideas. Then we'll review the leading practices for using a fusion approach to idea generation on a diverse team.

## Communication Barriers

Communication is the biggest challenge when trying to get diverse teams to dream up ideas together. Cultural differences heighten individuals' anxiety and uncertainty for speaking up. What you say and how you say it is strongly shaped by your cultural background. Culturally intelligent teams need to identify if and how these challenges exist for them.

### Language Fluency

The first communication barrier for many diverse teams is language fluency. For nonnative speakers, coming up with ideas and expressing them in a different language is extremely difficult. And when you add all the other cultural components, it can be downright overwhelming. Imagine what it's like to sit in a meeting as a nonnative speaker and be asked to share your idea on a topic that's just been introduced. Before you can share your idea, you may need to do the following:

- Translate the question or issue into your native language to be sure you grasp it; the more complex the idea, the more likely you'll do this, even if you're very comfortable in the language being used

- Construct a response to the question in your head using the language most comfortable for you
- Translate your response into the language being spoken and possibly rehearse it silently to be sure you're saying it right; even if you're extremely fluent, translation might be needed to construct the most cogent response

After doing all of this, you're finally ready to speak up. Chances are, though, that by now the meeting has moved forward without your idea. By this point, the confident, native speakers may well be talking over each other, and only the very confident, assertive nonnative speaker interjects an idea.

In addition, nonnative speakers are often confused by the idioms and insider language that flows freely between native speakers in the group. Many of the conversations in U.S. meetings include phrases like:

"What's up with Jerry?"

"He's going to be the fall guy."

"We're going to get nailed for this."

"I need you to step up to the plate."

"She runs a tight ship."

What in the world do those phrases mean if translated literally? An entirely different set of idioms is used in other contexts, even among English speakers. An Aussie might refer to someone as "flat out like a lizard drinking" (working very hard on a task), and a Brit might say, "That puts a real spanner in the works" (something that prevents something from happening). In addition, many organizations have insider vocabulary laced with acronyms that get thrown around and references to previous products or individuals that sound completely alien to an outsider or newcomer.

A good leader (and a culturally intelligent process) is aware of the language barriers that exist on a team and finds ways to create shared understanding among everyone. A culturally intelligent team creates the safety for diverse members to clarify and speak up when they don't understand what's being talked about.

## Communication Styles

Even when everyone is a native speaker of the same language, there are a number of other communication differences that influence dreaming up diverse ideas together. For example, direct eye contact signals attentiveness in some cultures, while it's a sign of rudeness in others. Some individuals come from a cultural orientation that feels ideas and emotions should be expressed openly, while others have been told to repress demonstrating their feelings. As trivial as these may sound, such differences directly shape team chemistry, trust, and productivity. Some of the most important work on intercultural communication styles comes from William Gudykunst and Stella Ting-Toomey, who identify four different communication styles found among different cultures.[9]

### DIRECT VS. INDIRECT

The degree to which communication is direct versus indirect is one of the biggest challenges I observe in many culturally diverse encounters. I'm from New York where we "say it like it is," and my daughter Emily has picked up my direct communication style. Last year, Emily and I were invited to dinner by a Chinese professor who was interested in meeting us. Emily is a vegetarian and on our way to dinner, I told her she needed to think about a respectful way of communicating her dietary preferences to our host. She said, "Why wouldn't I just tell her I don't eat meat?" We discussed the fact that that could be viewed as very disrespectful, particularly from a teenager who was invited to an exquisite restaurant chosen by our host. We brainstormed ways to communicate her dietary preferences without coming right out and declaring that she wouldn't eat meat. When our host began recommending dishes, Emily said, "What vegetable dishes do you recommend?" and our host immediately picked up on the cue and said, "Oh, are you vegetarian?"

The dominant communication style in cities like New York and countries like Israel and Germany is to share your ideas verbally and explicitly. In contrast, the more typical behavior in places like China and Kuwait is to rely more heavily upon what is not said. In these settings, the meaning of communication is derived from nonverbal cues and the context of the interaction—e.g., the relationships involved, where the meeting is held, and who is seated where. These nonverbal components are used to convey and interpret ideas. Team members with a preference for direct communication often view their indirect colleagues as offering too few ideas or taking too long to get them across. Meanwhile, indirect participants often view their direct counterparts as talking too much and not allowing enough time for reflection and interpretation. One North American described her experience on a global, virtual team saying, "I'm a direct person . . . I'm not as patient with this trying to read into what people are saying. And in some cultures, looking at body language is very important. Well, how do you do that over the telephone?"[10] The power of diversity for generating ideas can be quickly lost if the cultural differences in direct versus indirect communication are overlooked, something we measure on our CQ Assessments as low- versus high-context communication.[11]

## SUCCINCT VS. ELABORATE

The degree to which you prefer succinct, brief explanations versus elaborate descriptions is another stylistic difference that stems in part from the cultures of which you're part. The norm in Confucian Asian cultures is toward a more succinct style because more attention is devoted to the context and the nonverbal cues than to elaborate explanations. Silence and pauses are a regular part of succinct communication. Succinct communicators are more likely to share only what they deem relevant and necessary for the rest of the group.[12]

An elaborate communication style is more prevalent in Latin Europe and Latin America. Elaborate communicators may become nervous with too much silence and perceive silence and brevity as an indication that someone is disengaged, cold, or lacking confidence. Elaborate communicators go into more detail and like to talks things through. This is also the dominant approach in places like South Asia or in Middle Eastern contexts where a great deal of elaborate, verbal processing occurs.

Succinct versus elaborate is a communication difference that also occurs across functional cultures. The norm among engineers and IT professionals is to use a more succinct style that may seem very quiet and reserved to an outsider, whereas sales and HR professionals usually prefer a more elaborate approach to communication. Personality differences play a big part here as well. Your communication style is a mixture of your personality and your cultural orientation. The source of this stylistic difference (national culture, personality, functional difference, etc.) is less important than learning how to identify and address these communication differences when they surface in the diverse groups of which you're a part.

## CONTEXTUAL VS. PERSONAL

Another stylistic difference is contextual versus personal communication. A personal style of communication is concerned with helping people develop personal connections with each other. There's an emphasis on equality among group members and usually a level of informality to the interactions that occur. This would be the norm in many Western cultures. Some informal chitchat and friendly conversation is used to help people better connect.

But some cultures, such as Germanic ones, minimize small talk and get to tasks immediately. As always, treat generalizations about cultural norms carefully and use your interactions to get a read on the communication style that's most comfortable for an individual or group you encounter.

A personal approach to communication is usually found in more individualist and egalitarian cultures where who speaks when and how people are addressed isn't overly important. The personal style isn't necessarily meant to develop friendships but instead stems from a belief that people are more likely to speak up when they feel like they can personally relate to the other people sharing ideas.

The contextual style of communication is more formal and is more concerned with following the protocol of social and organizational differences between people. Waiting for the most senior people to offer their ideas first would be seen as extremely important to people from contextual cultures. In fact, most cultures that use a more contextual style of communication have different pronouns for how they speak to someone who is older or more senior. English has largely gotten away from formal pronouns like "thee" and "thou," so individuals from more contextually oriented cultures are often disoriented in finding the appropriate English words to use when speaking up with various team members.[13]

## INSTRUMENTAL VS. AFFECTIVE

The fourth communication style identified by Gudykunst and Ting-Toomey is instrumental versus affective. An instrumental style of communication, most prevalent in Western cultures, is to get things done. In many other parts of the world, the point of communication is to maintain relationship, and the tasks flow from that. This is often confusing to various teams because the personal communication style that is typical in the West is usually combined with an instrumental style. So an individual may seem to be extremely warm and personable, yet very focused upon task-oriented communication. The purpose of fostering interpersonal conversation was to accomplish a task. On the other hand, a North American might be disoriented by the more formal, contextual behavior of Kenyans in terms of how they interact, while at the same time observing a more affective style with elaborate stories about family and personal experiences.[14]

Is it any wonder that generating ideas from a diverse team is not as easy as it sounds? There's so much going on beneath the words, flip charts, and discussions. Take a moment and think about the members of a team you're part of. Which of these communication barriers are most relevant to your team? These can be another part of mapping your differences.

## Fusion Lab: Dream

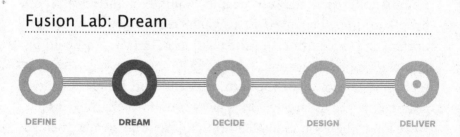

DEFINE    **DREAM**    DECIDE    DESIGN    DELIVER

Everyone wants to be heard. An intentional strategy is needed to give diverse participants culturally intelligent ways to voice their ideas. There are several practices you can use to effectively manage the process of generating ideas from a diverse team.

### 1. Redefine "Speak Up"

Many organizations emphasize the importance of everyone "speaking up," but leaders need to clarify what that means. In most cases, the objective is not to have everyone talking all the time, nor is it just to make everyone "feel" like they're part of the team. The objective is to gather ideas and innovations from every team member. Be sure to explain this to a diverse team and remind them of it regularly. The very words "speak up" sound like an assertive, verbal advancement of your ideas. Underscore that *participation* and *offering ideas* is what is needed most—but how that's done can vary according to the distinct preferences across your fusion team.

Have participants independently write down as many ideas as possible before a meeting. Then ask them to bring these to the meeting for systematic discussion and consideration. This method allows the less vocal group members to have their contributions considered alongside the ideas of those who readily speak up. Another option is for smaller groups of collectivists to meet together to develop ideas and then bring them jointly to the rest of the group. Or you may want to ask all the team members to submit their ideas ahead of time so that the group can review them without attaching specific personalities or functions to the ideas. The facilitator makes or breaks the effectiveness of these kinds of strategies. He needs to guide the group to review all the ideas that have been brought to the table and watch for group dynamics that impede the process.

TGIF meetings have been a part of Google's culture from the beginning. Every Friday, staff members can talk with leadership about any questions they have. At the headquarters in Mountain View, California, these meetings have usually been led by the founders, Larry Page and Sergey Brin. As the company has grown, fielding everyone's questions has become harder to manage—both because of the size of the staff and the intimidation some feel when asking their question in front of so many colleagues. As a result, Google developed a system called Dory, named after the memory-challenged fish in the movie *Finding Nemo*. Googlers who can't or don't want to ask a question publically can submit it to Dory. Then, others get to vote on whether it's a good question or not. The more thumbs-up votes a question receives, the higher it goes in the queue; tougher questions tend to get a lot of thumbs-up. At TGIF meetings, the Dory queue is put on the screen, and as Page and Brin go through the questions, they can't just pick and choose which ones to answer. They go through the list from top to bottom. Dory is a way for any team member to directly ask the CEO a tough question, and crowdsourcing helps vet the lame ones.[15] This is the kind of fusion strategy that better facilitates getting input from a diverse group of people.

## 2. Give Advance Warning

Let groups know ahead of time that you want their input. Not only does advance warning reduce the anxiety of participants who don't like to be put on the spot, but all team members are likely to have more thoughtful input if they spend some time thinking about it ahead of time. The more diverse the group involved in generating ideas, the more we should all think like introverts going to a cocktail party. Many introverts prepare for a cocktail party by rehearsing ahead of time the various conversation topics they can utilize with various guests. Speaking of introverts, on the whole, they prefer more time to process than extroverts do. So the strategies you're developing to leverage cultural diversity to drive innovation have a spillover effect to also better utilize the diverse personalities on your team.

For many individuals, providing a spontaneous response can be very intimidating, and even if they do respond, the social anxiety created may lessen both their self-confidence and the value of their contribution. In addition, nonnative English speakers will have more of a chance to think about how to construct a thoughtful contribution when they don't have to engage in the whole process on the spot. Native English speakers are usually more oriented toward quicker decision making, both because of the speed with which they can make sense of the ideas and because the language itself is oriented toward quick, succinct information. Cultural norms also influence the speed with which decisions get made. Cultures that are more dominantly individualist, competitive, and short-term—

oriented (i.e., focused upon immediate results and quick wins) typically make decisions more quickly than cultures that are more dominantly collectivist, cooperative, and long-term–oriented (i.e., focused upon long-term results even if it means short-term losses).

Send out a full agenda and all the relevant documents ahead of time. Make sure the materials are sent out far enough in advance for people to have time to review them, and be clear about how the meeting will be used.

## 3. Be Explicit About Expectations

If you expect everyone to offer ideas, make that clear. Even though I'm very aware that many individuals have been brought up in cultures where they were taught to avoid speaking up, my default operation is to go into a meeting, present an idea, and simply ask, "What do you think?" That approach won't work for many participants. And even those who are comfortable speaking up may not do so if they don't understand that they are expected to contribute to the conversation. In addition, the social loafers might sit back and let others do the work.

If every participant needs to offer something, be sure that's understood. You can say something like "I need to hear back from everyone by the close of business on Friday. You can either offer your input at our meeting this afternoon, by talking with me one-on-one, or by sending me an email."

## 4. Offer Multiple Ways to Give Input

Many times you're trying to generate ideas from a globally dispersed team. All the cultural challenges are magnified when you're trying to get ideas virtually; yet technology offers the chance to collect timely ideas from a much broader group than ever used to be possible. Treat a virtual meeting with the same level of commitment and planning that a physical meeting has: Send out an agenda and related materials ahead of time, expect participation and timely attendance, and follow ground rules for how people should participate. Here are a few specific guidelines for virtual meetings that are meant to generate ideas:

- Rotate the times of the calls so everyone shares the ideal and less ideal times to call in.
- Review the ground rules before each call (e.g., muting the mic except when speaking, not having side conversations, stating your name before speaking, not multitasking, no social loafing). Some of these sample ground rules are biased toward some cultures more than others, but it's appropriate to agree on some shared norms if you're going to use a fusion approach. Then the things that aren't stated allow individuals to retain their cultural preferences for how they engage.
- Pay attention to who has contributed and who hasn't. If one region is consistently quiet, do some proactive planning ahead of time to get the input of the people there (e.g., contact them beforehand and ask them to come prepared to share some ideas with the rest of the group). On the other hand, you may need to contact some of the most vocal participants and ask them not to speak until you call upon them.
- Don't mix remote and in-person meetings. If some participants are calling in independently, have everyone do so or you end up with "meetings within meetings." A group seated together will start their own conversation, and those calling in remotely won't know what is going on. This is particularly important if corporate is involved in the call. Regional teams often feel like they're just listening in on a meeting at corporate where the "most important" ideas are discussed, rather than having everyone participate equally in the meeting.

- Keep a virtual meeting focused and relatively short. It's hard enough to keep people engaged in any meeting but especially one that is done virtually.
- Allow for some brief socializing at the beginning for those participants who need that to break the ice.
- If this is an ongoing group, if at all possible, find a way to convene the group face-to-face. This goes a long way toward building trust—the crucial element we continue to raise as part of generating innovative ideas.

## 5. Use the Power of "Yes, and"

Finally, think like a stand-up comedian. When not on stage, Colleen Murray Peyton and Mark Sutton, from the Second City improv group, teach managers how to use the power of improvisation. The first rule of improvisation is just go with it. Never say no. Build upon an idea and take it further. Leadership guru Ken Blanchard and his son Scott participated in one of Murray and Sutton's sessions. In the session they attended, people were divided into groups of three, and everyone was assigned the task of planning a memorable company party. One person in each group was designated as the party planner, with the task of coming up with some creative party ideas. The other two group members were instructed to listen to each new idea, but then reject it and explain why.

### EXAMPLE OF "NO" RESPONSE:

**Idea:** "Let's do an '80s-themed party!"
**Response:** "No. That's overdone by too many other groups."

The negative responses had a chilling effect on the person pitching new ideas. Even the most enthusiastic people gave up after four or five of their ideas were turned down. They lost their ability to come up with anything in the face of all that negativity.

Next, Murray and Sutton instructed the groups to rotate roles. Now a new person in each group pitched ideas while the other two listened. But this time, instead of rejecting the ideas outright, the listeners were instructed to use a more subtle "yes, but . . . " response and share why the idea wouldn't work.

## EXAMPLE OF "YES, BUT" RESPONSE:

**Idea:** "Let's do an '80s-themed party!"
**Response:** "Yes, that would be fun. But I don't think that connects very well with our focus on the future."

This too was a frustrating experience for the idea givers, who quit after trying a few times and getting nowhere.

Finally, the groups were instructed to rotate roles again. This time, the two listeners were instructed to use the phrase "yes, and . . . " to acknowledge, affirm, and build on the idea.

## EXAMPLE OF "YES, AND" RESPONSE:

**Idea:** "Let's do an '80s-themed party!"
**Response:** "Yes! And we could ask everyone to bring what they think was the coolest invention from the '80s."

The "yes, and . . . " response made all the difference. Ideas flowed much more freely. The groups generated innovative, creative approaches that none of the individuals would have come up with on their own. The increase in energy and collaboration was palpable as the room buzzed with animated conversations, laughter, high fives, and every other behavior you would expect to see when people are genuinely engaged with each other.[16]

Various cultures and personalities respond to "yes, and" differently. But it's an excellent way to get a fusion of ideas flowing. The dreamers feel optimistic because they perceive a positive orientation that allows them to envision the possibilities and potential. And the more cautious or even pessimistic individuals perceive that this is not simply mindless brainstorming because the "and" approach is allowing for value-added direction, clarification, and deepened thinking.

Many Asian team members are already well accustomed to the "yes, and" strategy. Coming from a saving face culture where you avoid saying "no" as much as possible, they can lead your team through thinking about how to find a way to say "yes, and."

## Conclusion

Crest Whitestrips, a successful teeth-whitening product developed by Procter & Gamble, started from ideas that were generated from a diversity of people at P&G. The research and development team pulled together different cultures and units from across the company and tasked them with developing a disruptive approach to the high cost of paying a dentist to whiten teeth. Crest Whitestrips was the result—a kit with disposable plastic film strips that a consumer can use to whiten his teeth for relatively low cost and with relatively little effort. The film came from packaging work in the paper products area, the bleach technology came from fabric products, and the glue came from another application. This is a fusion innovation that did more than simply use the overlapping interests and strengths from the different cultures and units involved. It used the differences to create something entirely new. Recently, P&G and Google traded 20 staff members for a few weeks to benefit from the different perspectives they could offer and gain because both companies know that diversity is a treasure to be mined for truly innovative solutions.

Diversity offers one of the greatest challenges and opportunities for generating new ideas. Once a team has generated a diverse set of ideas, the next step is to decide which idea to pursue and how to get others on board—step 3 of the 5D process.

## DREAM: GENERATE DIVERSE IDEAS

Be clear about the kind of input needed, and create multiple ways for diverse team members to share ideas (i.e., use more than just a group brainstorming session).

✔ Write down the top five to ten ideas for solving the problem you are attempting to solve.

# CHAPTER 9

## DECIDE: SELECT AND SELL YOUR IDEA

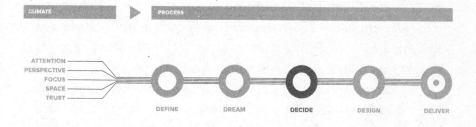

**M**y wife and I were recently looking for a new car. I convinced her to look at an Audi. During the first five minutes we talked to the salesman, he only looked at me and asked me questions about what I wanted in a new vehicle. After several minutes of him acting like my wife was invisible, I said, "Well, she's the one you need to convince because she's going to drive the car the most," at which point he said, "Well, Mrs. Livermore, what questions do you have for me?"

Linda responded, "Well, I'm more drawn to the Subaru. So how would you compare the two cars?" He replied, "Well, with all due respect, ma'am, there's no comparison whatsoever. I mean, I'm happy to sell you a Subaru if you want to go that route, but the Audi is a car that gives you immediate prestige and cachet the minute you get in it."

As soon as he said that, I thought, *Oh dude! You did* not *just say that to her.* My wife is one of the nicest people on the planet. Ask anyone who knows her, and one of the first things they'll describe about her is her kind, sweet demeanor. But this salesman's assumptions about what would be important to her struck a nerve. In response, she curtly replied, "I don't care about prestige and status whatsoever. In fact, that's precisely why I don't want the car. I'm not interested in driving around some pretentious vehicle that makes other people uncomfortable. I just need something reliable."

This was a very seasoned salesman. He told us he's been selling Audis for 40 years, and I'm sure he can safely assume that many women who look like my wife would be motivated by the kind of pitch he used with her. But instead of taking the time to find out what was important to her, he made a dangerous assumption and lost our business. Selling people on an idea or product requires insight into their motivations, values, and pain points.

Too many innovations stop at idea generation. But in order for ideas to be translated into solutions, you have to decide which idea to pursue and convince people to adopt it. Selecting an idea and selling it to others are two sides of the same coin. Part of how you determine the best idea to pursue involves anticipating how you will convince others that it successfully solves a problem. So we'll address both of these as part of the third part of the 5D process of culturally intelligent innovation—define and sell.

## The Power of the Idea

In a day when anyone can publish a book or any aspiring entrepreneur can set up a website and a business, the power of the idea, service, or product you're offering has never been more important. I'm always a bit nervous when people tell me they have a great idea but nobody else gets it. They can't figure out why no one else appreciates the brilliance of their breakthrough idea. I'm certainly inspired by the stories of authors, filmmakers, and inventors who are wildly successful despite early rejections of their ideas, so I'm not suggesting that there aren't times when individuals have good ideas that others overlook. Kodak rejected digital cameras as a cute idea that wouldn't go anywhere. Oprah Winfrey was fired as a TV reporter because her bosses disagreed when she thought the best journalism includes emotional connections. Howard Schultz, the CEO of Starbucks, was told no American would ever pay $4 for a cup of coffee. We regularly hear stories about wildly successful ideas that were initially rejected by funders, publishers, and managers. But too often, we use these unusual stories as justification for a lousy idea. There are times when few people see the brilliance of an idea that truly is innovative. But more often than not, if the consistent feedback to an idea is negative, it's likely the idea is flawed, or it could be that the idea is better suited for one market than another.

For example, imagine listening to an entrepreneur pitch an idea for a new Internet dating company. Online dating is a lucrative business because it uses the power of technology to meet the basic desire for companionship. As compared to the old days of lonely singles relying on newspaper ads and friends to make romantic introductions, the Internet offers a powerful solution for connecting people with individuals they may never otherwise meet. Some enterprising entrepreneurs have capitalized on this successfully. Even a single person living in a tiny town with very few people her age can suddenly explore potential dates across the country or even the world through online connections. That's the power of a good idea. It offers a compelling solution to a problem.

But the Internet dating business has become very crowded. How do you think investors would respond to an entrepreneur pitching an idea for a new Internet dating business? Imagine the pitch comes from a young woman who says her online dating service won't require a subscription and the focus will be on *narrowing* people's dating options rather than increasing them. My guess is that she wouldn't even complete her pitch before most investors would say, "No thanks. I'm out." But they would be missing out if the market was China. Gong Haiyan, who grew up on a rural farm in China, founded Jaiyuan, which is now China's largest Internet dating business. Jaiyuan grew out of Gong's understanding of the pain points uniquely experienced by Chinese singles, who have way too many options for potential dates. The appeal of Match.com in the United States is that users can *expand* their options for potential partners. In China, the appeal of Jaiyuan is the direct opposite. It's to *narrow down* the options. When a 23-year-old woman in Beijing logs on to a regular dating service, she sees there are 400,000 male users within her vicinity. But with Jaiyuan, she can reduce her options from 400,000 to a pool of 83 men in a matter of seconds. The filters allow her to look for partners according to any number of priorities, including things like blood type, height, and zodiac signs, some of the things that Jaiyuan discovered were important to many of its users.[1]

A powerful idea provides a new solution to a problem. New markets offer new problems and the need for new solutions. Diverse teams give you insights into the pain points and potential solutions that are best suited to diverse users. The prospective users might not always be aware the problem even exists, but eventually, they have to see the problem and understand how your idea solves it. And the solution offered needs to relieve the pain points related to the identified problem. No amount of slick marketing or smooth talking will help an innovation that starts with a weak idea.

## Smart, Empowered Teams

The best ideas come from diverse teams of smart people who are empowered to act on their varied talents and ideas. Many leadership books and articles promote the importance of hiring people who are smarter than management, but few leaders have the self-confidence to do this. Google, however, claims that finding smart people who have powerful ideas is a central part of its recruiting strategy. Google hires "people who are smart enough to come up with new ideas and crazy enough to think they just might work."[2]

Smart, empowered teams are the best way to come up with successful products. Customers won't tolerate bad products. Product excellence built from smart ideas is the only way for an innovation to be successful. But managers have to be listening to the diverse perspectives on their teams in order to benefit from them.

When Rick Wagoner became chairman of General Motors, the world's largest car company was on the receiving end of constant ridicule and criticism for offering nothing new. In response, Wagoner issued a mandate that 40 percent of all new GM products must be innovative. Anything that looked reasonably radical got the green light, regardless of whether it was truly a good idea.

One of the innovations that emerged was the Pontiac Aztek, an early attempt at a lean, crossover vehicle, which many view as the biggest failure in recent automotive history (see Figure 9-1). Several GMers voiced concerns about the design of the Aztek. It failed market research so badly that prototype respondents said things like, "Can they possibly be serious with this thing? I wouldn't take it as a gift."[3] But Don Hackworth, the leader of the product development team, forged ahead and said, "Look. We've all made up our minds that the Aztek is gonna be a winner. It's gonna astound the world. I don't want any negative comments about this vehicle. None. Anybody who has bad opinions about it, I want them off the team."[4]

**Figure 9-1. Pontiac Aztek**

The Aztek was launched in 2000 with a great deal of fanfare, and GM described it as the most versatile vehicle on the planet. Sales were projected to be 75,000 annually, but the real numbers were just over 27,000 a year for the first three years. Five years after the launch, GM discontinued the Aztek entirely. The car had started with a bad idea and no amount of sales and marketing could overcome that. The leadership behind the Aztek failure was described as totalitarian and browbeating, squelching dissent. If everyone on your team is thinking alike, it means that somebody isn't thinking or that you have no diversity on your team. The Aztek is a visible reminder of what happens when companies don't empower and listen to the smart people they hire.

## Test the Idea

To test the strength of your idea, begin by sharing it informally. Tell a diversity of friends and colleagues about it, preferably individuals who will be frank with you about their opinion. If they reject it but you're still convinced it's a good idea, keep working on it and come back to them again. If they at least respond with "Hmm . . . now that's interesting," run it by an entrepreneur or investor. See if other creative thinkers see potential in your idea. Make revisions based upon the input you receive before ultimately deciding to pursue the idea.

Most truly innovative ideas are rarely accepted immediately, so don't give up too soon. In fact, if everyone is too quick to accept your idea, you may need to reconsider whether it's truly innovative. But your energy should go toward utilizing the diverse responses you receive to come up with the best solutions for the points of resistance.

Occasionally, you should forge ahead even if no one else affirms the idea, but those instances are few and far between. Penelope Trunk from *Inc.* magazine says, "Dumping an idea you love is as brave as running with an idea you love."[5] Decide which idea to pursue based upon the pain point it addresses and the benefits it offers if successfully implemented.

## Getting Internal Buy-In

Once you decide to pursue an idea, you have to get other internal stakeholders on board. Nowadays, many organizations around the world have moved toward a matrix structure where buy-in more often comes through influence, not authority. How do you get people to support an innovative idea when you can't require them to do so?

I was talking about this one day with Bill McLawhon, head of leadership development at Facebook. It's hard to find a flatter organization than Facebook, where the number one way to gain influence is through results. People notice whether you're having impact or not, and that's all that really matters. One of the many provocative posters on Facebook's campus says "Whine less. Code more." The iconic stories around Facebook are about individuals who took a risk, went after something, and made a big impact. The number of hours you log and your activities are irrelevant. Howard Schultz of Starbucks, who is a board member at Facebook, says, "The future belongs to people who are willing to get their hands dirty."[6] Facebook rewards impact, not effort. Impact is all that matters. It doesn't matter where you are, where you work from, or what time of day you work . . . just ship it.

McLawhon tells me that getting people to pay attention to your idea at Facebook requires a high level of emotional intelligence and self-awareness. One of Mark Zuckerberg's guiding principles for the company is "Treat people with extraordinary respect." McLawhon says, "We have very few assholes at Facebook. You never hear people shouting at each other and bullying rarely happens. If they do, they're gone!"

But the way you express respect, influence your peers, and get people to adopt a new idea is highly conditioned by culture. I asked McLawhon about that because Facebook is rapidly expanding its employee base internationally. The company has created a flow of information, strategies, and ideas that stream from everywhere to everywhere. That means that not only do people in Mumbai pick up ideas from Menlo Park but also that Menlo Park and Mumbai get ideas from Buenos Aires. McLawhon says, "We want to find the right individuals globally who are culturally synchronous with both their local context and Facebook. It won't work if they can't bridge both cultures."[7]

A fusion paradigm is required to anticipate the best ways to communicate ideas to various stakeholders across different cultures. The majority of organizations around the world operate with a much higher level of hierarchy than what exists at Facebook. How do you pitch an idea laterally or from the bottom up if you're in a more top-down environment? The Hay Group interviewed leaders around the world to identify the key competencies necessary to influence and accomplish results when you have limited formal authority. They found that the keys to bottom-up influence are empathy, conflict management, influence, and self-awareness.[8] Ideas that emerged from lower ranks received attention higher up when the individuals pitching them learned how to find the pain points of management and offered solutions for relieving the pain. In addition, the individuals allowed the managers to get the credit for the ideas.

In the olden days, you could convince people to get on board by making bold claims about an idea: "Research proves X." Today, people can fact-check you on their smartphones faster than you can get through your PowerPoint presentation. So how do you influence your peers? It depends upon their cultural background, their personality, and the situation. But bear in mind that effectively building alliances internally requires spending the time to get to know who the key players are, understanding how they're motivated and what their preferences are, and knowing how the decision will be made to accept your idea or not. And it involves getting to the key players' hearts. This is one of the reasons I'm cautious when someone tells me she has a great idea but no one else buys into it. If you can't convince people internally that the innovation is worth pursuing, will you be able to do so with the potential users?

All workplaces are inherently political and full of cultural dynamics. The first place to use your cultural intelligence is in developing a plan for internal buy-in. The power rests with certain individuals and departments, and getting their buy-in is going to be critical. Tap the diversity on your team to come up with a plan for selling your idea internally just as intentionally as you do for selling it externally.

## Getting User Buy-In

The most essential part of the third step (Decide) in the 5D process is considering how to convince the user to support your innovation. IATA, the international trade association for 92 percent of the commercial airlines in the world, has led the way in many aviation innovations, but the group's greatest challenge comes in getting the governments and airlines all working together. How do you convince airlines as diverse as Lufthansa, Emirates, United, and Ethiopia Airlines to all agree?

In 2004, only 20 percent of airlines were using e-ticketing. Giovanni Bisignani, the CEO of IATA at the time, insisted on 100 percent adoption in four years. No one thought it was possible, but by 2008 it happened. The paper ticket became a thing of the past, and the innovation of e-ticketing saved airlines $3 billion a year and alleviated passengers' anxiety of losing their tickets or experiencing unpleasant headaches to change an itinerary.

How did IATA do it? It came from a strategic process of building alliances with airport commissioners, government officials, and airline executives. Everyone from senior management to entry-level associates at IATA was part of building the necessary alliances. IATA's diverse staff engaged with local officials and airline personnel around the world to better understand the barriers to e-ticketing, and they used the insights gained to eventually convince them of the benefits unique to their situation. The IATA teams used cultural intelligence to identify the key problems for respective stakeholders and offer a customized pitch. Some airlines needed little help or convincing, while others had never issued a single electronic ticket and needed help overcoming the technical barriers. Still others resisted the innovation because channeling all ticketing through digital means seemed too risky compared to the tried and true reliability of paper tickets. Bisignani took it on himself to convince the legacy airline carriers to adopt the innovation. The big airlines had been complaining about the unfair competition coming from low-cost carriers, so Bisignani pitched e-ticketing as a core strategy for addressing this. E-ticketing would simplify the business, which in turn would save the airlines money and help them survive the growing competition from disruptive entrants. He told them they had to adapt if they were going to compete. Bisignani is convinced that without the switch to e-ticketing, the legacy carriers would have found it impossible to compete with the budget airlines.

Governments also had to be sold on the idea. Governmental support of aviation in Kuwait, the Emirates, and Qatar has led to incredibly effective hubs. Bisignani used this as an example of why governments could make or break the future of aviation success in their countries. And with 9/11 still fresh in governments' minds, Bisignani's primary point of persuasion with government leaders was safety and security, since e-ticketing would help governments more carefully vet and track a passenger's travels. As he talked with various stakeholders, Bisignani made e-ticketing "their" idea for solving "their" problem, which made them much more motivated to get on board.

## Clearly Identifying the User

Part of selling your idea to the outside world requires extreme clarity about who your user is. For IATA, there are a variety of users, including governments, airports, airlines, and travelers. For a company like Google, the primary users aren't the paying customers. Most of us don't pay Google, but Google designs its products and services for users, not customers. When Google acquired Motorola in 2012, one of the first meetings was to review the features and specifications for all of Motorola's phones. Motorola's leaders kept referring to the customer's requirements, most of which seemed alien to what Google believed about what someone wants from a phone. Suddenly, people at the meeting realized that Google and Motorola were talking about two different "customers." Google was thinking of the individual who uses the phone, while Motorola was thinking about the mobile carrier. Eric Schmidt and Jonathan Rosenberg say, "At Google, our users are the people who use our products, while our customers are the companies that buy our advertising and license our technology. When there are conflicts between the two, we design for the user."[9]

But Google doesn't assume the user knows what he wants or needs. Like Apple, Google eschews traditional approaches to market research and relies instead on its diverse teams to understand what consumers want. Apple and Google trust their vision and want to create the best experience possible for their users.

Schmidt and Rosenberg say, "If your customers are asking for it, you aren't being innovative when you give them what they want; you are just being responsive. That's a good thing, but it's not innovative . . . For something to be innovative, it needs to be new, surprising, and radically useful."[10] It also means you have to know your users extremely well. And it makes the importance of having a strong, diverse team all the more important so that you have firsthand insights into the needs and interests of your users. Brian Moynihan, CEO of Bank of America, personally chairs the bank's diversity and inclusion council. He believes there's a direct link between the bank's diversity efforts internally and customer satisfaction. He says, "When internal diversity and inclusion scores are strong, and employees feel valued, they will serve our customers better, and we'll be better off as an organization."[11]

## Adapting the Pitch for the User

IATA used a pretty basic sales principle in getting all its respective users to adopt e-ticketing: The pitch was designed based upon the needs and problems of the respective users. But it's amazing to me how often this is overlooked. From the guy pitching the Audi to my wife to sales reps for multibillion-dollar companies, there's often far too little creativity and adaptation put into how to pitch an idea to the prospective user. The principles reviewed in Chapter 3 on perspective taking are essential for doing this well.

Bisignani's greatest leverage point in selling and implementing his ideas during his 10 years leading IATA was his knack for becoming an insider with top influential leaders in the world. This is a guy who had dinner with U.S. Secretary of Homeland Security Janet Napolitano one evening, then headed off to Iraq the next day to help that country get the airplane parts it needed to fly passengers safely. And he was open about that. He dined with the Gandhi family when he was in India, he regularly spent time with Singapore's Prime Minister Lee Kuan Yew, and much to the dismay of some, he shared meals with Mugabe of Zimbabwe and Gaddafi of Libya. But don't confuse Bisignani's social, gregarious personality for being overly diplomatic and politically correct. Everybody thought he was crazy for having dinner with dictators. One of his most famous speeches was entitled "Throw a Bomb in the Church!", which emphasized the need for a complete revolution in aviation; and there were times when he intentionally went against cultural norms to accomplish IATA's objectives. How was he able to win the confidence and become a confidant of such diverse, oppositional leaders and convince them to adopt the innovations he believed were essential for aviation to overcome the challenges of the 21st century?

Bisignani's ability to build alliances to drive innovative results across the most global industry of all—aviation—is rooted in his simultaneous commitment to building trusting relationships and bringing strategic impact quickly. This characterizes well the fusion approach to innovation. It uses differences to drive innovative solutions. Bisignani describes himself as the "confessor." He told me, "Everyone seems to tell me their secrets." And he managed to get the CEOs of competing airlines to become comrades. The airline industry is one of the most fiercely competitive industries in the world, so how did he get the executives of United Airlines, British Airways, Singapore Airlines, Ethiopia Airlines, Emirates, and dozens more to work together collegially? He did it by getting them focused on their most important shared value—safety! Everyone is willing to work together for the sake of safety, and any airline in the world will share a part with another airline to ensure that passengers arrive safely. Alongside building relationships and trust, Bisignani was ruthlessly committed to driving change and accomplishing results quickly. The crisis of 9/11 and all that ensued thereafter for governments and airlines meant decisive change was needed quickly. The move toward e-ticketing was one of many innovations Bisignani and his team led in a relatively short period of time, and it hinged on getting stakeholders on board from the beginning. He identified their pain points and drew upon his diverse team of leaders around the world to understand how to successfully pitch the innovation of e-ticketing as a way to relieve their pain.

When listening to a new idea, most recipients are trying to determine whether you understand their situation and needs. They want to know if you've come prepared and whether you're open to some adaptations if needed. This will reveal whether the personal connections made are solely a manipulative tool for getting buy-in or whether you genuinely want to solve a problem for them.

David Maister, author of *Managing the Professional Service Firm*, says there are three things a corporate buyer considers when meeting with you to hear you pitch your idea:

- *Did you come prepared?*

  "If you ask us basic information you could have found on our website, I'm not impressed and I feel like this is basically a canned approach."

  A Word document that outlines how the innovative idea uniquely meets the customer's needs may be far more impressive than a slick brochure, video, or PowerPoint. In fact, sketching the idea on a napkin over lunch or on a whiteboard may be better yet.

- *Can I interrupt you?*

  "I'd prefer to have you sit down and have a conversation with me than to lower the lights and show me your canned presentation."

  If going through a presentation is essential, the buyer may want to see if he can interrupt you. If you can't veer from your preplanned slide deck, it's going to be difficult for him to feel confident that you can be flexible in working with his unique needs.

- *Are you seeking to understand our condition?*

  "Is this simply a sales pitch to talk me into your existing products and services? Or are you truly listening to our situation and willing to think about creative solutions?"

  You may be asked to submit a proposal. But the ultimate decision will be based upon trust. Ideally, a proposal is simply following up what was already discussed together.[12]

The purpose of the pitch isn't necessarily to convince others to immediately adopt your idea. It's to pique their interest and begin a conversation, and it may be part of what helps you determine which exact idea to pursue. In his book *To Sell Is Human,* Daniel Pink writes, "In a world where buyers have ample information and an array of choices, the pitch is often the first word, but it's rarely the last."[13]

## Fusion Lab: Decide

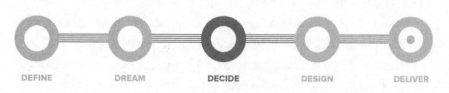

DEFINE    DREAM    DECIDE    DESIGN    DELIVER

There are a number of critical strategies that will guide you to select which idea to pursue and help you garner the support of others. As with many of these practices, many of them apply to any innovative project, but they're particularly relevant to innovating across cultures. Consider the fusion strategies that follow to decide and sell your idea.

### 1. Encourage Bottom-Up—Intervene Top-Down

Most innovation comes from the grass roots. That's why companies like Pixar want their administrative assistants engaged in the creative process alongside the film directors. But one of the biggest cultural differences on diverse teams is the varied cultural preferences for top-down versus flat approaches to leadership and decision making. A fusion approach utilizes both.

Alibaba in China, HCL Technologies in India, Banco Galicia in Argentina, and Pixar in the United States are all companies that have created an environment that fosters bottom-up innovation. They understand that the more ideas and decisions that bubble up from the bottom of the organization, the more innovation is likely to occur. However, the leaders in all these companies also exert strong and timely direction. Linda Hill from Harvard Business School and her coauthors write: "Even in most highly innovative organizations, hierarchy is alive and well. But it's used as needed and very selectively."[14] Top-down direction is most useful when it provides the needed boundaries and constraints for ensuring that an innovation moves from idea to implementation. Helping the team select an idea and reminding them of the objective, budget, timeline, and other constraints is one of the most important ways directive leadership can be used on a highly diverse team.

In addition, top-down intervention is important when someone is violating the rules of engagement or when power is unequal. There are times when the leader may need to intervene to neutralize power differences such as when an idea has been chosen simply because of political reasons rather than what's best for accomplishing the shared goal. Power differences can emerge from dominant cultures, from those with more tenure in the organization, or from those who bring more insider knowledge. This is one of the times top-down intervention is needed. The team needs to hear from everyone to ensure the innovation is informed by their diverse perspectives.

Unleashing the innovative potential versus harnessing the energy of a diverse team is one of the most important dynamics that occurs in a fusion approach to innovation. Culturally intelligent leadership that encourages bottom-up decision making and intervenes top-down is essential if a team is going to successfully decide which idea is best and get the buy-in that's needed.

## 2. Vote

In many cases, a diverse team organically reaches consensus about which idea to pursue. But when conflict and indecision are keeping the team from making a decision, consider voting. Voting helps you move forward and prevents you from bulldozing ahead with an idea that is supported only by the most vocal participants. It creates some potential disadvantages because it inevitably creates some winners and losers, but at least it provides some legitimacy to competing ideas. Randall Peterson from London Business School found that under conditions of high conflict, majority rule was better than consensus for getting decisions made and generating satisfaction with the decision.[15]

To gain the best from a fusion approach, keep in mind the norms of your team and the values of your participants for how you conduct the vote. In some cases, you might be able to go around the room and have participants simply state their vote. In other cases, votes might need to be written down anonymously or have different subteams cast their vote as a unit.[16]

## 3. Map Reactions to the Idea and Pitch

Use the diversity across your team to anticipate the reactions of other stakeholders and to determine the best way to garner support. Team members from more collectivist cultures may want to involve their sponsors and constituencies as part of the decision-making process, whereas those from individualist cultures may be more comfortable selling the decision of the group to the constituencies after it's been decided. A fusion approach allows these preferences to coexist rather than insisting everyone do the same thing. One way to do this is by giving everyone ample information and time so that the collectivist participants or stakeholders can be approached before the decision is finalized. The input that ensues can be part of what is used to make the decision, and it may also be an effective way to garner early buy-in by giving everyone the chance to participate in the decision. You can also make team decisions contingent on the approval of key stakeholders. Another fusion approach is creating enough time in the process that a tentative decision can be made with opportunity for collectivist cultures to consult with their key stakeholders before the final decision is made. In addition, a realistic timeline is needed so that individualists can have a clear sense of when they will be able to begin gathering support, part of which will be knowing that a decision is final.[17]

## 4. Insist on Clarity

People want to know what you're selling and the value proposition you're offering. There are differences in *how* you clearly sell the idea—direct versus indirect, expressive versus nonexpressive, and the amount of detail that is deemed useful. But clarity is a shared value across followers in all cultures.

In fact, clarity is something people want from leadership, regardless of their cultural background. The GLOBE Leadership Study looked at similarities and differences in what people want from leaders. Followers from some cultures want leaders who are visionary and charismatic, while others want leaders who are more low-key and who micromanage the day-to-day processes. There's no such thing as a one-size-fits-all leadership style. But one thing that followers across all the cultures want is *clarity*.[18]

To sell your idea, you need to help others clearly see their situation in fresh and revealing ways to help them identify problems they didn't know they had. Highlighting problems has to be done carefully. Fear and negativity might gain attention initially, but that's not a sustainable form of motivation. Thus, the emphasis should move rather quickly from the problem to the way your idea provides a solution. Help them visualize a positive outcome by eliciting positive emotions.

Use your diverse team to effectively curate information—collecting and organizing vast amounts of information in a clear, organized way. Anyone has access to information, but the sheer volume can be overwhelming. Curating through massive troves of information and presenting the most relevant and clarifying pieces is essential. There's a great deal of research on how our cultures organize things differently, so be sure to draw upon the diversity of your team to consider a variety of approaches for clearly selling the idea to various audiences. Use a fusion approach that blends communicating with bullet points, narrative descriptions, and images.

## 5. Recruit Early Adopters

Finally, recruit early adopters who want to be at the front edge of an innovation. Some cultures, organizations, and individuals thrive on being first, but most prefer to know that someone else has tried it. A fusion approach gets early adopters to get buy-in from both groups—inviting those who want to be the pioneers and using the experience of the pioneers to convince cultures that are more risk-averse.

Many companies in Asia have been reluctant to invest in Internet advertising and e-commerce because it's relatively novel. However, as more reputable companies have gotten on board and as the offerings have expanded beyond only the options offered from Google and Facebook to also include Alibaba of China and Rakuten of Japan, many Asian companies are now spending much more money on web-based business.

When creating a movement, getting the first follower is often the most important step. It turns the crazy loner into the leader. It has to capture the imagination of someone willing to take a risk but also has to be so compelling that others want in when they view it. Who's most likely to be your early adopter? How can you work with them to pitch the idea to others?

## Conclusion

Today, one of the biggest innovations IATA is pitching to its stakeholders around the world is a universal screening process. We've all come to tolerate long lines, invasive screening, and different rules as we board flights from one city to the next. IATA's innovation strategy involves addressing the varied roadblocks that exist across different stakeholders (e.g., governments, airports, airlines, and regulators), and accounting for the cultural differences in terms of how to safely and respectfully screen individuals and attend to the respective cultural concerns that vary from one place to the next. We can only hope IATA succeeds at its proposed innovation, which would reduce the wait time for security screening to 15 seconds anywhere in the world.

Technology offers more opportunities than ever before to get ideas in front of a global audience. It also means there's never been more competition for the countless ideas out there. A crucial part of culturally intelligent innovation is selecting the best idea and getting others to support it. That leads us to the next crucial stage in the process—design and testing. What does a culturally intelligent approach to innovation do that's unique with this familiar phase of innovation?

## DECIDE: SELECT AND SELL YOUR IDEA

Deliberate together until you have an idea that everyone views as "mine" and "ours." This requires bottom-up initiative and top-down direction.

✔ Decide which idea to pursue and write down alternative pitches for at least three different groups of users.

# CHAPTER 10

## DESIGN: CREATE AND TEST FOR DIVERSE USERS

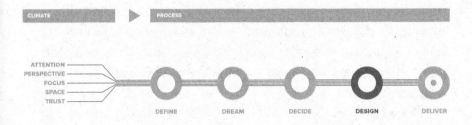

In today's image-conscious world, the way an innovation is designed and tested can easily make or break its success. Gerber's infamous faux pas when introducing baby food to the West African market stemmed from assuming that a cute baby face on the label would sell baby food anywhere. Gerber saw an opportunity to provide middle-class consumers in places like Ghana and Liberia with the convenience and nutritional benefits of baby food. The company launched its product at a very low price with lots of promotions including free samples, but very few people picked up the samples and even fewer purchased the baby food. Sales flopped until the company realized that most West African grocery distributors place pictures of what's inside the package on their labels. Therefore, selling a jar with a baby on the label didn't work.

Gerber isn't the only company with a design failure. Bic's design failure started with presuming that women wanted their own fashionable pink pens, sold as Bic for Her. If some women (and some culturally intelligent men) were on the design team, the company could have avoided receiving sarcastic reviews like this one from

Amazon's listing: "I bought these pens to write down my grocery list, barefoot in the kitchen. But the packaging was so hard to open, I had to wait until my husband came home from work just to open it." Similarly, when Men's Warehouse started marketing traditional guayabera shirts to Hispanic men in the United States, the Latino community revolted with comments like: "We'd never wear those kinds of shirts to the office. What are you thinking?"

A culturally intelligent approach to innovation requires developing a design and testing process that accounts for cultural differences in form and function. What a user in one culture may find efficient, another may find clunky. A website that seems clear and contemporary to a Swiss user may seem cheap and boring to a Japanese one.

There are a number of useful resources devoted to the topic of design and prototyping. The purpose here is to address the central ideas of design and testing through the lens of cultural diversity. Design and testing are part of the same step in the 5D process. The more diverse your potential users, the more important it is that design and testing occur as a symbiotic, cyclical process: design and test . . . design and test . . . design and test. Each design iteration should factor in the input from the latest testing.

## Be User-Focused

The golden rule of design and testing is to know the user. This requires the foundational skill of perspective taking covered in Chapter 3. It's why a diverse team is one of your best resources. When the people working on the project reflect the values and needs of the users, a better solution will emerge. And the more a team utilizes its diversity in the design and testing process, the greater the likelihood the innovation will be useful to a diversity of users.

It's surprising how often the golden rule of user-focused design and testing is overlooked in the innovation process. Design and testing can quickly resort to what psychologists call the mirror image fallacy, where you assume others want what you want. Assuming users want the same features you do is dangerous for any innovation given the unique tastes and personalities of individuals everywhere. But it's especially problematic when different cultures are involved. When Microsoft first used the "mailbox" icon, it required a lot of explaining to global users, for whom mail is not delivered in anything that resembles the quintessential U.S. suburban mailbox. And the word "paste" in Microsoft Word was translated as "stuck" in Chinese, which made for a clunky, confusing design. There are a couple of ways to avoid these design mistakes.

## Test with a Diverse Team

How did Bic end up causing such an uproar by creating a pen specifically for women, "designed to fit comfortably in a woman's hand" and available in an attractive barrel design in pink and purple? Many products are designed specifically for one gender or the other and go unnoticed. There are pink video games, pink guns, and pink sports jerseys. There are also camouflaged backpacks, windbreakers, and pens. It's unlikely many would have noticed if Bic had simply made pink pens available; the problem was that the product was saying, "Pink stuff is for girls!" Neutral stereotypes generally have some predictive value (e.g., women are more likely to use a pink pen than men), but when you explicitly state them, they become offensive. This is what happens when you design an innovation solely based upon homogenous assumptions. Even the use of data and focus groups doesn't replace the hard work of interacting with users and letting them test different iterations of the solution.

It's difficult to imagine that the people who made the decision to launch Bic for Her were the same women expected to buy the pens. And that's why a majority of consumer brand launches fail. The true concerns and values of the user have been overlooked or misunderstood. Entrepreneurs rarely make this kind of mistake because they usually start a business to solve their own problems and they understand those problems well. As a result, their innovations rarely look as silly as the Bic for Her line.[1]

A quick visit to Bic's global website reveals a number of interesting things about the company's leadership. Led by CEO Mario Guevara and Chair Bruno Bich, the company is predominantly white and male. There appears to be virtually no ethnic diversity among the leadership and only a few women leaders. Given the pressure on today's companies to at least give lip service to diversity, it's striking that a review of Bic's website and annual report finds virtually no reference to the value of diversity and inclusion. It's hard to imagine Bic for Her would have happened if women and staff from a variety of backgrounds had had more voice and influence in the innovation. The Bic for Her story displays the subtle costs that accrue for organizations that continue with business as usual while the world at large becomes much more multifaceted and diverse.

The design mantra of "know your user" means better understanding the way culture shapes what users want. And when you have a culturally diverse team and create ways for members to voice their diverse perspectives, you have a built-in laboratory for seeing the differences in how people respond to design. A diverse team gives you a different set of eyes. This is a critical part of what moved Lego from the verge of bankruptcy to being the world's leading toy company. CEO Jorgen Vig Knudstørp credits a great deal of Lego's turnaround to deep ethnographic understanding conducted by the organization's diverse team, which studied how kids around the world play. One of the innovations that emerged was a product line for girls called Lego Friends. Compared to the situation at Bic, Lego's innovation emerged from understanding approaches to play that were unique to girls (e.g., giving them options for both shopping malls they could build and jungle animals they could rescue). Also, the Lego Friends line was marketed without being explicit about gender stereotypes (boys can play with them too!). As a result, the product line has caught on with girls in markets from China to Germany to the United States, and it all began by utilizing the diversity on the research team.[2]

## Test Up Close

Design also has to be informed by observing users up close. This is why A. G. Lafley, the CEO of P&G, insists on in-home visits with consumers when he travels internationally. He doesn't want to make decisions based solely on market research done by consultants and R&D teams. When he visited Istanbul, he sat with a Turkish woman in her house and watched her wash dishes and clothes. He talked to her for about 90 minutes and asked her to try out new products P&G was developing. Such in-home visits improve his understanding of consumer needs and send a message to all his executives. If the CEO of an $80 billion company has time to spend a couple of hours in a home in Istanbul, maybe you do too.[3]

For many years, Toyota struggled to compete with Honda and Chrysler in the North American minivan market. So the company decided to redesign its minivan, the Sienna. Yuji Yokoya was tasked with the job. Yokoya had been successful leading the design efforts for several Toyota vehicles for Japan and Europe, but he had never designed a vehicle for North America, and he decided he needed to spend time there.

He drove the Sienna model through all 50 U.S. states, all 13 Canadian provinces and territories, and all across Mexico. His on-the-ground experiences in North America gave him insights that would have been entirely missed if he had simply researched market trends and North American demographics from an office in Japan. For example, he discovered that many Canadian highways have a higher crown than U.S. roads—bowed in the middle, presumably to deal with snow. That led him to see the importance of a design that dealt with the inevitable drift that happens as a van drives along the sloped road.

Crossing a bridge over the Mississippi River, a gust of wind nearly caused Yokoya to lose control. Going along an open highway with trucks passing by gave him additional insights into the kind of stability needed. Driving around the narrow streets of Santa Fe, New Mexico, he noted the poor turning precision of the existing model.

One of the biggest differences between Japanese and North American cultures is the way people eat. Japanese rarely eat on the go. If a Japanese family is driving and gets thirsty, they're more likely to stop and get small drinks that they finish before getting back in the van. But North Americans bring their food and drinks along, often filling up large drink containers to get them across long distances. In fact, Yokoya learned that many U.S. drivers wanted at least two drinking compartments for each passenger. The result was 14 cup and bottle holders in the newly designed Sienna as well as flip-up trays for food.

The Japanese culture thrives on minimalism, so the original Toyota minivan was designed smaller than competitors' vans. But when Yokoya stood in a Home Depot parking lot watching people load 4' x 8' plywood sheets in the back of their pickup trucks and Honda Odysseys, he knew the North American version of the Sienna needed to be longer.[4]

One might think that taking the time to travel through every Canadian province and U.S. state is a bit extreme. But it was this attention to detail that led to a design that made the new Sienna so successful in the North American market. The contrast with what happened with GM's Aztek is striking; testing for the Aztek was done quickly by a homogenous team and user input was ignored. All too often, innovative ideas and even full-scale vision statements are drafted in isolation by leadership teams without getting substantial input from the intended users. Be sure testing includes the target users, not simply global professionals with MBAs who think they understand the needs of the users. And consider the socioeconomic status of the targeted users and get their input as you design and test. Testing directly with targeted users takes more time, but in the long run it ends up with an innovation design that truly addresses the user's needs. Lego's Knudstorp says, "If you want to understand how animals live, you don't go to the zoo, you go to the jungle."[5]

## The Power of Color: Black Means White and White Means Black

Does food taste different based upon its color? Yes! William Lidwell, a thought leader in design and innovation, describes a research study done with different colors of gelatin. Test subjects were asked to taste four different colors of Jell-O—red, yellow, green, and blue. All four kinds had exactly the same flavor, but the subjects didn't know that. When blindfolded, subjects couldn't tell any difference in the taste. But those who saw the different colors consistently identified the following flavors with each one:

The red Jell-O is sweet. It tastes like strawberry.

The yellow is sour. It tastes like lemon.

The green is tart. It tastes like green apple.

The blue is odd. It tastes something like coconut.[6]

In reality, they were all exactly the same flavor. But the color "changed" the taste. It would be interesting to see how the responses would differ if this study was conducted cross-culturally.

The flavors attributed to certain colors would likely change, with different colors associated with different localized tastes.

When the Sichuan earthquake happened in China in 2008, a few multinational corporations changed their Chinese home pages to black to pay respect to the 60,000 lives lost in the disaster. But white is the color of mourning in China, not black. In Chinese culture, black more typically symbolizes evil, corruption, or illegal activity. Many Chinese consumers probably understood the good intentions behind the black home pages, but this kind of design mistake can be costly. It also sends a message of a company that is out of touch with its consumers. Worse yet was when United Airlines gave white carnations—a colored flower typically reserved for funerals—to its passengers on its first flight from China to the United States.

As with any cultural norms and descriptions, it's dangerous to stereotype all people in a culture as having a unified experience with a color. Different personalities also respond to colors differently. But here are some general guidelines related to color in a few major cultures globally:

* Red is the color of love in many cultures. Traditional Chinese brides wear red, and red roses are the most common gift on Valentine's Day. But red also indicates emergencies and warnings in many places around the world. Red must be used carefully because it elicits very strong reactions from many cultures around the world.
* Green has become associated with the environmental movement in many places globally. But traditionally, it was considered the color of Islam and the national color of places like Egypt. In contrast, green is often a symbol of sickness in many Asian cultures, and historically, a Chinese man wearing a green hat was revealing that his wife had been cheating

on him. In North America, green is often associated with wealth and money since paper currency is green.

* White is perceived as a color of purity and innocence in many Western cultures. But it's the color of mourning in most Confucian Asian cultures. Likewise, in India, family members wear white after the death of a loved one. A Westerner seeing a woman wearing white is likely to think of a bride whereas some Asians may see a person who is in mourning.[7]

You don't need to master the distinct meanings of colors for every culture you work with. That's impossible. But a culturally intelligent approach to design consciously accounts for the varying ways color can be perceived. And you need to ensure that your design process gathers input from users from a diversity of backgrounds to understand the varying responses to the colors used. Ask team members, users, and local experts for their advice on colors.

## Example: Website Design and Testing

Innovative design is necessary across any kind of organization and industry—whether it's automotive engineers designing a new vehicle, nurses creating a new way to chart medicines, or airline personnel coming up with more efficient boarding procedures. But in order to get more specific, let's look at an example that nearly every 21st century organization and user encounters on a daily basis—websites. How should cultural differences influence the design and testing of your website?

Just ask a group of friends how they like your new website and you'll quickly see how much personal taste dictates people's opinions about design. The more diverse your friends, the more varied the opinions will be. Dianne Cyr has done some of the most extensive research focused on consumers' website preferences related to cultural differences. Her research consistently shows that consumers prefer to visit and interact with sites that are made specifically for them. And the more consumers believe a website reflects their interests and priorities, the greater their trust, satisfaction, and e-loyalty.[8]

Users from a hierarchical orientation are subconsciously screening a website for things like expertise, authority, and official credentials. Intranet sites used inside hierarchical companies are expected to have different sections for managers versus nonmanagers. In addition, hierarchical cultures tend to prefer sites with a formal layout and more vivid visuals. Limited choices and restricted access to information are favored. Visual elements that resonate with the pulse of the region are valued. In contrast, egalitarian-oriented cultures prefer informal layouts with clear access and multiple choices for how to navigate through the site. Flexible interactions that guide the user in case of errors are valued. Visual elements that are more universal are preferred, and Western users increasingly value minimal text and more images.[9]

Coca-Cola's website in Kuwait, a very hierarchical context, organizes information using a formal layout. There are limited choices for people to make when visiting the site. The images used are powerful and guide the user through the site. In addition, the site portrays an image of flashiness and wealth for people who are loyal to the Coca-Cola brand. But Coke uses a different design and structure for its website in Ireland, a culture with an egalitarian orientation. The search functionality encourages exploration and allows for multiple options for how a user navigates and engages with the site. The image portrayed is one of fun, friendship, and community. Portraying an image of extravagance and opulence would be a turnoff to the majority of consumers in Ireland.

A website designed for an individualist culture may highlight individual successes and youthfulness as a result of the company's offerings, whereas one designed for a collectivist culture may high-light wise leaders and represent community and societal interests. The layout of a website serves as a communication bridge between the organization and the user. The goal of culturally intelligent design is to understand different cultural perspectives holistically while not stereotyping cultures or making tacit assumptions about user preferences.

An organization's trustworthiness and credibility is instinctively judged within seconds of viewing a website. Research points to the importance of a global approach to the back-end design for web-sites (e.g., the programming and platform used behind the scenes) and local customization to the front-end design so that website visitors see a design that reflects their needs and tastes.[10] Test early iterations of the design with a diversity of users and consider their feedback before finalizing it. The fusion approach to innovation is ideally suited for this.

Any organization with a web presence can be global, so all or-ganizations need to give some consideration to how the design and content of their websites communicate across cultures. Incorpo-rating cultural considerations in the design process increases the aesthetic value, perceivable quality, and behavioral intention in the users.[11]

## Determine the Relative Importance of Design

Branding and design companies try to convince you that the design of your product or the overall image portrayed by your branding will be the most important differentiator as you compete globally. But the importance of design is relative to a couple of additional factors.

First, if you're in a market or entering one where there's already a great deal of competition, design is often the key factor that differentiates you from a crowded field of options. Fen Hiew is a business and IT strategy consultant who works with several global companies. He says that when positioning yourself in contrast to several competitors who offer nearly identical products or services, design is the primary way to get people to notice you. Take, for example, the meteoric prominence accomplished by Airbnb, the online portal connecting homeowners with short-term renters who want to stay in a home rather than a hotel. Websites and companies offering personal residences for rent existed long before Airbnb came along. But Airbnb entered the market with a simple, beautiful design that allows the user to easily search the exact features wanted in a rental with brilliant pictures of the properties. Airbnb's people would argue that the services they offer are different from what one would get from competitors like Vacation Rental By Owners (VRBO) or travelmob, and perhaps there are some slight differences. But for the user, the primary offering is the same—the chance to rent directly from a homeowner. Therefore, design was a critical differentiator for Airbnb and helped the company disrupt the entire hotel industry.

However, if your innovation stems from a core capability that no one else has or from offering a service that is not available from others, your primary value proposition rests less in the design and more in your distinctive offering. Design still has relevance. You can't show up with a homemade website or with a prototype that's clunky; but your design has less importance to a user than it does when you're offering an existing service that is abundantly available. Your value proposition is more strongly connected to your new offering or competency than to your design. Airbnb entered a very crowded space of travel websites and booking alternatives, so design and image was critical. However, when Amazon first entered the market offering online retail, it faced very little competition. An innovation that was almost solely conducted online meant Amazon certainly had to give some attention to design. But for Amazon, the distinctive offering—allowing people to make purchases securely and in a glitch-free manner—was a far more important part of what it was offering consumers than the visual design itself. The big allure of Amazon was not its "look" but offering an innovative way to buy books (and now far more!) that was financially secure.

Design had less importance to Amazon's early success than to Airbnb's. Determine what level of sophistication is needed in designing your innovation and the degree to which the visual design is important. As you test different versions of your innovation, notice the relative importance of design for different users. Then utilize your diverse team to consider several strategic questions as a way to create a culturally intelligent design and prototype.

## Fusion Lab: Design

| DEFINE | DREAM | DECIDE | **DESIGN** | DELIVER |

Culturally intelligent innovation requires a conscious plan for how to design and test an innovation for a diversity of users. Take time to consider and respond to the following questions when designing and prototyping your innovation and make the most of your diverse team to come up with a fusion design.

### 1. What Needs Does It Meet?

Do you have to create the need (e.g., the iPod or Starbucks), or is there already pent-up demand for this innovation? What cultures will have the hardest time seeing the need? How will the needs influence the way you design it? Taking the time to identify the *felt* and *real* needs of your target users can help inform the way you design the innovation.

When Coke started putting personal first names on individual cans of Coke as part of its Share a Coke campaign, I didn't really see the point. *If I want a can of Coke, why do I care if my name is on it?* But then, with a name like David, I've never had a very hard time finding personalized products with my name on them. Yet the personalized Coke cans were a huge hit in places like South Africa. For the first time, individuals with names like Buhle or Da Silva could buy something with their names on it. Some people on Coke's global team suggested a different approach for Millennials in the United States, in which college students could go to a Coke machine on campus and personalize a can of Coke to say whatever they wanted.

This is the benefit of a fusion approach to culturally intelligent innovation. It offers a built-in resource for understanding diverse users' needs. Consumers in Johannesburg are unlikely to request personalized Coke products, and college students won't likely ask for a way to personalize their Coke cans. But studying consumers' behavior and listening to a diverse team that included South Africans and U.S. Millennials led to a fusion design for the Share a Coke campaign.

To understand user needs, observe and interview users in the context where the innovation will be used (e.g., in the home where they will use the detergent or in the workplace as they're doing their job). Describe what you'd like to do and get input at all the design stages. It's important to have visuals and demos. Many users react far more strongly to visual demonstrations than to verbal or written ones. This is all the more true for users in high-context cultures where experiencing the design as realistically as possible is important.

## 2. What Prior Knowledge Is Assumed?

Assuming too much or too little knowledge can derail the innovation. Does the consumer know how to use it effectively, and what kind of instruction and support needs to be offered?

As usual, you will be ahead of the game if you utilize the diversity on your team to understand the knowledge gaps. What seems obvious to one individual may not seem that way to someone else at all. Be sure to benefit from those who have no insider knowledge to see what implicit assumptions and tacit knowledge may be guiding your design process. What's intuitive to one user may not be to another. In a market where people prefer certainty (high uncertainty avoidance), explicit information is going to be all the more important. The reverse is true for users coming from cultures that are reticent to have things too planned out and controlled (low uncertainty avoidance).

Most groups default to an emphasis on the common knowledge shared across the group and fail to glean unique insights from each other. In order to use the fusion process successfully, you need to keep coming back to amplifying your differences and using them to guide your decisions. Continually emphasizing the divergent perspectives, experiences, and values on your team primes you to think divergently and to come up with more creative, realistic solutions for more users.

## 3. What Does the Design Communicate?

Rigorously assess what the design communicates to various cultures. This should include at least the following:

- What does the color communicate? How does it make you feel?
- What do the images say? Might there be hidden meaning to these images you aren't aware of?

- If you're using symbols, what do they communicate in different cultures?
- How have you accounted for language differences?
- How does the level of functionality influence users from different cultures?

Many prospective users will not have a conscious reaction or opinion to these kinds of questions, so tap your diverse team to think about how to creatively explore these questions. In today's image-conscious world, it's never been more important to attend to the very strong, visceral reactions users have to design—good, bad, and indifferent. Design and test . . . design and test . . . design and test.

## 4. With Whom Should You Test?

Time constraints and efficiency often cause teams to skip testing with actual users. This often happens because teams dangerously assume that they already know the user and can just test internally. But even if the innovation emerged from market research and user input, the user needs to actually experience the prototype and offer feedback.

Even if you have a diverse team, you still need to test with users who haven't been part of your internal process. Users are excellent at reacting to concrete, visible designs. They bring important "folk knowledge" to the innovation that may have otherwise been overlooked by the design team. And involving users in the prototyping process is an effective way to get greater buy-in and build anticipation. The user is not always right, so the input needs to be factored in with all the other considerations. But take the time to thoroughly test the prototype with users. Also, be sure the test-users reflect the diversity of the long-term intended users. Beware of allowing one individual or organization to solely represent an entire culture or market. The more input you get, the better. And when you choose to dismiss user feedback, be able to convince your team why the feedback isn't relevant.

## 5. What Level of Sophistication Is Needed for the Prototype?

Brainstorm different prototype options and choose a level of sophistication or fidelity that will give you the best way to test the innovation without investing too much time and effort. Not only is an overly sophisticated prototype costly, but it can communicate to the sample user that this is already a done deal rather than something that will truly be shaped by user input. Also, the more minimalist the initial prototype, the easier it is to adapt it based upon user input. By scaling back on the bells and whistles from the start, you can avoid a lot of hassle, spending, and planning.

Low-fidelity prototypes are quick and cheap and are usually done as paper mock-ups. This provides an opportunity for quick user reactions and elicits suggestions. Many feel that this works best when sketched out in the moment rather than being written up ahead of time. The speed of low-fidelity prototypes makes it easier to get a lot of feedback quickly. Dan Roam's book *The Back of the Napkin* is packed full of strategies for successfully communicating innovative ideas, services, and products through stick figures on a napkin.

Medium-fidelity prototypes are typically simulations that are done on a digital device. They demonstrate some but not all features of the intended system. A medium-fidelity prototype provides a more sophisticated, albeit still limited, experience for the user and provides a more nuanced test. Just beware that these prototypes can be costly and can cause things to get bogged down quickly. But depending upon the culture (e.g., those who prefer a high level of certainty), it may be important to go to a medium-fidelity level for prototyping. Medium-fidelity prototypes are best for fine-tuning design.

Only in rare cases is a high-fidelity prototype the way to go. However, in some cultures where it is important to visualize precisely what the new product or service is going to be like, it may be necessary to have something that is close to the level of sophistication that is intended in the end product.

## Conclusion

Most people need to tangibly experience an innovation to be able to provide input on it. And you'll be better able to anticipate the many variables of executing the innovation long-term by having taken the time to develop and test a prototype. The process of the design is as important as the response you get from it. The time you spent defining a shared mental model (Chapter 7) will pay off when you get to this stage in the process. You'll need to continually revisit the shared mental model to address the inevitable conflicts and setbacks that will occur.

If during testing you find that users are focused primarily on one part of your innovation, consider scrapping the rest of it and focus on that. Some businesses that fumble have one small segment that really works but are unwilling to let go of the other segments that don't. You have limited time and resources, so channel your energy around what works best for your users.

As you design and test your idea, keep it simple and listen to the feedback you receive. There's nothing more valuable than learning from how people respond to your innovation.

### DESIGN: CREATE AND TEST FOR DIVERSE USERS

Watch a diversity of users test a prototype, and adapt the design accordingly. Look for what features they focus on most and least.

✔ List the diverse users who will test your prototype.

# CHAPTER 11

## DELIVER: IMPLEMENT GLOBAL SOLUTIONS

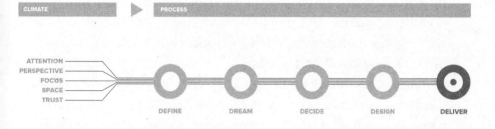

One of the U.S. companies we work with at the Cultural Intelligence Center recently merged with a German organization. Prior to the merger, both companies had similar organizational values and reputations for being disruptive innovators. The greatest point of internal conflict after the merger was a difference in how the companies prioritized speed versus attention to detail. The German company was used to highly detailed project plans that required extensive deliberation and review. For the Americans, the norm was to implement things as quickly as possible, even if it wasn't perfectly fine-tuned. Even the U.S. engineers, who typically thought of themselves as the more detail-oriented members of their teams, said they were forever telling their new German colleagues, "We can't possibly anticipate every 'what-if' scenario that's going to happen. We need to get our plans to about 80 percent and then get it out to market and make corrections as we go." The Americans were consistently frustrated by what they saw as unnecessary delays, and the Germans were chafed by what they viewed as careless expediency.

In one study that examined the contrast between how Germans and Americans work, a German participant said, "Americans work two to three times faster than Germans, they are very goal oriented, but if the plan does not work, they will completely throw it overboard after three months. It is much more difficult to change a plan in Germany once it has been implemented."[1] Both approaches to speed and detail can lead to successful innovation. An even better approach can emerge from fusing detailed processes with a focus on expediency. Diversity makes or breaks the success of implementing an innovation.

Great ideas mean nothing if they can't be effectively implemented. More than 50 percent of technological innovations end up never being successfully implemented. It's estimated that more than $500 billion is wasted by companies each year by failing to effectively implement the innovations they develop.[2]

The ideas that change the world are built around the not so sexy implementation plans that translate ideas into real-life solutions. Diversity is unlikely to impede implementation as long as you develop a plan for implementation. And if you've consciously managed the diversity throughout each step of the 5D process, you will be much better positioned to implement effectively.

## Barriers to Implementation

There are a number of things that stand in the way of diverse teams delivering innovative solutions. These barriers exist for any team, but as always there are additional variables to consider for diverse teams.

### Technical Knowledge/Skills Gap

Some innovations require users to gain new technical knowledge and skills. For early adopters and users who are comfortable with ambiguity, this isn't usually a problem. They welcome the chance to try something new. But for others, learning something new is tedious, stressful, and at the very least time-consuming. The degree to which project engineers adopt new technological innovations is directly related to the level of complexity involved in doing so. If the new technology is significantly more complicated than what it is replacing, the engineers are unlikely to adopt the innovation. Individuals coming from short-term–oriented cultures where the emphasis is upon quick wins and speed are more likely to be frustrated by the learning curve required to implement a complicated innovation than those who come from long-term–oriented cultures.[3]

## Skepticism and Resistance to Change

The decision to adopt and implement an innovation is typically made by those higher in the hierarchy than the innovation's targeted users.[4] This raises another barrier that is particularly relevant to implementing across cultures. The targeted users might not be convinced they really need the innovation, particularly in egalitarian cultures like Australia and Israel, or among Millennials, where resistance to management mandating a new change may be even more of an issue. Reluctance might be a result of skepticism, an unwillingness to change, or simply a sense that management doesn't really get it. But management often tells staff members that they need to adopt the innovation anyway.

Utilize the diverse ideas and perspectives to think about how the innovation can best be developed *and* implemented. Forecast what types of resistance may occur and highlight the diversity of input that was utilized for developing the innovation. Use your fusion team to come up with different implementation plans for different users.

Some personalities and cultures have a disposition toward viewing anything new suspiciously. This can be particularly true in certain professional cultures. Faculty are often socialized all throughout their academic careers to look for gaps and insufficiencies in existing research or in student work. As a result, many faculty members view new approaches suspiciously and look for inadequacies. Implementing innovations with individuals coming from this kind of perspective requires a much more thorough, rational process.

Some innovations may require individuals to make changes they don't want to make. Perhaps they have to start working more or less autonomously or have to coordinate more with others, things that may go against their preferred working style and cultural values. In one study, a group of doctors and nurses were asked to implement an innovative approach for working with people with diabetes. The approach was based upon the idea that patients have a level of expertise about their condition that most health care professionals don't have. Since the patients actually live with diabetes on a day-to-day basis, the innovation was built around equipping them to better diagnose and treat their own symptoms. The medical personnel bought into the idea conceptually, but when it came down to it, the approach went against the whole foundation of how they had been trained. They were the experts and they were paid to tell patients what to do. Their view was shaped from how they had been trained and it's what patients expect from their doctors. The innovation couldn't be successfully implemented because of the underlying, subconscious values and norms among the key implementers—the doctors, nurses, and patients.[5]

## Time Consumed

Even if an innovation is said to save people time, it typically requires additional time and effort to make the switch. Effective implementation often requires training, troubleshooting, and an investment of time and support, which in turn initially reduces performance. Even the most beneficial innovation is likely to result in poorer team performance in the short run. And although managers and targeted users might know that an innovation will eventually lead to better performance, many are reluctant to accept the lag in performance required to get there. Given the emphasis on speed and being the first to market, the time required to adopt a new innovation can be a threat for effective implementation, particularly for Westerners. The more that this is intentionally addressed in the implementation phase, the better.[6]

This is one of the ways the diverse team of which I'm a part has really helped me. I'm very task-oriented and I put a high value on productivity. But over the last few years, I've better appreciated the immense strength that has come from attending to many of my colleagues' more thorough, process-oriented approach that takes more time but ends up leading to better solutions.

## Procrastination

One of the biggest barriers to implementation is procrastination. And according to Piers Steel, a leading researcher on motivation, procrastination typically stems from one of three things: low expectancy, low value, or impulsiveness. Low expectancy is limited confidence in the success of a proposed innovation. Low value means you see little reward from implementing the idea. Impulsiveness refers to the distractions of other priorities and requests that keep you from moving an innovation from idea to implementation.[7] A fusion team may benefit from taking time to discuss the way these three procrastination factors vary on your team. Have each person rate the level of value and expectancy she attributes to seeing this innovation launched. Also, identify which distractions are most prevalent for various members. In polychronic cultures where individuals are expected to attend to family members and authority figures at their beck and call, they may be faced with a different set of distractions than those who come from cultures where you're left alone to work unless there's a real emergency.

One of the best ways to address procrastination is to come back to the shared mental model developed at the beginning of the 5D process (Chapter 7). Working from a shared goal helps keep the vision alive throughout the slog of implementation. An understanding of how the procrastination factors play differently on your team provides a greater level of patience with each other while also keeping you focused on the shared outcome.

A paradox that confronts every innovation team is that growth creates complexity, and complexity threatens growth. Oliver Wendell Holmes, Jr., a former U.S. Supreme Court justice, famously said, "I wouldn't give you a fig for simplicity on this side of complexity; I would give my right arm for simplicity on the far side of complexity." Diversity fuels a more complex ideation and design process that is essential for developing truly transformative solutions. But on the other side of that complexity, simplicity is needed for effective implementation. This creates opportunities for an organization like the one formed by the U.S.–German merger I discussed at the beginning of this chapter. Together, the two original companies can offer a fusion of their U.S. and German strengths. The German team is predisposed to giving the necessary attention to detail and complexity that leads to better innovative outcomes, and the U.S. team is better oriented toward wading through the complexity to offer a measure of simplicity to the user. And together, they are developing a fusion culture and resulting innovations that emerge from sophistication and complexity while also offering users solutions that appear simple and user-friendly; thus far, the results of their collaborative efforts exceed what they forecasted in sales.

## Case Study: ERP Implementation—Chinese vs. Australian Company

Enterprise Resource Planning (ERP) is a software solution used by many global companies to synchronize all of their standard business operations into one integrated system. Implementing ERP usually costs millions of dollars, but many large companies perceive it as an investment that's essential for long-term sustainability and growth. Most ERP projects take more time and money than anticipated, most of which is due to inefficient planning and an inability to coordinate the efforts across different functions, personalities, and cultures.

Graeme Shanks and his colleagues examined the impact of cultural differences on ERP implementation at Elevatorco, a large elevator company in China, versus the impact at Oilco, one of Australia's fastest growing oil refineries.[8] (See Table 11-1.) At the time of the study, Elevatorco had annual sales of $450 million. It had 20 percent of the market share for elevators in China and an annual growth rate of 15 percent. The company decided to implement an ERP system after senior management saw how much money was being spent to maintain multiple information systems across the company. Data redundancy was a big problem, and the technical sophistication of the IT staff was limited.

### Table 11-1. ERP Implementation at Chinese vs. Australian Company

| ELEVATORCO: Chinese elevator company | OILCO: Australian oil refinery |
|---|---|
| **Shared Objective:**<br>• Large-scale implementation of ERP systems<br>**Shared Success Factors:**<br>• Top management support<br>• Diverse functions and users were part of the testing and implementation | |
| **Unique Implementation Strategy:**<br>• External expertise<br>• Clear goals and data accuracy to guide implementation | **Unique Implementation Strategy:**<br>• Internal champions<br>• Intentional change management process |

Oilco owned approximately $2 billion in assets. It is the Australian subsidiary of one of the largest multinational oil companies in the world, with a network of 1,800 locations across Australia. Similar to Elevatorco, the leadership at Oilco saw the need for an integrated information system to reduce costs, align efforts across all locations, and improve the speed and quality of the service offered to customers. Oilco needed a sophisticated ERP system so it could process up to 35,000 transactions an hour and handle more than 1,000 orders per day.

Both Elevatorco and Oilco believed that the implementation of an efficient, integrated ERP system was essential for their long-term success. Both projects were large-scale implementations of ERP systems and both used an incremental, staged process of implementation. The commitment and support of top management was a key success factor for both companies. In addition, both companies benefited from implementation teams that had a fusion of IT people and end users, a diversity that, when managed well, is essential for successful implementation of new software systems.

But there were some key differences between the ERP implementation approaches that reflect the different cultures. For Oilco, having champions across various business units who supported the ERP project was critical. The champions didn't have formal authority, but they were individuals who informally promoted the value of the ERP implementation among their peers. But champions were irrelevant at Elevatorco. In the Chinese context, the top manager is the only champion who really matters; whether other individuals think the project is important has little bearing on the success of the innovation. In fact, a subordinate who feels the need to champion a cause in a Chinese context might be seen as a threat to the formal authority figures.

Change management was another crucial factor at the Australian company. The project team knew they needed a specific plan for getting buy-in across the company and considered the specific organizational dynamics that should influence how the implementation would be rolled out. In a traditional Chinese company, however, organizational processes are typically communicated top-down. Senior leadership imposes processes, and therefore a conscious plan for change management is less likely to be a critical success factor. There tends to be higher trust in senior leadership to do what's best for everyone involved.

Elevatorco described external expertise as critically important for implementing ERP across the company, whereas that was not a key part of the implementation strategy employed by Oilco. Chinese culture typically places a higher importance on external expertise than Australian culture does.

In addition, the Chinese company was much more explicit about the importance of clear goals and data accuracy than the Australian company was. This reflects the cultural differences in the importance of certainty between Australians and Chinese people, with Chinese typically being more concerned about reducing uncertainty and ambiguity than Australians. And the importance of clear goals also reflects a more methodical process-orientation that often emerges from a Confucian approach to work and projects rather than the results-orientation that is more predominant in many Anglo-dominated contexts such as Australia.[9]

The contrast of these two companies' implementation of ERP highlights some of the recurring differences that emerge in delivering innovative solutions. It's dangerous to make too much out of these two isolated scenarios. And a fusion approach would do some of both—create value and expectancy from having champions and from senior leadership. But to ensure that an idea is effectively implemented, a diverse team needs to draw upon the differences of its members to organize themselves for the most successful implementation.

## Fusion Lab: Deliver

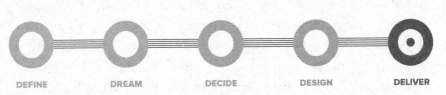

DEFINE　　　　DREAM　　　　DECIDE　　　　DESIGN　　　　**DELIVER**

Successfully implementing ideas from and for a diversity of cultures rests in taking time to develop a plan for delivery. A fusion approach to implementation requires attention to the following areas.

### 1. Formalize Leadership

In order to successfully implement an idea, leadership is essential. This sounds obvious but I see countless situations where this is overlooked. Many companies that have adopted a global matrix model of leadership overlook the importance of formalizing leadership, particularly for a temporary team or project. Leaders of fusion teams need to consider the bottom-up/top-down paradox of fusion leadership (Chapter 9). Formalizing this kind of leadership includes the factors that follow.

#### *PROJECT LEAD*

Most teams need someone who is given explicit authority to lead the team. Even in a very egalitarian environment, it becomes confusing and disorienting if people aren't clear who is ultimately responsible for managing the project. But this is especially relevant for teams that involve individuals coming from a more hierarchical orientation to leadership—most of the world! At the same time, the project lead has to know when and how to allow various regions or functional experts to take the lead. After all, when you bring together a group of highly talented people, many individuals within the team may bring more expertise about the project than the team leader has. And nothing disengages some participants more quickly than a failure to share the leadership, ownership, and credit with others. It's critical for the project lead to have high CQ to leverage the most from the diverse parties involved.

*SENIOR LEADERSHIP SUPPORT*

One of the team leader's main responsibilities is ensuring that the project team has the full support of key stakeholders across the organization. It's critical to get input and backing from the highest levels of leadership possible. Even if the idea originally came from senior leadership, don't take their ongoing support for granted. Find out what kind of budget and personnel they're willing to devote to the project. Perhaps the greatest test of their support is to find out what kind of time they will personally invest in the project.

In addition, the managers in any functional area affected by the innovation must support the project in order for it to succeed. The team's objectives must be seen as a priority among all related departments or it will be too difficult for individual team members to find the time and resources necessary to complete their tasks. When the team has enough high-level support, senior managers can ensure that people within the organization understand the team's objectives and how they fit with the big picture.

*CHAMPIONS*

In some cases, particularly in egalitarian cultures like Oilco, it is important to recruit champions across various departments. This isn't a formalized role; rather, it's the individuals who are sold on the idea and its value and share that with others. Successful implementation is often most at the hands of the individual contributors who are ultimately the ones making the idea happen. Some cultures and personalities want a great deal of voice in how the implementation occurs, while others simply need to have clear communication about if and how this will directly have an impact upon their area. A fusion approach includes champions to better engage those motivated by hearing peers promote the forthcoming innovation.

## 2. Agree on Timing

Few things create more intercultural conflict during the implementation than different time orientations. This most offen occurs over different expectations about deadlines and the amount of time it should take to reach a decision and implement a process.

I like speed. I rarely slow down. And I apply that same propensity for speed to how I make decisions. I want to work it through, analyze the details, and then reach a decision. The same goes for how I prefer to work on a project. I want to get at it quickly, work hard, and bring it to completion so we can move on to the next thing. One of my Asian colleagues prefers a much more thorough, detailed process than my typical flow. Her preferred way of working is to go through 12 to 15 iterations of a project with ongoing analysis and revisions before finalizing it, sometimes starting all over with a different approach multiple times along the way. We've discussed this difference in our approach and the potential strengths of each. We've reached a fusion solution that agrees on not having fewer than three and more than five iterations of something we're working on. This isn't just a compromise. We've found that we actually come up with better outcomes following this approach, which requires both of us to give up something from our preferred way of working. She drills deeply into the complexities, and I keep us focused on moving forward. Together, we include and transcend our preferences.

For individuals and cultures that don't value punctuality and follow-through as much, be sure they understand how a delay will impede the overall project (assuming it will). If they understand that the deadline isn't simply an artificial target set by someone consumed by efficiency, they will be more motivated to meet it.

Describe the implications of a delay in relational terms. How will it break down trust?

Individuals and cultures that don't value detailed processes, deliberation, and multiple drafts can be motivated to adjust their sense of timing if they understand that several iterations will yield more benefits, save time in the long run, build trust, and offer a more sustainable approach. Discuss how to develop timelines based upon expectations that meet the objective and account for how to make the most of the diverse participants involved in the project. Various participants have important information the leader lacks about certain variables that should influence the timing. Other personalities and cultures resist imposed deadlines if they perceive the leader hasn't accounted for the other responsibilities and constraints being faced by everyone involved.

## 3. Define Your Communication and Conflict-Resolution Process

Create a specific process for how communication will occur and when, and the process for how decisions will be made. How often will you meet? What is the purpose of those meetings? What kind of communication protocol is needed? The more diverse your team, the more explicitly you need to spell this out. Include things like what should/shouldn't be communicated by email, when you should copy others, and who should be included in what meetings. Also take the time to articulate a conflict resolution process.

What kind of communication updates will be needed for your team? Develop a very explicit plan that allows for the coexistence of cultural differences on your team:

- What should be communicated?
- How?
- To whom?
- How often?

By communicating appropriately right from the start, you can avoid rumors and misinformation, raise awareness of the team's objectives, and build relationships that will be needed to move through the inevitable conflict that will occur. Team members themselves must remember to talk with appropriate people within their departments about what the team is discussing and deciding. Revisit the differences you mapped at the beginning of the process (Chapter 7) and discuss each team member's preferences for addressing conflict (giving and/or receiving). Some prefer discussing points of conflict informally over a coffee break, while others prefer doing so in a formal meeting. Don't just assume your interpersonal skills are going to be enough to work through this. Agree upon a fusion process that allows different approaches to coexist while also committing to a few essential rules of engagement that everyone agrees to follow.

## 4. Motivate and Monitor Follow-Through

Implementation requires ongoing accountability, motivation, and follow-through. The problem is that we often assume *What motivates me, motivates others.* Culture plays a strong role in how we're motivated. Stop and consider what kind of value completing this project has for the other parties involved. Look at the different cultural value orientations on your team. What are the benefits for meeting the deadline (or the consequences for not doing so)? Extrinsic motivators like financial rewards may play a part in motivating someone to get something done on time, but a far more sustainable motivation is when there's intrinsic interest in the project and a desire to be part of something like this in the future.

Some individuals on a diverse team are most concerned about a project lead who keeps the process on track—following up on specific tasks and project requirements. Others are more concerned about a leader who maintains the interpersonal dynamics and relationships with everyone. A fusion team accounts for both preferences as a way to keep everyone engaged in the project. Developing consensus about the process, working on the tasks together, and regularly talking it all through might seem inefficient to some, but it's actually how projects most effectively get completed in most cultures. A fusion team prioritizes relationships alongside task completion. Beware: Pretending to build a relationship simply to get something done will be sniffed out right away. The intent has to be genuine.

An important part of motivation is a conscious awareness that progress is being made. In one study, a team of researchers told a group of hotel maids that their daily work cleaning rooms provided them with a vigorous form of calorie-burning exercise. Another group of maids were not given this information. The maids who learned about the benefits of their physically demanding work lost more weight than their peers who were not told this. Simply being conscious of the health benefits led to more weight loss.[10] Being aware of the progress being made while working on a project yields positive benefits for sustaining motivation.

Monitoring follow-through also means helping team members handle the constraints that come along—time limitations, budget reductions, and other hurdles, which may or may not have been anticipated. Constraints aren't all bad. They can be a powerful driver of innovation, but they need to be handled thoughtfully and strategically.

## 5. Launch and Do a Post–Implementation Review

At last, the innovation is launched. Depending upon the timeline and prototyping model developed, the launch may happen incrementally or all at once. Determine what kind of fanfare, if any, is appropriate for the various markets involved. And be sure to have all hands on deck for the inevitable glitches.

Highlight the diverse inputs that led to the innovation. And before you move on to the next project, create a deliberate plan to audit the implementation process and assess it in light of the goal defined at the beginning of the process. Expect that the innovation will need further refinements, and make the most of the mistakes and glitches to develop improved iterations.

## Conclusion

As a team matures from being a bold disrupter to becoming a more well-established part of the organization, there's a danger that it will lose some of its innovative power. There's a need for systems, processes, policies, etc., to drive efficiency and sustainability. On the other hand, the very systems and processes set up to implement innovation can run in conflict with remaining innovative. Before you know it, a good day at the office is one where everyone is working hard and checking off their to-do lists and emptying their email inbox rather than solving real problems and creating value. The challenge for leaders is to retain a founder's entrepreneurial mentality, which includes a bias toward action, a long-term vision, an obsession with customers and frontline operations, and an aversion to bureaucracy.[11]

We need look no further than our personal lives to be reminded of many great ideas that never go anywhere. Productive teams generate far more ideas than they should pursue. Dreaming up new ideas is the fun part. But exercising the discipline to develop a plan and follow it through to completion is the only way an idea actually goes anywhere. The satisfaction of seeing an innovation implemented is a great payoff for all the hard work.

## DELIVER: IMPLEMENT GLOBAL SOLUTIONS

Create a deliberate plan for a timely launch while building in flexibility for unexpected delays and diverse approaches to implementation.

✔ Write down an explicit process for decision making and conflict resolution.

**P**eople often ask me, "So how did you end up in this work?" I'm never quite sure how to respond to that question. The easy answer is that my professional and academic pursuits led me across international borders, which inevitably brought me face-to-face with cultural differences. I needed a way to navigate those differences. But cultural intelligence was not simply a practical solution for me. It became a necessity in order to hold together the increasingly complex, diverse world I was encountering. For me, cultural intelligence was as much a discovery as a pursuit. And in some ways, cultural intelligence found me.

I grew up in a fundamentalist environment and I never left the continent until college. All my childhood friends and classmates looked pretty much like me. My global perspective was limited to what I learned from missionaries who came to stay in our home or speak at our church. The closest I got to an international meal was my mom's chop suey or a faux Mexican dish at a church potluck.

Yet today, I rarely go through passport control without answering the question, "Why do you travel so much?" My closest friends come from dozens of different cultures and faiths, and my kids love an authentic Thai curry as much as I do. There's a great deal about where I began that I still treasure. But the privilege of seeing through the eyes of people from different cultural backgrounds has made the world a much more colorful, interesting place. It's a continual source of inspiration to me in my own creative work. I long to share that gift with others.

Senior executives across the world agree that finding effective cross-cultural personnel is a top management challenge.[1] And CEOs from 60 countries agree that creativity is the number one leadership competency of the future.[2] Leading companies need talent who are creative and adept at working across different cultures. Culturally intelligent innovation offers a way to awaken the sleeping giant within diverse teams. A fusion approach that intentionally utilizes diversity leads to the best, innovative solutions.

## Diversity × CQ = Innovation

Diversity is everywhere and it's a treasure trove, rich with innovative solutions waiting to be mined. When you work with culturally diverse people, you get another set of eyes—or better yet, several more sets of eyes. Seeing the world through other eyes can either be a constant source of tension and conflict or it can offer you a broader, wider, fuller view of the world.

Map and amplify your differences, seek to understand them, and find ways for them to coexist so that you can draw upon them to offer the most innovative solutions for a diversity of users.

Cultural intelligence is having the skills to work effectively in situations characterized by cultural diversity. Cultural Intelligence (CQ) includes four capabilities:

*CQ Drive: Your interest, drive, and confidence to adapt to multicultural situations*

The culturally intelligent see the positive benefits of diversity. Their focus is upon the innovative potential that exists from being on a diverse team.

*CQ Knowledge: Your understanding about how cultures are similar and different*

The culturally intelligent understand their team members' values and where they're coming from. This is essential for leveraging the informational diversity that exists on a diverse team.

*CQ Strategy: Your awareness and ability to plan for multicultural situations*

The culturally intelligent are aware of how cultural differences influence the way team members approach a task. They consciously plan for how to engage effectively with their diverse colleagues and customers.

*CQ Action: Your ability to adapt appropriately when working and relating interculturally*

The culturally intelligent operate with a sense of authenticity while understanding that some adaptation is essential to make the most of a diverse team.

Diversity alone doesn't lead to innovation, but cultural intelligence and diversity together are a multiplying force. Diversity and low CQ leads to higher levels of frustration and reduced productivity. But diversity and high CQ leads to far brighter outcomes than homogenous teams can ever experience.

## The Climate for Culturally Intelligent Innovation

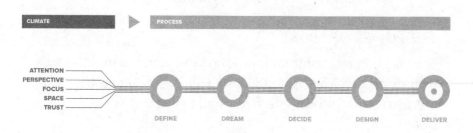

The field of social psychology offers powerful insights for creating a climate that nurtures innovation among culturally diverse groups.

## THE POWER OF ATTENTION

Your mind is your most powerful asset for innovation. By consciously paying attention to innovation and the diverse perspectives around you, you're primed to come up with better, innovative solutions.

## THE POWER OF PERSPECTIVE TAKING

Learning to see from another point of view is a fascinating, critical part of developing innovative solutions that truly address the pain points of potential users. Don't assume others want what you want.

## THE POWER OF FOCUS

Distraction and multitasking are the enemies of creativity. If you can discipline yourself to give your undivided attention to solving the problem at hand, you've further created the ideal climate for tapping diversity to promote innovation.

## THE POWER OF SPACE

Take control of your space in whatever way you can to help promote the right ecosystem for innovation to thrive. Your surroundings are the incubator for generating and implementing new ideas.

## THE POWER OF TRUST

Trust is a nonnegotiable for innovation to occur, and building trust with diverse colleagues and clients requires an intentional plan. Calculate how to most effectively build trust across your diverse team.

# The 5D Process for Culturally Intelligent Innovation

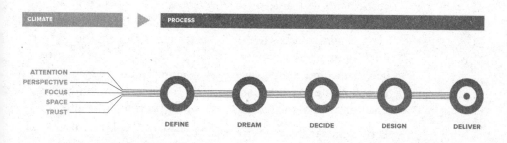

Once you've created the climate for culturally intelligent innovation—personally and/or on a team—you're ready to walk through the 5D process for culturally intelligent innovation. The process is ideally suited to a fusion approach to diversity where instead of allowing one culture to dominate, you transcend and include your differences while unifying around a common goal. (See Table Ep-1.)

**Table Ep-1. : Summary of 5D Process of Culturally Intelligent Innovation**

| | Challenges for Diverse Teams | Fusion Approach |
|---|---|---|
| *Define:* Align Diverse Expectations and Goals | Individuals who are uncomfortable with ambiguity (high uncertainty avoidance) may want to overanalyze the objectives and create a level of detail that leaves little room for flexibility and new insights.<br><br>Individuals who are comfortable with ambiguity (low uncertainty avoidance) may devote too little time to achieve clarity on what exactly the project is setting out to do and assume everyone is on the same page when they aren't. | The deliberation and discipline of achieving objectives that the entire team owns allows for greater flexibility along the way when inevitable adjustments are needed.<br><br>1. Map your differences<br>2. Compare your expectations<br>3. Take each other's perspective<br>4. List what you have in common<br>5. Define a common goal |

*(continued)*

| | Challenges for Diverse Teams | Fusion Approach |
|---|---|---|
| *Dream:* Generate Diverse Ideas | Participants with an individualist orientation may perceive individuals who don't speak up as lacking the confidence and competence to participate and as being uncommitted to the project.<br><br>Participants with a collectivist orientation may perceive teammates who voice a lot of ideas as being egocentric, power hungry, or unwilling to follow someone else's lead. | The time devoted to understanding differences and creating alignment (during the *Define* stage) provides the relational glue to generate diverse ideas from individuals who will do so differently.<br><br>1. Redefine "speak up"<br>2. Give advance warning<br>3. Be explicit about expectations<br>4. Offer multiple ways to give input<br>5. Use the power of "Yes, and" |
| *Decide:* Select and Sell Your Idea | Individualists are quicker to decide which idea to pursue and may immediately start working on convincing others to buy-in.<br><br>Collectivists may want more time to process the decision on which idea to pursue and want consensus not only from the team but from other stakeholders who will be invested in the innovation. | A fusion approach assertively blends the different perspectives on which idea (or ideas) to pursue and uses something like assertive inquiry to make decisions. Instead of saying something like, "Don't you think . . ." or, "Wouldn't you agree . . . ," team members say, "Could you help me understand . . . " or, "How does what you're saying overlap, if at all, with what I suggested?"[3]<br><br>1. Encourage bottom-up, intervene top-down<br>2. Vote<br>3. Map reactions to the idea and pitch<br>4. Insist on clarity<br>5. Recruit early adopters |

|  | Challenges for Diverse Teams | Fusion Approach |
|---|---|---|
| *Design:* Create and Test for Diverse Users | Direct communicators are vocal about their satisfaction/dissatisfaction with a prototype. Indirect communicators may say nothing or only imply their opinion.<br><br>The more unfamiliar the innovation, the more varied the responses you will get—from early adopters to late adopters and everyone in between. | Utilize the diversity on your team to anticipate the varied responses you receive to your proposed design. Anticipate how to handle criticism and determine in advance whether you're open to further adapting the innovation.<br><br>1. What needs does it meet?<br>2. What prior knowledge is assumed?<br>3. What does the design communicate?<br>4. With whom should you test this?<br>5. What level of sophistication is needed for the prototype? |
| *Deliver:* Implement Global Solutions | Some individuals resist defining concrete milestones and hard deadlines for fear of letting down the team.<br><br>Some team members project their speed preference (either direction—moving too quickly or too slowly) upon the project. | Effective implementation requires that each individual and department continue to see beyond personal and departmental interests to realize the fusion of opportunities if everyone strives together to reach the milestones.<br><br>1. Formalize leadership<br>2. Agree on timing<br>3. Define your communication and conflict-resolution process<br>4. Motivate and monitor follow-through<br>5. Launch and do a post-implementation review |

When you encounter someone with a different opinion, the impulse is to think: *Why in the world do you see it that way?* That is really to ask: *Why can't you see it like I do?*

In those moments when you see things differently from those around you, you have a few choices: You can hold on to your view, defend it, protect it, and argue for its superiority. You can also let go of your view and entirely acquiesce to the view of others—or you can allow your perspective to be broadened, enriched, expanded, and deepened.

Culturally intelligent innovation begins with changing our impulse from *Why can't you see it like I do?* to *Help me see what I might be missing!* Together, we can each transcend and include our individual perspectives and upbringings to see the world more fully. We can work together to come up with innovative solutions to solve problems big and small. And that's why I do what I do.

This book has been years in the making—not the writing itself, but the research, reading, conversations, and observations that are behind it. I've been reflecting about these ideas for a long time, but not alone. Even though someone's name has to be listed as the author, I only take partial credit (and all the blame) for the book.

A diversity of people from varied organizations and cultures graciously read and offered feedback to a very early draft of the book, including Soon Ang, Gary Cormier, Rick DeVos, Amri Johnson, Andy Ouderkirk, Susan Sullivan, Sandra Upton, and Linn Van Dyne. Figuring out what to do with their extremely varied perspectives and feedback forced me to apply the very fusion process I wrote about. I learned so much from the input I received and appreciate the gift of their time and feedback.

I receive far too much credit for the growth in cultural intelligence that is happening globally. There's a growing community of academics and practitioners who are moving the cultural intelligence work forward in so many corners of the world, and none of that would be possible without our amazing team at the Cultural Intelligence Center. They put up with my frenetic travel and my endless new ideas, and they personally embody a team that learns to pursue culturally intelligent innovation together.

It's been a joy to develop another book with the wonderful team at AMACOM. Rosemary Carlough is forever chasing me somewhere around the world to discuss a new opportunity, and Therese Mausser continues to use her own cultural intelligence to expand the number of languages into which the cultural intelligence books have been translated. My editor, Stephen S. Power, provides the ideal mix of respecting my expertise and perspective while also pushing me to make what I write better, clearer, and more useful. And Erika Spelman has a unique ability to retain my voice while using her editorial precision to clean up my messy writing (she even let me start this sentence with "and"!).

Emily and Grace, my "kids" who are quickly becoming young adults, have taught me more about creativity and innovation than anyone else ever has. As they get ready to leave home and spread their wings, I watch with immense anticipation for how their diverse ideas will continue to make the world a better place.

Finally, my wife, lifelong companion, and love, Linda, has listened to my endless deliberations about cultural intelligence, innovation, and much more when we're supposed to be having a romantic dinner together or taking a relaxing walk around the lake. But she generously listens, prods, challenges, and most of all assures me that she'll be with me to the end, no matter what.

# APPENDIX A: CULTURAL INTELLIGENCE —WHAT'S YOUR CQ?

**W**hy is it that some people seem extremely comfortable interacting with others who come from different cultures, while others seem like a fish out of water in those circumstances? Is it merely a matter of who has experience and who doesn't, or is there something more to it? This is the area that has piqued my interest for the last several years, and it is the foundation of our research on cultural intelligence, or CQ—the capability to be effective in any culture.

The world includes gifted musicians, athletes, economists, and writers. In the same way, some people are culturally intelligent— that is, they have the gift of effectively interacting and working with people from diverse cultures. But cultural intelligence isn't a natural-born trait. It's a set of capabilities that almost anyone can develop and learn.

## Who Are the Culturally Intelligent?

Individuals with high CQ can effectively adapt to various multicultural situations. They possess strength in four distinct CQ capabilities: CQ Drive, CQ Knowledge, CQ Strategy, and CQ Action (see Figure A-1). All four capabilities are needed, because focusing on one without the others may actually result in increased cultural ignorance rather than enhanced cultural intelligence. This is because CQ requires an overall repertoire of adaptive capabilities.

## Figure A-1. Four CQ Capabilities

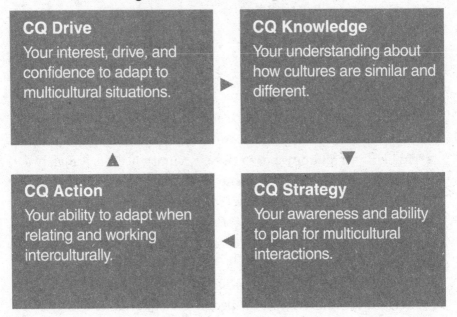

**CQ Drive**
Your interest, drive, and confidence to adapt to multicultural situations.

**CQ Knowledge**
Your understanding about how cultures are similar and different.

**CQ Action**
Your ability to adapt when relating and working interculturally.

**CQ Strategy**
Your awareness and ability to plan for multicultural interactions.

Here's a brief description of these four CQ capabilities and some examples of how they relate to working and relating cross-culturally.

### 1. CQ Drive: Having the Interest, Confidence, and Drive to Adapt Cross–Culturally

CQ Drive refers to whether or not you have the confidence and drive to work through the challenges and conflict that often accompany intercultural work. The ability to be personally engaged and to persevere through intercultural challenges is one of the most novel aspects of cultural intelligence. Many intercultural training approaches simply *assume* that people are motivated to gain cross-cultural capabilities. Yet employees often approach diversity training apathetically, and employees headed out on international assignments are often more concerned about moving their families overseas and getting settled than they are about developing cultural understanding. Without ample motivation, there's little point in spending time and money on training.

Doug, an American with a multinational firm who was sent to manage a team in Bangkok, describes how little attention he paid to the cultural training he received before moving to Thailand. It wasn't that he didn't care. It's just that he was overwhelmed getting ready for the move, and he found the training overly theoretical and too focused upon cultural stereotypes. But he definitely wanted to succeed.

CQ Drive includes intrinsic motivation—the degree to which you derive enjoyment from culturally diverse situations; extrinsic motivation—the tangible benefits you gain from culturally diverse experiences; and self-efficacy—your confidence that you will be effective in an intercultural encounter. All three of these motivational dynamics play a role in how you approach multicultural situations. Stop and examine your motivation for doing cross-cultural work. Your CQ Drive is strongly related to your effectiveness in new cultural contexts.

## 2. CQ Knowledge: Understanding Intercultural Norms and Differences

CQ Knowledge is the cognitive dimension of cultural intelligence. It refers to your level of understanding about culture and culture's role in shaping the way to interact when different cultures are involved. Your CQ Knowledge is based upon the degree to which you understand the idea of culture and how it influences the way you think and behave. It also includes your overall understanding of the ways cultures vary from one context to the next.

When Doug got to Bangkok, he quickly discovered that leading and motivating his mostly Asian team wasn't coming easily. Although he had a reputation for being a phenomenal negotiator, his negotiations kept getting stalled. Even though he had extensive management experience, he was losing confidence in his ability to be a good leader in his new location.

One of the most important parts of CQ Knowledge is a macro understanding of cultural systems and the cultural norms and values associated with different societies. In order to lead effectively, you need to understand ways that communication styles, predominant religious beliefs, role expectations for men and women, etc., can differ across cultures. In addition, general knowledge about different types of economic, business, legal, and political systems that exist throughout the world is important. And you need a core understanding of culture, language patterns, and nonverbal behaviors. This kind of knowledge helps build your confidence when working in a new cultural environment.

The other important part of CQ Knowledge is knowing how culture influences your effectiveness in specific domains. For example, being an effective global leader in business looks different from being an effective leader of a multicultural university. And working across borders for an information technology company requires a different application of cultural understanding than working across borders for a charitable organization or on a military initiative. This kind of specialized, domain-specific cultural knowledge, combined with a macro understanding of cultural issues, is a crucial part of leading with cultural intelligence.

CQ Knowledge is the area that is most often emphasized in typical approaches to intercultural competency. A large and growing training and consulting industry focuses on teaching people about cultural values. While valuable, however, the understanding that comes from CQ Knowledge has to be combined with the other three capabilities of CQ or its relevance to the real demands of leadership is questionable and potentially detrimental.

## 3. CQ Strategy: Making Sense of Culturally Diverse Experiences and Planning Accordingly

CQ Strategy refers to your level of awareness and ability to strategize when crossing cultures. This capability involves slowing down your activity long enough to carefully observe what's going on inside your own and other people's heads. It's the ability to think about your own thought processes and draw upon your cultural knowledge to understand a different cultural context and solve problems in that situation. It includes whether we can use our cultural knowledge to plan an appropriate strategy, accurately interpret what's going on in an intercultural situation, and check to see if our expectations are accurate or need to be adjusted.

Doug has always used a leadership style focused on developing individuals to pursue their personal goals and to "lead themselves." He was aware that this was a countercultural approach in Asia, but he had no interest in becoming a highly directive leader. Thus, he had to develop a strategy for how to be true to himself while effectively leading a team with values that differed from his.

Seasoned leaders often jump into meetings and new situations with little planning. This often works fine when meeting with colleagues or clients from a similar cultural background. By drawing on emotional intelligence and leadership experience, we can often get away with "winging it" because we know how to respond to cues and how to talk about projects. When meetings involve individuals from different cultural contexts, however, many of the rules change. Relying upon our ability to intuitively respond to cues in these more novel situations is dangerous. That's where CQ Strategy comes in.

CQ Strategy includes planning, awareness, and checking. Planning is taking the time to prepare for an intercultural encounter—anticipating how to approach the people, topic, and situation. Awareness means being in tune with what's going on in one's self and others during the interaction. And checking is the monitoring we do as we engage in interactions to see if the plans and expectations we had were appropriate. It's comparing what we expected with our actual experience. CQ Strategy emphasizes implementation, and it's the lynchpin that connects understanding cultural issues to actually being able to use that understanding to manage effectively.

### 4. CQ Action: Changing Verbal and Nonverbal Actions Appropriately When Interacting Cross–Culturally

Finally, CQ Action is your ability to act appropriately in a wide range of cultural situations. It influences whether you can actually accomplish your performance goals effectively in light of different cultural situations. One of the most important aspects of CQ Action is knowing when to adapt to another culture and when *not* to do so. A leader with high CQ learns which actions will and won't enhance effectiveness, then acts upon that understanding. Thus, CQ Action involves flexible behaviors tailored to the specific cultural context.

Doug is grateful for staff who are fluent in English. He's learning some basic Thai to get along, but at times, he feels like he has to relearn English, too. His assistant needs very explicit, step-by-step directions. On the rare occasion when she makes a request, Doug has the hardest time figuring out exactly what she's asking for.

CQ Action includes the capability to be flexible in verbal and nonverbal actions. It also includes appropriate flexibility in speech acts—the exact words and phrases we use when we communicate specific types of messages (e.g., offering negative feedback directly or indirectly, or knowing how to appropriately make a request).

While the demands of today's intercultural settings make it impossible to master all the dos and don'ts of various cultures, there are certain behaviors that should be modified when we interact with different cultures. For example, Westerners need to learn the importance of carefully studying business cards presented by those from most Asian contexts. Also, some basic verbal and nonverbal behaviors enhance the extent to which others see us as effective. As an example, the verbal tone (e.g., loud versus soft) in which words are spoken can convey different meanings across cultures. In addition, although it is not necessary for an outsider to master the intricacies of bowing in Japan, appropriate use of touch *is* something to bear in mind. In sum, almost every approach to intercultural work has insisted on the importance of flexibility. With CQ Action, we now have a way to enhance flexibility.

## Improving Your CQ

Your CQ can improve. It's something all people can develop and learn, assuming they are interested in doing so. Here are a few basic ways to get started.

### REFLECT ON YOUR CQ

Begin with a commitment to consider your capabilities for working and relating across cultures. By thinking through the four capabilities of CQ, consider which areas are strongest and weakest for you.

*CQ Drive:* What's my level of interest in cross-cultural issues?

*CQ Knowledge:* To what degree do I understand how cultures are similar and different?

*CQ Strategy:* Am I aware of what's occurring in a cross-cultural situation, and am I able to plan accordingly?

*CQ Action:* Do I know when I should adapt and when I should *not* adapt my behavior cross-culturally?

Each of us is stronger in some of these areas than others. Zero in on one specific CQ capability to begin increasing your overall CQ.

*ASSESS YOUR CQ*

There are a variety of academically validated CQ assessments that have been proven to predict the degree to which you are able to function effectively in intercultural contexts (see Figure A-2). The *CQ Self-Assessment* is a great way to begin developing awareness by reflecting on your intercultural abilities. As a next step, the *CQ Multi-Rater Assessment* can be used as a 360-degree instrument that allows bosses, peers, direct reports, clients, and sometimes even family members to assess you according to the four CQ capabilities and the subdimensions of each. Find more information about these and other CQ assessments at www.culturalQ.com.

**Figure A-2. Assess your CQ.**

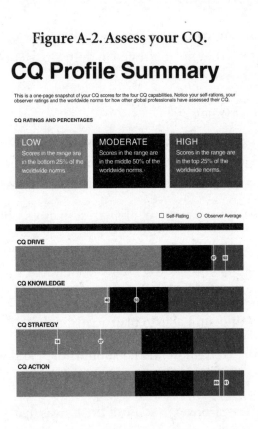

# CQ Profile Summary

This is a one-page snapshot of your CQ scores for the four CQ capabilities. Notice your self-ratings, your observer ratings and the worldwide norms for how other global professionals have assessed their CQ.

**CQ RATINGS AND PERCENTAGES**

| LOW | MODERATE | HIGH |
|---|---|---|
| Scores in the range are in the bottom 25% of the worldwide norms. | Scores in the range are in the middle 50% of the worldwide norms. | Scores in the range are in the top 25% of the worldwide norms. |

☐ Self-Rating   ○ Observer Average

CQ DRIVE

CQ KNOWLEDGE

CQ STRATEGY

CQ ACTION

## GET HANDS-ON EXPERIENCE

There's no substitute for on-the-job training when it comes to improving your CQ. The ideal scenario is when you have a chance to travel internationally and get immersed in a local culture. Whether you're traveling for work, pleasure, or as a charitable volunteer, be sure to wander from the touristy spots. Even if you're staying at the Shangri-La in downtown Bangkok, you can jump on a bus and suddenly be immersed in true local culture. This gives you a whole different insight into Thai culture than what you get from the hotel lobby or Starbucks.

There's an abundance of opportunities for hands-on experiences closer to home too. Chances are, there are growing numbers of people from different cultures living nearby. For example, the 2010 U.S. Census data reported that the United States now has more than 50 million Hispanics—more than the entire population of Spain. Although many Hispanic Americans live in coastal cities or close to the southern border, my little Midwest city in Michigan has grown from 3 percent Hispanic 15 years ago to 17 percent Hispanic today. If you're in a community where there's still relatively little ethnic diversity, seek out interactions with people who come from a different subculture religiously, politically, or generationally. Or gain some hands-on experience by pulling together a cross-functional team with people from marketing, engineering, and IT.

Working together with people from these kinds of diverse "subcultures" can also play a role in increasing your CQ. Individuals who are part of culturally diverse groups are more likely to have high CQ than those who remain isolated with individuals like themselves. It sounds obvious, but it's amazing how often work groups and people in social gatherings miss out on the rich resources available to them through hands-on experiences with diverse colleagues and friends.

## *PUT TOGETHER A PERSONAL DEVELOPMENT PLAN*

Once you have a good idea of where your greatest CQ strengths and weakenesses lie, you can put together a development plan for improving your CQ. The research on CQ has revealed several demonstrated strategies for how to use your CQ strengths and how to enhance other CQ capabilities (Drive, Knowledge, Strategy, and Action). Many of these strategies may not strike you as rocket science (name your biases, study a new language, manage your expectations, etc.), but they've been shown to increase your effectiveness in culturally diverse situations. We often overlook some of the obvious ways to tap into things we already do to also improve the ways we interact and work cross-culturally. See *The Cultural Intelligence Difference* by David Livermore (AMACOM, 2011) for dozens of strategies to improve each CQ capability.

Identify something you can do in the next week to help you improve in one of the four CQ capabilities. How about in the next month? Six months? Year? Write down your plan, share it with others, and have them offer you feedback.

## *TAKE A CLASS*

Learning about culture through books and classes is *not* a sure way to improve CQ. In fact, someone who learns about culture only academically may actually have lower CQ than someone who hasn't taken any formal courses on culture and diversity. Cerebral understanding about culture without the corresponding motivation and strategy can actually be detrimental to your overall CQ. You might *think* you are culturally intelligent but actually have little common sense for how to apply the cultural knowledge you've learned academically.

However, when combined with the other CQ capabilities, studying about culture and global events through a class—either a formal university course or a workshop offered by your organization—can improve your CQ. This benefit can be tapped even from a class that doesn't directly relate to culture and diversity. Simply exercising the brain to think critically and strategically can play a role in how you improve your overall CQ. When you devote focused attention to studying the role of culture in the world and interact with others about it, it's another powerful way to enhance your cultural intelligence.

## A Better Way

Despite millions of dollars spent on cultural sensitivity training and diversity programs, little has improved in the way many individuals and companies are actually behaving when it comes to working across borders—whether with the person in the cubicle next door or a client 12 time zones away.

Respect and sensitivity are nonnegotiable values, but we have to go beyond those ideals to actually find ways to successfully adapt to various cultural situations while still remaining true to ourselves. The cultural intelligence research and model is uniquely suited to address this need.

Begin by finding out what your CQ is, or more importantly, which of your CQ capabilities are strongest and weakest. Then gain the benefits that come from improving your CQ while simultaneously treating people with respect and dignity—and, in turn, make the world a better place for all of us.

To learn more about cultural intelligence, visit www.culturalQ.com, or read *Leading with Cultural Intelligence* and *The Cultural Intelligence Difference*.

# APPENDIX B: GLOSSARY OF CULTURAL VALUE DIMENSIONS

This book often makes mention of cultural value dimensions that help distinguish one culture from another. Extensive material has been written about several cultural value dimensions, but for those unfamiliar with the terms, here are some brief definitions of 10 of the most important cultural value dimensions.

**INDIVIDUALISM–COLLECTIVISM**
**Individualism:** Emphasis on individual goals and rights
**Collectivism:** Emphasis on group goals and personal relationships

**POWER DISTANCE**
**Low Power Distance:** Emphasis on equality; shared decision making
**High Power Distance:** Emphasis on differences in status; decisions made by superiors

**UNCERTAINTY AVOIDANCE**
**Low Uncertainty Avoidance:** Emphasis on flexibility and adaptability
**High Uncertainty Avoidance:** Emphasis on planning and predictability

**COOPERATIVE–COMPETITIVE**
**Cooperative:** Emphasis on collaboration and nurturing behavior to get results
**Competitive:** Emphasis on competition, assertiveness, and achievement to get results

## TIME ORIENTATION
**Short-Term:** Emphasis on immediate outcomes (success now)
**Long-Term:** Emphasis on long-term outcomes (success later)

## CONTEXT
**Low Context:** Emphasis on explicit communication (words)
**High Context:** Emphasis on indirect communication (tone, context)

## BEING–DOING
**Being:** Emphasis on quality of life
**Doing:** Emphasis on being busy and meeting goals

## UNIVERSALISM–PARTICULARISM
**Universalism:** Emphasis on rules; standards that apply to everyone
**Particularism:** Emphasis on specifics; unique standards based on relationships

## NEUTRAL–AFFECTIVE
**Neutral:** Emphasis on nonemotional communication; hiding feelings
**Affective:** Emphasis on expressive communication; sharing feelings openly

## MONOCHRONIC–POLYCHRONIC
**Monochronic:** Emphasis on one thing at a time; work and personal life kept separate
**Polychronic:** Emphasis on many obligations; comfortable with interruptions; work and personal combined

See Table 7-1 in Chapter 7 for a fusion approach to using cultural value differences. Also, to learn more about cultural value dimensions, check out *Cultures and Organizations* by Geert Hofstede, Gert Jen Hofstede, and Michael Mikov; *Foreign to Familiar* by Sarah A. Lanier; *Riding the Waves of Culture* by Fons Trompenaars and Charles Hampden-Turner; and *The Silent Language* by Edward T. Hall.

In addition, Chapter 5 of my book *Leading with Cultural Intelligence* (2015, 2nd edition) covers these 10 cultural value dimensions in greater detail, along with examples of cultural clusters where each value preference is the norm and strategies for leading in light of these differences.

## Introduction

1. Mark Berniker and Josh Lipton, "A Call for More Diversity on Silicon Valley Tech Boards," *CNBC-Technology*, December 25, 2013, http://www.cnbc.com/id/101295498.

2. Marco della Cava, "Google's Diversity Chief Started Crusade Young," *USA Today*, November 5, 2014, 2B.

3. See my books *Leading with Cultural Intelligence* (New York: AMACOM, 2015) and *The Cultural Intelligence Difference* (New York: AMACOM, 2011).

## Chapter 1—Diversity is.

1. Amri Johnson, personal conversation, December 5, 2012.

2. Gören measures cultural diversity using a formula he built that calculates the degree of linguistic and ethnic differences across the country. Erkan Gören, "Economic Effects of Domestic and Neighbouring Countries' Cultural Diversity," April 23, 2013. In *ZenTra Working Paper in Transnational Studies*, No. 16/2013. http://dx.doi.org/10.2139/ssrn.2255492, accessed August 21, 2014.

3. Bernadine Racoma, "Top Ten Culturally Diverse Cities in the World," May 4, 2013, http://www.daynews.com/latest-news/2013/03/top-10-culturally-diverse-cities-in-the-world-15031, accessed August 15, 2014.

4. C. Kluckhohn and W. H. Kelly, "The Concept of Culture," In R. Linton, ed., *The Science of Man in the World Crisis* (New York: Colombia University Press, 1945), 78-105.

5. Geert Hofstede, Gert Jan Hofstede, and Michael Minkov, *Cultures and Organizations: Software of the Mind* (New York: McGraw-Hill, 2010), 89-134.

6. Rosabeth Moss Kanter, "Some Effects of Proportions on Group Life: Skewed Sex Ratios and Responses to Token Women," *American Journal of Sociology* 82 (1977), 965-990.

7. Katherine Y. Williams and Charles A. O'Reilly III, "Demography and Diversity in Organizations: A Review of 40 Years of Research," *Research in Organizational Behavior*, Volume 20 (Greenwich, CT: JAI Press, 1998), 81.

8. Economist Intelligence Unit, *Values-Based Diversity: The Challenges and Strengths of Many* (London: Economist Intelligence Unit, January 23, 2014), http://www.economistinsights.com/sites/default/files/EIU_SuccessFac tors_Values-based%20diversity%20report.pdf.

9. David Livermore, "How Facebook Develops Its Global Leaders: Conversation with Bill McLawhon," *People and Strategy* 36 (2013), 24-25.

10. Economist Intelligence Unit, 11.

11. Jo Ann Lublin, "Bringing Hidden Biases into the Light: Big Businesses Teach Staffers How 'Unconscious Bias' Impacts Decisions," *Wall Street Journal*, January 9, 2014, http://online.wsj.com/news/articles/SB1000142405270230 37544045793085626690896896.

12. *Kumbuya* is a word that is often used satirically to refer to naïve, optimistic views of everyone just getting along (my intended use of the term). Its origins are as a spiritual song first recorded in the 1920s and later used as a standard campfire song for many religious and scouting groups.

13. Williams and O'Reilly, 77-140.

14. Economist Intelligence Unit, "CEO Briefing: Corporate Priorities for 2006 and Beyond," *The Economist*, http://a330.g.akamai. net/7/330/25828/20060213195601/graphics.eiu.com/files/ad_pdfs/ceo_ Briefing_UKTI_wp.pdf, 3.

15. See David Livermore, *Leading with Cultural Intelligence* (New York: AMA-COM, 2015) for a fuller explanation of the four capabilities of cultural intelligence, the results predicted by high CQ, and the citations of the dozens of studies that validate these findings.

16. K. Y. Ng, S. Ang, and L. Van Dyne, *Speaking Up in the Culturally Diverse Workplace: The Role of Cultural Intelligence and Language Self-Efficacy*. Paper presented at the American Psychological Association, Washington, DC, August 2011.

17. E. W. Morrison and F. J. Milliken, "Organizational Silence: A Barrier to Change and Development in a Pluralistic World," *Academy of Management Review* 25 (2000), 706-725.

18. Sara Ellison and Wallace Mullin, "Diversity, Social Goods Provision, and Performance in the Firm," *Journal of Economics & Management Strategy* 23(2) (Summer 2014), 465-481.

19. Sheryl Sandberg and Adam Grant, "Women in the Boardroom and Bedroom," *The Straits Times*, March 9, 2015, A18.

20. Salvatore Parise, Eoin Whelan, and Steve Todd, "How Twitter Users Can Generate Better Ideas," *MIT Sloan Management Review*, June 1, 2015, http://sloanreview.mit.edu/article/how-twitter-users-can-generate-better-ideas/, accessed June 5, 2015.

21. Sylvia Ann Hewlett, Melinda Marshall, and Laura Sherbin, "How Diversity Can Drive Innovation," *Harvard Business Review*, December 2013.

22. Marco della Cava, "Google's Diversity Chief Started Crusade Young," *USA Today*, November 5, 2014, 2B.

## Chapter 2—The Power of Attention

1. Ellen Langer, "Mindful Learning," *Current Directions in Psychological Science* 9 (2002).

2. Linda Hill, Greg Brandeau, Emily Truelove, and Kent Lineback, *Collective Genius: The Art and Practice of Leading Innovation* (Cambridge, MA: Harvard Business Press Review, 2013), 11.

3. Winifred Gallagher, *Rapt: Attention and the Focused Life* (New York: Penguin, 2009), 2.

4. Susan Smalley and Diana Winston, *Fully Present: The Science, Art, and Practice of Mindfulness* (Philadelphia: Lifelong Books, 2010), 134.

5. John F. Pratto, "Automatic Vigilance: The Attention Grabbing of Negative, Social Information," *Journal of Personality and Social Psychology* 61, 1991, 380-391.

6. Barbara Fredrickson, *Positivity: Groundbreaking Research Reveals How to Embrace the Hidden Strength of Positive Emotions, Overcome Negativity, and Thrive* (New York: Crown, 2009).

7. Gallagher, 78-79.

8. Ibid., 62.

9. Hill et al., 74-76.

10. Ibid., 74-93.

11. John A. Bargh, Mark Chen, and Lara Burrows, "Automaticity of Social Behavior: Direct Effects of Trait Construct and Stereotype Activation on Action," *Journal of Personality and Social Psychology* 71(2), 1996, 230-244.

12. Martin Lindstrom, *Brandwashed: Tricks Companies Use to Manipulate Our Minds and Get Us to Buy* (New York: Crown Business, 2011), 43-44.

13. Boris Groysberg and Katherine Connolly, "Great Leaders Who Make the Mix Work," *Harvard Business Review*, September 2013, https://hbr.org/2013/09/great-leaders-who-make-the-mix-work.

14. http://www.economist.com/news/united-states/21611122-southern-speech-still-draws-unwanted-attention-mind-drawl-yall.

15. Mahzarin Banaji and Anthony Greenwald, *Blindspot: Hidden Biases of Good People* (New York: Delacorte Press, 2013); Kindle edition, "Who Likes the Elderly" section, Loc 1028.

16. P. Herbig and S. Dunphy, "Culture and Innovation," *Cross Cultural Management: An International Journal* 5(4), 1998, 13-21.

17. S. A. Shane, "Cultural Influences on National Rates of Innovation," *Journal of Business Venturing* 8, (1993), 59-73; S. A. Shane, S. Venkataraman, and I. MacMillan, "Cultural Differences in Innovation Championing Strategies," *Journal of Management* 21(5), 1995, 931-952.

18. Shumpeter, "The Scale-Up Nation: Israel Is Trying to Turn Its Davids into Goliaths," *The Economist*, December 14, 2014, 70.

19. TNS/EOS Gallup Europe, "Entrepreneurship—Flash Eurobarometer 160" (Brussels: Commission of the European Communities, 2004).

20. "Patent Fiction: Are Ambitious Bureaucrats Fomenting or Feigning Innovation?" *The Economist*, December 13, 2014, 73-74.

21. R. Inglehart and C. Welzel, *Modernization, Cultural Change, and Democracy: The Human Development Sequence* (New York: Cambridge University Press, 2005).

22. Herbig and Dunphy, 13-21.

23. Gerard J. Tellis, Jaideep C. Prabhu, and Rajesh K. Chandy, "Radical Innovation Across Nations: The Preeminence of Corporate Culture," *Journal of Marketing* 73, January 2009, 3-23.

24. Ibid.

25. Ibid.

26. Eric Schmidt and Jonathan Rosenberg, *How Google Works* (New York: Grand Central Publishing, 2014); Kindle edition, "The CEO Needs to Be the CIO" section, Loc 2750.

## Chapter 3—The Power of the Empty Chair | Perspective Taking

1. Adam G. Galinsky, Joe C. Magee, M. Ena Inesi, and Deborah H. Gruenfield, "Power and Perspectives Not Taken," *Psychological Science* 17, December 2006, 1068-1074.

2. Daniel Sobol, "Far-Fetched Ideas Are Fun but Innovation Usually Starts Small," http://www.fastcodesign.com/1670073/far-fetched-ideas-are-fun-but-innovation-usually-starts-small, accessed May 22, 2013.

3. Ibid.

4. Esther Duflo, "Improving Immunization Coverage in Rural India," http://economics.mit.edu/files/5579, accessed June 20, 2013.

5. Milton Bennett, "Towards Ethnorelativism: A Developmental Model of Intercultural Sensitivity," in R. Michael Page, ed., *Education for the Intercultural Experience* (Yarmouth, ME: Intercultural Press, 1993), 41-43.

6. James Allworth, "Empathy: The Most Valuable Thing They Teach at HBS," *Harvard Business Review Blog Network*, May 15, 2012, http://blogs.hbr.org/2012/05/empathy-the-most-valuable-thing-they-t/, accessed September 8, 2014.

7. George Deeb, "Why Big Companies Struggle with Innovation," *Entrepreneur*, August 22, 2014, http://thenextweb.com/entrepreneur/2014/08/22/big-companies-struggle-innovation/.

8. Daniel Pink, *To Sell Is Human: The Surprising Truth About Moving Others* (New York: Riverhead Books, 2012), 74.

9. Adam D. Galinsky, William M. Maddux, Debra Gilin, and Judith White, "Why It Pays to Get Inside the Head of Your Opponent: The Differential Effects of Perspective Taking and Empathy in Negotiations," *Psychological Science* 19(4), April 2008, 378-384.

10. Anna Ringstrom, "One Size Doesn't Fit All: IKEA Goes Local for India, China," *Reuters*, March 7, 2013, http://in.reuters.com/article/2013/03/07/ikea-expansion-india-china-idINDEE92603L20130307, accessed September 5, 2014.

11. Ibid.

12. Arnold Burns, "Proximity and Particularism," *Ethical Perspectives*, October 1996, 157-160.

13. Jamil Zaki, "Sympathy Can Heighten Conflict," *Scientific American*, June 7, 2012, http://www.scientificamerican.com/article/sympathy-can-heighten-conflict/, accessed September 4, 2012.

14. Emile Bruneau and Rebecca Saxe, "The Power of Being Heard: The Benefits of 'Perspective-Giving' in the Context of Intergroup Conflict," *Journal of Experimental Social Psychology* 48(4), July 2012, 864.

15. D. Dougherty and T. Heller, "The Illegitimacy of Successful Product Innovation in Established Firms," *Organization Science* 5, 1994, 209.

16. Grant McCracken, *Chief Culture Officer: How to Create a Living, Breathing Corporation* (New York: Basic Books, 2011), 120.

17. Tina Seeling, *inGenius: A Crash Course in Creativity* (San Francisco: Harper One, 2012), 117.

18. McCracken, 122.

19. Lev Grossman, "The Man Who Wired the World: Mark Zuckerberg's Crusade to Put Every Single Human Being Online," *Time*, December 15, 2014, 35.

20. Ibid.

21. Nicholas Epsley, *Mindwise: How We Understand What Others Think, Believe, Feel, and Want* (New York: Knopf, 2014), 164.

22. Evan Thomas, "Why It's Time to Worry," *Newsweek*, December 13, 2010, 35.

23. U. R. Hulsheger, N. Anderson, and J. F. Salgado, "Team-Level Predictors of Innovation at Work: A Comprehensive Meta-Analysis Spanning Three Decades of Research," *Journal of Applied Psychology* 94(5), September 2009, 1128-1145.

24. Ralph Waldo Emerson, *The Complete Works of Ralph Waldo Emerson*, Volume 12 (New York: Houghton Mifflin & Co., 1904), 10.

## Chapter 4—The Power of 90 Minutes | Focus

1. David Foster and Matthew Wilson, "Reverse Replay of Behavioural Sequences in Hippocampal Place Cells During the Awake State," *Nature* 440, March 30, 2006, 680-683.

2. Jake Brutlag, "Speed Matters," *Google Research Blog*, June 23, 2009, http://googleresearch.blogspot.com/2009/06/speed-matters.html, accessed May 14, 2012.

3. O. Ayduk Y. Shoda, and W. Mischel, "Longitudinal Links Between Preschool Ability to Delay Gratification and Adult Life Outcomes," unpublished data, Columbia University, 2006. Quoted in Y. Shoda, D. Cervone, and G. Downey, *Persons in Context: Building a Science of the Individual* (New York: Guilford Press, 2007), 200-212.

4. B. J. Casey et al., "Behavioral and Neural Correlates of Delay of Gratification 40 Years Later," *PNAS* 108(36), 2011, 14998-15003.

5. Ibid.

6. Winifred Gallagher, *Rapt: Attention and the Focused Life* (New York: Penguin, 2009), 153.

7. Jeff Dyer, Hal Gregersen, and Clayton Christensen, *The Innovator's DNA: Mastering the Five Skills of Disruptive Innovators* (Cambridge, MA: Harvard Business Review Press, 2011), 82.

8. Malcolm Gladwell, *Blink: The Power of Thinking Without Thinking* (Boston: Back Bay Books, 2007), 10-11.

9. Kirk Warren Brown and Richard M. Ryan, "The Benefits of Being Present: Mindfulness and Its Role in Psychological Well-Being," *Journal of Personality and Social Psychology* 84(4), 2003, 822-848.

10. Gallagher, 153.

11. Salvatore Parise, Eoin Whelan, and Steve Todd, "How Twitter Users Can Generate Better Ideas," *MIT Sloan Management Review*, June 1, 2015, http://sloanreview.mit.edu/article/how-twitter-users-can-generate-better-ideas/, accessed June 5, 2015.

12. Daniel Pink, *To Sell Is Human: The Surprising Truth About Moving Others* (New York, Riverhead Books, 2012), 95.

13. Clayton Christensen, James Allworth, and Karen Dillon, *How Will You Measure Your Life?* (New York: HarperCollins, 2012), 100-101.

14. Dyer, Gregersen, and Christensen, 79-80.

15. Ibid., 68-69.

16. Ibid., 69.

17. Ibid., 79.

18. David Rock, *Your Brain at Work: Strategies for Overcoming Distraction, Regaining Focus, and Working Smarter All Day Long* (New York: HarperBusiness, 2009), 20.

19. Richard Wiseman, *59 Seconds: Change Your Life in Under a Minute* (New York: Anchor Books, 2009), 19.

20. Adam Lashinsky, "Jeff Bezos: The Ultimate Disruptor," *Fortune*, December 3, 2013, 100-110.

21. Wiseman, 19.

## Chapter 5—The Power of Trees | Space

1. Winifred Gallagher, *The Power of Place: How Our Surroundings Shape Our Thoughts, Emotions, and Actions* (New York: HarperPerennial, 1993), 210, 213.

2. Ibid.

3. Marc Fried, *The World of the Urban Working Class* (Cambridge, MA: Harvard University Press, 1973).

4. Daniel Kripke, D. J. Mullaney, et al., "Phototherapy of Non-Seasonal Depression," in C. Shagrass, R. C. Josiassen, et al., eds., *Biological Psychiatry* (New York: Elsevier, 1985), 45-49.

5. Gallagher, 17-18.

6. Ibid., 209.

7. Ibid., 29-30.

8. R. J. Wurtman, M. J. Baum, and J. T. Potts, Jr., eds., *The Medical and Biological Effects of Light*, Vol. 453 (New York: New York Academy of Sciences, 1985), 195-212.

9. G. Franta and K. Anstead, "Daylighting Offers Great Opportunities," *Window & Door Specifier-Design Lab*, Spring 1994, 40-43.

10. J. H. Heerwagen, J. A. Johnson, P. Brothers, R. Little, and A. Rosenfeld, "Energy Effectiveness and the Ecology of Work: Links to Productivity and Well-Being," *Proceedings of the 1998 ACEEE Summer Study* (Washington, DC: American Council for an Energy-Efficient Economy, 1998), 8.123-8.132.

11. Gallagher, 55.

12. P. A. Bell and T. C. Greene, "Thermal Stress: Physiological Comfort, Performance, and Social Effects of Hot and Cold Environments," in G. W. Evans, ed., *Environmental Stress* (New York: Cambridge University Press, 1982), 173.

13. Eric Schmidt and Jonathan Rosenberg, *How Google Works* (New York: Grand Central Publishing, 2014); Kindle edition, "Keep Them Crowded" section, Loc 490-491.

14. Ibid.; Kindle edition, Loc 490-508.

15. Susan Cain, *Quiet: The Power of Introverts in a World That Can't Stop Talking* (New York: Crown Books, 2012), 76.

16. Gallagher, 185.

17. Johann Wolfgang von Goethe, *Theory of Colors* (Cambridge, MA: MIT Press, 1970), 347.

18. Thomas Wehr, "Seasonal Affective Disorders: A Historical Overview," in Norman Rosenthal, ed., *Seasonal Affective Disorders and Phototherapy* (New York: Guilford Press, 1989), 78-92.

19. *The Challenges of Working in Virtual Teams: Virtual Teams Survey Report* (New York: RW3 Culture Wizard, 2010).

## Chapter 6—The Power of Trust

1. Christine Caldwell, "Tomorrow's Global Leaders," *People and Strategy* 36(3), 2013, 46-51.

2. Fenny Ang, " 'Do I Trust You More if I Think You Are Culturally Intelligent?' An Investigation on Trust-Building Between Expatriate Leaders and Host Country Nationals and the Role Cultural Intelligence Plays in the Trust-Building Process" (Ph.D. thesis, University of South Australia, 2012).

3.  Betsy Model, "The Virgin Knight," *Cigar Aficionado*, September/October 2007, http://www.cigaraficionado.com/webfeatures/show/id/The-Virgin-Knight_6219/p/2, accessed December 19, 2014.

4.  "Former Korean Air Executive Apologizes for Nut Rage," *BBC News*, December 12, 2014, http://www.bbc.com/news/world-asia-30444228.

5.  Mahzarin Banaji and Anthony Greenwald, *Hidden Biases of Good People* (New York: Delacorte Press, 2013); Kindle edition, "Infants" section, Loc 1949.

6.  B. Pelham, M. C. Mirenberg, and J. T. Jones, Why Susie Sells Seashells by the Seashore: Implicit Egotism and Major Life Decisions, *Journal of Personality and Social Psychology*, 82, 2002, 469-487.

7.  C. Aberson, M. Healy, and V. Romero, "In-Group Bias and Self Esteem: A Meta-Analysis," *Personality and Social Psychology Review*, 4, 2000, 157-173; M.B Brewer, "In-Group Bias in the Minimal Intergroup Situation: A Cognitive-Motivational Analysis," *Psychological Bulletin*, 86, 1979, 307-324.

8.  Susan Segrest, "Coke Executives on How to Navigate a Complex Global Environment," November 19, 2014, http://www.coca-colacompany.com/stories/coke-executives-on-how-to-navigate-a-complex-global-business-environment#TCCC, accessed November 19, 2014.

9.  Ibid.

10. Adapted from D. R. Ilgen, J. R. Hollenbeck, M. Johnson, and Dustin Jundt, "Teams in Organizations: From Input-Process-Output Models to IMOI Models," *Annual Review of Psychology* 56, 2005, 517-543.

11. Eric Schmidt and Jonathan Rosenberg, *How Google Works* (New York: Grand Central Publishing, 2014); Kindle edition, "Intro to Talent-Hiring Is the Most Important Thing You Do" chapter, Loc 1235.

12. Henri Tajfel, "Experiments in Intergroup Discrimination," *Scientific American* 223, 1970, 96-102.

13. A. Bandura, *Self-Efficacy: The Exercise of Control* (New York: Freeman Press, 1997).

14. R. A. Guzzo, P. R. Yost, R. J. Campbell, and G. P. Shea, "Potency in Groups: Articulating a Construct," *British Journal of Social Psychology* 32, 1993, 87-106.

15. M. A. Campion, E. M. Papper, and G. J. Medsker, "Relations Between Work Team Characteristics and Effectiveness: A Replication and Extension," *Personnel Psychology* 49, 1996, 429-452.

16. R. D. Goddard, "A Theoretical and Empirical Analysis of the Measurement of Collective Efficacy: The Development of a Short Form," *Educational and Psychological Measurement* 93, 2002, 467-476.

17. Cristina Gibson, "Do They Do What They Believe They Can? Group Efficacy and Group Effectiveness Across Tasks and Cultures," *Academy of Management Journal* 42(2), 1999, 138-152.

18. Amy C. Edmondson and Kathryn S. Roloff, "Leveraging Diversity Through Psychological Safety," *Rottman Magazine*, Fall 2009, 48.

19. Ibid., 47-51.


## Chapter 7—Define: Align Diverse Expectations and Goals

1. Jeffery Liker, *The Toyota Way: Fourteen Management Principles* (New York: McGraw-Hill, 2004), 72.

2. Ibid., 129.

3. Noel Tichy, *Managing Strategic Change: Technical, Political, and Cultural Dynamics* (New York: Wiley-Interscience, 1983), 103; Noel Tichy, *The Leadership Development Program* (presented paper, Building the Leadership Engine meeting, Ann Arbor, Michigan, 2002).

4. R. Nouri, M. Erez, T. Rockstuhl, S. Ang, L. Leshem-Calif, and A. Rafaeli, "Taking the Bite Out of Culture: The Impact of Task Structure and Task Type on Overcoming Impediments to Cross-Cultural Team Performance," *Journal of Organizational Behavior* 24, 2014, 739-763.

5. David Teece, "Business Models, Business Strategy and Innovation: Long Range Planning," *International Journal of Strategic Management* 43, 2010, 172-194.

6. Nouri et al., 739-763.

7. David Livermore, *Cultural Intelligence: Improving Your CQ to Engage Our Multicultural World* (Grand Rapids, MI: Baker, 2009); David Livermore, *Serving with Eyes Wide Open* (Grand Rapids, MI: Baker, 2012).

8. Michele Gefland, Jana Raver, L. Nishii, L. Leslie, J. Lun, B. Lim, et al., "Differences Between Tight and Loose Cultures: A 33-Nation Study," *Science* 27, May 2011, 1100-1104.

9. Maddy Janssens and Jeanne Brett, "Cultural Intelligence in Global Teams: A Fusion Model of Collaboration," *Group and Organization Management* 31(1), February 2006, 137.

10. Andrew Ouderkirk, personal communication, February 17, 2015.

11. Isaura Barrera, Robert M. Corso, and Dianne Macpherson, *Skilled Dialogue: Strategies for Responding to Cultural Diversity in Early Childhood* (Baltimore: P.H. Brookes, 2003), 17-22.

12. Stephen Covey, *The Third Alternative: Solving Life's Most Difficult Problems* (New York: Free Press, 2011), 41.

13. Ibid., 42.

14. Clayton Christensen, *The Innovator's Solution* (Cambridge: Harvard Business Press, 2003).

15. George Doran, "There's a S.M.A.R.T. Way to Write Management's Goals and Objectives," *Management Review* 70(11), 1981, 35-36.

16. Judith Orasanu, "Shared Mental Models and Crew Decision Making," *Cognitive Science*, Technical Report 46 (Princeton, NJ: Princeton University, 1990).

## Chapter 8—Dream: Generate Diverse Ideas

1. Susan Segrest, "Coke Executives on How to Navigate a Complex Global Environment," November 19, 2014, http://www.coca-colacompany.com/stories/coke-executives-on-how-to-navigate-a-complex-global-business-environment#TCCC, accessed November 19, 2014.

2. Ronald Burt, "Network-Related Personality and the Agency Question: Multirole Evidence from a Virtual World," *American Journal of Sociology* 118(3), 2012, 543-591.

3. B. A. Nijstad, W. Stroebe, and H. F. M. Lodewijkx, "The Illusion of Group Productivity: A Reduction of Failures Explanation," *European Journal of Social Psychology* 36, 2006, 31-48.

4. Linn Van Dyne and Richard Saaverda, "A Naturalistic Minority Influence Experiment: Effects on Divergent Thinking, Conflict, and Originality in Work Groups," *British Journal of Social Psychology* 35, 1996, 151-167.

5. A. Mojzisch, L. Grouneva, and S. Schulz-Hardt, "Biased Evaluation of Information During Discussion: Disentangling the Effects of Preference Consistency, Social Validation, and Ownership of Information," *European Journal of Social Psychology* 40, 2010, 946-956.

6. Garold Stasser and William Titus, "Pooling of Unshared Information in Group Decision Making: Biased Information Sampling During Discussion," *Journal of Personality and Social Psychology* 48(6), June 1985, 1467-1478.

7. H. C. Wang, S. R. Fussell, and L. D. Setlock, "Cultural Difference and Adaptation of Communication Styles in Computer-Mediated Group Brainstorming" (Proceedings, ACM Conference on Human Factors in Computing Systems, 2009).

8. K. Y. Ng, S. Ang, and L. Van Dyne, *Speaking Up in the Culturally Diverse Workplace: The Role of Cultural Intelligence and Language Self-Efficacy*, (paper, American Psychological Association, Washington, D.C., August 2011).

9.  W. Gudykunst and S. Ting-Toomey, *Culture and Interpersonal Communication* (Newbury Park, CA: Sage), 99-116.

10. P. Shachaf, "Cultural Diversity and Information and Communication Technology Impacts on Global Virtual Teams: An Exploratory Study," *Information and Management* 45(2), 2008, 136.

11. Edward Hall, *The Hidden Dimension* (New York: Anchor Books, 1969), 122-145.

12. Gudykunst and Ting-Toomey.

13. Ibid.

14. Ibid.

15. Eric Schmidt and Jonathan Rosenberg, *How Google Works* (New York: Grand Central Publishing, 2014); Kindle edition, "It Must Be Safe to Tell the Truth" section, Loc 2355.

16. Ken Blanchard and Scott Blanchard, "What Improv Can Teach Your Team About Creativity and Innovation," *Fast Company*, http://www.fastcompany.com/3021450/what-improv-can-teach-your-team-about-creativity-and-collaboration, accessed November 20, 2013.

## Chapter 9—Decide: Select and Sell Your Idea

1.  Evan Osnos, *Age of Ambition: Chasing Fortune, Fame, and Faith in the New China* (New York: Farrar, Straus, & Giroux, 2014), 52.

2.  Eric Schmidt and Jonathan Rosenberg, *How Google Works* (New York: Grand Central Publishing, 2014); Kindle edition, "The CEO Needs to be the CIO" section, Loc 2769.

3.  "Complete Acquiescence: Bob Lutz Reveals How the Pontiac Aztek Happened," *Car and Driver*, October 14, 2014, http://blog.caranddriver.com/complete-acquiescence-bob-lutz-reveals-how-the-pontiac-aztek-happened/.

4.  Ibid.

5.  Penelope Trunk, "How to Tell if You Have a Good Idea," *Inc.*, http://www.inc.com/penelope-trunk/how-to-tell-if-you-have-a-great-idea.html, accessed October 15, 2014.

6.  David Livermore, "How Facebook Develops its Global Leaders: Conversation with Bill McLawhon," *People and Strategy* 36, 2013, 24-25.

7.  Ibid.

8.  Ruth Malloy, "Managing Effectively in a Matrix," *Harvard Business Review Blog*, August 10, 2012, http://blogs.hbr.org/2012/08/become-a-stronger-matrix-leade/, accessed October 10, 2014.

9.  Schmidt and Rosenberg; Kindle edition, "Think Big" section, Loc 2822.

10. Ibid.; Kindle edition, "What Is Innovation" section, Loc 2687.

11. Boris Groysberg and Katherine Connolly, "Great Leaders Who Make the Mix Work," *Harvard Business Review*, September 2013, https://hbr.org/2013/09/great-leaders-who-make-the-mix-work.

12. David Maister, *Managing the Professional Service Firm* (New York: Free Press, 1997), 69-70.

13. Daniel Pink, *To Sell Is Human: The Surprising Truth About Moving Others* (New York, Riverhead Books, 2012), 158.

14. Linda Hill, Greg Brandeau, Emily Truelove, and Kent Lineback, *Collective Genius: The Art and Practice of Leading Innovation* (Cambridge, MA: Harvard Business Press Review, 2013), 40.

15. Randall S. Peterson, "Can You Have Too Much of a Good Thing? The Limits of Voice for Improving Satisfaction with Leaders," *Personality and Social Psychology Bulletin* 25, 1999, 313-324.

16. Maddy Janssens and Jeanne Brett, "Cultural Intelligence in Global Teams: A Fusion Model of Collaboration," *Group and Organization Management* 31(1), February 2006, 140.

17. Ibid.

18. R. J. House, P. J. Hanges, M. Javidan, P. W. Dorfman, and V. Gupta, *Culture, Leadership, and Organizations: The GLOBE Study of 62 Societies* (Thousand Oaks, CA: Sage, 2004).

## Chapter 10—Design: Create and Test for Diverse Users

1. David Vinjamuri, "Bic for Her: What They Were Actually Thinking (As Told by a Man Who Worked on Tampons)," *Forbes*, April 30, 2012, http://www.forbes.com/sites/davidvinjamuri/2012/08/30/bic-for-her-what-they-were-actually-thinking-as-told-by-a-man-who-worked-on-tampons/, accessed October 21, 2014.

2. Jonathan Ringen, "How Lego Became the Apple of Toys," *Fast Company*, February 2015, 77.

3. Chris Gibbons, "The Top Team," *Acumen*, October 2013, 35.

4. Jeffrey Liker, *The Toyota Way: 14 Management Principles from the World's Greatest Manufacturer* (New York: McGraw-Hill, 2004), 228-230.

5. Ringen, 76.

6. William Lidwell, *The Meanings of Color, Lecture 1. How Colors Affect You: What Science Reveals* (Chantilly, VA: The Teaching Company, 2013).

7. Thomas J. Madden, Kelly Hewett, and Martin S. Roth, "Managing Images in Different Cultures: A Cross-National Study of Color Meanings and Preferences," *Journal of International Marketing* 8(4), 2000, 90-107.

8. D. Cyr, "Modeling Web Site Design Across Cultures: Relationships to Trust, Satisfaction, and E-Loyalty," *Journal of Management Information Systems*, 4 (4), 2008, 47-72.

9. A. Marcus and E. Gould, "Crosscurrents: Cultural Dimensions and Global Web User-Interface", *Interactions* 7, 2000, 32-46.

10. Nitish Singh, Hongxin Zhao, and Xiarui Hu, "Analyzing Cultural Information on Web Sites: A Cross-National Study of Web Site Comparison of China, India, Japan, and the U.S.," *International Marketing Review* 22(2), 2005, 109-125.

11. S. Eristi, "Cultural Factors in Web Design," *Journal of Theoretical and Applied Information Technology* 9, 2009, 82-90.

## Chapter 11—Deliver: Implement Global Solutions

1. Norbert Hedderich, "When Cultures Clash: Views from the Professions," *Die Unterrichtspraxis*, 1999, 161-165, translated into English at http://www.dartmouth.edu/~german/German8/Typical.html.

2. Katherine J. Klein and Andrew P. Knight, "Innovation Implementation: Overcoming the Challenge," *Current Directions in Psychological Science* 14(5), 2005, 245.

3. L. Aiman-Smith and S. G. Green, "Implementing New Manufacturing Technology: The Related Effects of Technology Characteristics and User Learning Activities," *Academy of Management Journal* 45, 2002, 421-430.

4. Klein and Knight, 244.

5. E. T. Adolfsson, B. Smide, E. Gregeby, L. Fernstro, and K. Wikblad, "Implementing Empowerment Group Education in Diabetes," *Patient Education and Counseling* 53, 2004, 319-324.

6. Klein and Knight, 244.

7. Piers Steel, *The Procrastination Equation: How to Stop Putting Things Off and Start Getting Stuff Done* (New York: HarperCollins, 2010), 17-39.

8. G. Shanks, A. Parr, B. Hu, B. Corbitt, T. Thanasankit, and P. Seddon, "Differences in Critical Success Factors in ERP Systems Implementation in Australia and China: A Cultural Analysis," *Proceedings of the 8th European Conference on Information Systems*, Vienna, Austria, July 3-5, 2000.

9. Ibid.

10. Alicia Crum and Ellen J. Langer, "Mind-Set Matters: Exercise and the Placebo Effect," *Psychological Science* 18(2), 2007, 165-171.

11. Scott Leibs, "Bound Up in Complexity," *Inc.*, October 2014, 114.

## Epilogue

1. Economist Intelligence Unit, "CEO Briefing: Corporate Priorities for 2006 and Beyond," *The Economist*, http://a330.g.akamai.net/7/330/25828/20060213195601, graphics.eiu.com/files/ad_pdfs/ceo_Briefing_UKTI_wp.pdf, 3.

2. IBM, "Capitalizing on Complexity," *IBM 2010 Global CEO Study* (Armonk, NY: IBM, 2010), 3.

3. Christopher Argyris, *Organizational Traps: Leadership, Culture, Organizational Design* (New York: Oxford University Press, 2012).

neutral stereotypes, 195
Nigeria, 8
noise, 93–94
nondominant groups, 60
Novartis, 25, 36–37, 87
NTT, environment, 34

objectives, strategic
   questions in developing,
   150
observing, 61–62
office environment, 87
Oilco, 216–219
older people, bias against
   working with, 37
online dating, 175
open office plan, 95
opinions, sharing, 153–154
Orasanu, Judith, 150
organizations, ROI of high
   CQ for, 22–25
Ouderkirk, Andrew,
   142–143
out-groups, 8
owner, acting like, 129–130

Page, Larry, 165
pain point, finding, 50
Palestinians, vs. Israelis, 60
particularists, 114
   vs. universalists, 142, 252
patience, 70
Pelham, Brett, 109
personal communication
   style, 162–163
personal development plan,
   248
personal space, 95
personalities, and
   innovation, 38–44
perspective taking, 54,
   147–148, 232
   checking for accuracy,
   65–66
   improving, 61–66
   as personal, 57–61
   vs. perspective giving,
   60–61

responsible use, 59
perspectives
   from diversity efforts, 12
   transcending, 58–59
Peterson, Randall, 189
Peyton, Colleen Murray, 169
Pink, Daniel, *To Sell Is
   Human*, 54, 187
Pixar, 187–188
polychronic cultures, 77, 89,
   142, 252
post-implementation
   review, launch of, 225–226
Powell, Nik, 106
power
   of color, 199–201
   of ideas, 174–178
   of space, 101–102
   of "Yes, and," 169–171
power distance, 141, 251
PricewaterhouseCoopers,
   36–37
priorities, 83, 85, 211
problem finding, focus for,
   79–82
procrastination, 215–216
Procter & Gamble, 31
   Crest Whitestrips, 170
production blocking, 155
professional behavior, 32
Project Implicit, 46
project lead for teams,
   220–221
prototypes, sophistication
   level needed, 209–210
psychological safety,
   121–122
punctuality, 70

quality of life, 89
questioning, 81–82
*Quiet* (Cain), 95

reality, diversity and, 1
red, cultural meanings, 200
regional perspectives, top
   diversity challenges, 10
reliability, trust and, 115

religion, 9–10, 41
representation, 15–16
reputation, trust and,
   115–116
respect, 157, 179, 249
return on investment, from
   diversity efforts, 1
revenue streams, 19
risk, 105–106
   tolerance for, 43
Roam, Dan, *Back of the
   Napkin*, 209
Rock, David, 83
Rogers, Jim, 37
Rosenberg, Jonathan, 45, 95,
   111, 183

safety, psychological,
   121–122
Saito, Atsushi, 153
SAP, 138
Schmidt, Eric, 45, 95, 111,
   183
Schultz, Howard, 175, 179
Schulz-Hardt, Stefan, 155
self-awareness, 16–17
self-control, 69
   focus and, 70–72
sensitivity, 249
shame, 14–15
Shane, Scott, 38–39
Shanks, Graeme, 216
shared competency, 120
shared mental model,
   130–133, 151, 215
silence, 162
similarity, and trust, 109
Singapore, 39, 136
skepticism, 213–214
skills gap, 212–213
SMART goals, 149
social categorization theory,
   8
social loafers in
   brainstorming session, 155
social norms, 136
socialization, and spaces, 89
Sonnefeld, Jeffrey, 1